THE RENAISSANCE

EXCLUDING DRAMA

GREAT WRITERS STUDENT LIBRARY

Editor: James Vinson
Associate Editor: D. L. Kirkpatrick

THE RENAISSANCE

EXCLUDING DRAMA

INTRODUCTION BY
ELIZABETH STORY DONNO

M

First published 1983 by
THE MACMILLAN PRESS LTD
London and Basingstoke
Associated Companies throughout the world

ISBN 0 333 28342 2   hard cover edition

ISBN 0 333 28343 0   paperback edition

Printed in Hong Kong

CONTENTS

EDITOR'S NOTE

The entry for each writer consists of a biography, a complete list of his published books, a selected list of published bibliographies and critical studies on the writer, and a signed critical essay on his work.

In the biographies, details of education, military service, and marriage(s) are generally given before the usual chronological summary of the life of the writer; awards and honours are given last.

The Publications section is meant to include all book publications, though as a rule broadsheets, single sermons and lectures, minor pamphlets, exhibition catalogues, etc. are omitted. Under the heading Collections, we have listed the most recent collections of the complete works and those of individual genres (verse, plays, novels, stories, and letters); only those collections which have some editorial authority and were issued after the writer's death are listed; on-going editions are indicated by a dash after the date of publication; often a general selection from the writer's works or a selection from the works in the individual genres listed above is included.

Titles are given in modern spelling, though the essayists were allowed to use original spelling for titles and quotations; often the titles are "short." The date given is that of the first book publication, which often followed the first periodical or anthology publication by some time; we have listed the actual year of publication, often different from that given on the title-page. No attempt has been made to indicate which works were published anonymously or pseudonymously, or which works of fiction were published in more than one volume. We have listed plays which were produced but not published, but only since 1700; librettos and musical plays are listed along with the other plays; no attempt has been made to list lost or unverified plays. Reprints of books (including facsimile editions) and revivals of plays are not listed unless a revision or change of title is involved. The most recent edited version of individual works is included if it supersedes the collected edition cited.

In the essays, short references to critical remarks refer to items cited in the Publications section or in the Reading List. Introductions, memoirs, editorial matter, etc. in works cited in the Publications section are not repeated in the Reading List.

INTRODUCTION

One of the traditional dates for the beginning of the English Renaissance is 1485, a date commemorating the defeat of Richard III at the Battle of Bosworth Field and inaugurating with Henry VII the more than century-long rule of the Tudors. Such a chronological starting point neatly accords with the political rule of a single dynasty in the 16th century; it also neatly accords with the emergence of intellectual forces that shape so much of the literary output for the next two centuries. But it offers problems in that certain writers (like Stephen Hawes, Alexander Barclay, and "Beastly" John Skelton, as Pope calls him) either in terms of technique or of subject matter seem to have at best a transitional if not indeed a medieval cast. Moreover, the problem of dating is intensified by the curious curve of literary development in the century. Those poets at the court of Henry VIII who introduced the "sweet new Italian style," as the critic Puttenham characterized them, represent a spot of brilliance just as the humanists connected to his court represent an intellectual ferment that we associate with the devolving concepts of the Renaissance, but this is followed by a poetic lag or slacking of achievement that has notoriously been labelled the "Drab Age." Then at the end of the 1580's there is a sudden proliferation of writers who are, in C. S. Lewis's terms, "golden" in manner and in matter. After the turn of the century they are succeeded by others pursuing different literary styles and approaches in a fragmenting of humanistic values until these values may be said to be reconstituted in Milton's *Paradise Lost*.

In turning to a recovery of classical authors, with an accompanying recovery of their critical tenets, the generation of humanists for whom we have adequate records looked to both the Greeks and the Romans, though the recovery of the Greek language came slowly (the first Regius professorship of Greek was established in 1540) and had a relative short duration in the century as a discipline stirring much general academic enthusiasm, a fact decried by Elizabethan dons. John Colet (1467?–1519), an early humanist and the founder of St. Paul's School, which became a prototype of later grammar schools, did not endeavour to learn Greek until he was in his fifties, but he did spark interest in the development of a historical interpretation of the Bible in his lectures at Oxford and later in London. His influence on Erasmus in countenancing a rejection of the medieval schoolmen was marked, and although his interests were primarily theological, by his styling the writings of the Middle Ages as "blotterature," he typifies the reactions not only of the first but also of the second generation of 16th-century humanists.

Thomas Linacre, both a physician and a grammarian, translated a number of Greek works into Latin, achieving special applause for his renderings of Galen. His Latin grammars were also popular; one went through 50 editions in the century though Colet rejected a text prepared for St. Paul's School in favour of one prepared by his headmaster, William Lily, which was then revised by both Colet and Erasmus. This composite work became the authorized grammar in 1540, and generations of schoolboys conned it word for word, giving point to the jesting incorporation of phrases from it into literary works (for example, the opening scene of Act IV of *The Merry Wives of Windsor*). With later doctoring, it was destined to continue as a textbook well into the 19th century.

The most important of English humanists both in his own right and in his close association with the internationally acclaimed Erasmus was Thomas More. Early in his career he shared with him a joyous enthusiasm for Lucian, that arch-scoffer at religion, and together they prepared Latin translations of a number of his dialogues which were published in 1506. More's most famous Latin work is, of course, the *Utopia*, which he himself generally referred to as *Nusquam* (though modern commentators like to emphasize the possible play on the meanings of the Greek *eu* (good)-place and *ou* (no)-place. Modern commentators also have wrestled with the intention of the piece: does it offer a serious pattern for rectifying social and economic abuses or is it a *jeu d'esprit* with some serious overtones in the vein of an Erasmian counterpart, the *Praise of Folly* (*Encomium Moriae*)? Interpretations are multiple, frequently reflecting the political bias of the commentator. Publication of the *Utopia* in 1516 was a major factor in establishing More's international reputation as a humanist; for readers of the vernacular there was a translation in 1551 by Ralph Robinson. Of his productions in English, the *History of Richard III* (also in a Latin version) is an impressive (though unfinished) example of a rhetorical projection of an eminent figure from recent history, in which More weights the argument so skilfully that the image of the malevolent crookbacked usurper (according to Erasmus, one of More's shoulders was higher than the other) dominated the histories down to the time of Horace Walpole's *Historic Doubts*—and later.

Though not an Englishman by birth but perhaps so by his own predilection and that of his humanist friends, Erasmus deserves consideration because of his enormous impact on intellectual and educational theories during the century. One of the characteristics of the Renaissance was a recovery of the art of rhetoric which in the later Middle Ages had succumbed to the dominance of dialectic. And to this recovery Erasmus contributed greatly. He also tirelessly plundered Greek and Latin and Christian authors to compile an ever increasing collection of adages that became a staple for writers, secular and religious, who delighted to lard their works with telling maxims. This practice was to bear special fruit at the end of the century in the early essays of Bacon, which, as has been observed, represent an elaboration of related wise sayings on a particular topic. Erasmus's *De copia* is a manual proving the means of attaining a copious or "facundious" style. It provides a store of examples taken from the entire spectrum of classical authors and gives directions on how to order these into a commonplace book (or "tables") that can be dipped into by the student seeking an effective comparison or metaphor, aphorism or anecdote. Writers from John Lyly to Andrew Marvell might as readily as Hamlet have said, "My tables—meet it is I set it down." Though written for St. Paul's School, this text had an international audience: there were about 180 printings during the century issuing from 21 different cities.

Some scholars label individuals like Colet, More, and Erasmus as "Christian humanists" because of their efforts to justify the study of pagan writers by stressing the compatibility of the moral outlook of their works with Christian doctrine. (There is here perhaps a sideswipe at the image of the indulgent Italian Renaissance glorying in a sensual paganism, though it too, as with the rest of contemporary Europe, was Christian.) And, indeed, of the humanists already mentioned, all but More studied in Italy.

After the Henrician reformation, the religious situation and, consequently, the mood change. There is, first, an attempt by the government during Edward's short reign (1547–53) to impose Protestant doctrine on a not altogether willing populace; then there is a right-about-face to Catholicism during Mary Tudor's even shorter stint as queen (1553–58), with the result that during her reign many of the ardently reformed sought exile in Switzerland or the Low Countries. After Elizabeth's accession, these Marian exiles felt free to return, and return they did, but having come under the influence of Calvinism and other reformed doctrines, they were imbued with even stronger Protestant fervor.

Such radical changes in such a short period made an immense alteration in the social and political scene, with a corresponding effect on literature. There was now a range of religious attitudes within the Church as well as without – reformers within, reformers without – and much of the literary energies of the period were spent on doctrinal and related political issues even as was to be the case in the next century. But those who had participated in the pendulum swing of religious alteration, while they endorsed humanistic principles, gave both priority and emphasis to their religious beliefs. The general mood in England becomes increasingly Protestant, increasingly anti-papal. On the part of these second-generation humanists there was a corresponding rejection of literature that emanated from Catholic countries, particularly from Italy. One describes the dangerous translation of Italian books: "They open not fond but common ways to vice but such subtle, cunning, new, and divers shifts to carry young wits to vanity and young wits to mischief, to teach old bawds new school points, as the simple head of an Englishman is not able to invent, nor never was heard of in England before, yea, when papistry overflowed all."

At midcentury, two humanists both ardent Protestants – Thomas Wilson and Roger Ascham – writing now in the vernacular, follow up the educational approach of Erasmus. Like him they look largely to Cicero and Quintilian. Thus they too stress the art of rhetoric as the means to attain eloquence and accept the triple ends of oratory – teaching, delighting, and persuading – as pertinent to any mode of discourse. Wilson's two textbooks, one on logic and one on rhetoric, with a wealth of examples, were well known to the imaginative writers of the Elizabethan period, and Ascham's *Schoolmaster*, published posthumously in 1570, though it discusses educational theory, offers critical *obiter dicta* that became general.

The compatibility of this rhetorical approach with the critical doctrines of Horace, particularly as set forth in the *Ars poetica*, meant that for most critical thinkers the poet, who in Horatian terms both teaches and delights, easily merged with the orator. Another effect of Horatian ideas was an incipient neo-classicism. Thus the principle of decorum (suiting the manner to the matter) was linked to a theory of literary kinds (epic, satire, etc.) and to the three styles (low, middle, and high) considered appropriate to each kind. Above all, the idea that literature should be didactic was widely endorsed in theory. Still, many authors, particularly those writing for a popular audience, went their own exuberant ways despite these prevailing tenets.

Curiously, it was not until the last two decades of the century that criticism achieved an independent status and then largely as a defensive against attacks on the immorality of the theatre and wanton Italian romances by stern-minded puritans. Sir Philip Sidney's *Apology for Poetry* (or *Defense of Poesy* as one edition is called) is the most urbane example of this critical response. Written c. 1583 but not published until 1595, it was, nonetheless, well known to the literary world through circulation in manuscript. Sir John Harington, for example, echoes it in the preface to his translation of Ariosto's *Orlando Furioso* (1591).

The first thing one ought to note about the *Apology* is that it is organized as a forensic oration, designed to persuade an audience of his suit that poetry is to be defended because it is superior to all other disciplines, in particular those of history and philosophy. (Whether he himself believed this is doubtful, but it is the posture he adopts in arguing his case.) By poetry, Sidney, as with many others of the period, includes all work that is fictive in nature, whether written in prose or verse. This explains his calling the *Cyropaedia* "an absolute heroical poem," because Xenophon presents a *feigned* image of Cyrus rather than a "true" portrait such as the historian Justin presents. Whereas the other arts necessarily imitate nature, the poet alone is able to conceive of things better than any that exist or of things that never existed, being inhibited only by the confines of his own wit and imagination. Consequently, in what Sidney hopes is not too saucy a comparison, the poet or "maker" is likened to that Heavenly Maker who made the natural world and then made man in his own image. ("Nature," as Sir Thomas Browne was to say, "is the art of God.")

In adopting the Greek term "maker" (*poetes*) as opposed to the Latin seer (*vates*), Sidney like other Elizabethans is stressing the craftsmanship of the artist shaping his artifact. He has little time for the Platonic doctrine of inspiration. Given the Renaissance admiration for the practical Romans who also discounted it, this is not surprising. Furthermore, with the supply of rhetorical manuals, acknowledged as useful alike for poet, orator, and preacher, the emphasis is on the Sidneian means – art, imitation, exercise. "Make me a poet," the ten-year-old Drayton begs his tutor, and the notion that one could "become" a poet is general though with some, perhaps because of their self image, there is also due concern for innate ability (*natura* or *ingenium*); Ben Jonson is an instance.

The focus of Sidney's argument is to establish poetry as the most efficient of the disciplines directing men to "right doing." Other disciplines are (tactically) reduced to "serving sciences" arranged in a hierarchy that culminates in the ethical-political concerns of men. It is the poet who best ministers to these concerns. By freely creating notable images, he teaches even as he induces delight, and by an empathetic means he persuades men to adopt "right action." Poetry – that is, the fictive – is seen as pragmatic. It is also seen as fulfilling the triple ends of classical oratory or eloquence. When in the *confirmatio* or proof of his case Sidney attempts to answer the charges that have been levelled at poetry from Plato on down, he is dazzlingly adroit, arguing by affirmation, concession, denigration, and denial. The intention of his *Apology* is to persuade the "poet-whippers"; in his own terms, the result shows perhaps more good will to poetry than good reasons, but it persuaded many of his contemporaries.

Amidst the numerous apologetic treatises, the one novel approach to criticism before the end of the century is provided by Puttenham in his *Art of English Poesy*, published in 1589 but much of it written earlier. In contrast to many of his contemporaries, he considers poesy to include only what is written in verse and not what is fictive at base. Particularizing the Horatian dictum that poets were the first civilizers of the world, he denominates them the first philosophers, the first rhetoricians, the first astronomers, etc., but, uniquely, he drops the moral posture to accept the end of poetry as providing solace and delectation. The *Art of English Poesy* was, notably, one of only three *English* literary works to be catalogued in 1605 in the new Bodleian Library.

The "courtly makers" who introduced Puttenham's "sweet new Italian style" – Wyatt, Surrey, and other "uncertain authors" – also introduced the sonnet form which had become a rage in Italy following Petrarch's infinite variety and skill in handling amatory lyrics in praise of his beloved Laura. (Since he was crowned in Rome in 1341 with the laurel – *lauro* – which ties in nicely with her name, the notion arose that the lady celebrated in his love poetry may have served only as a poetic peg, a situation certainly obtaining with many later imitators who took up the fashion of sonneteering.) His collection known as *Canzoniere* or *Rime sparse* (i.e., scattered rhymes) includes forms other than the sonnet (sestinas, madrigals) and subjects other than his varied psychological response to love such as those having a patriotic, moral, or religious cast. During his lifetime Petrarch was imitated, even plagiarized, and in the two centuries after his death Petrarchism became a veritable craze – some imitating his language or his manner, some composing *centoni* – poems made from bits and pieces of other poets – and some interlarding their poems with Petrarchan lines. His influence had no geographic boundary.

Both Wyatt and Surrey used Petrarch and the Petrarchists (particularly Serafino and the French Marot) for translation and/or adaptation; while Wyatt approximates the Italian form of the sonnet (an octave rhyming abba abba and a sestet of three rhymes), for some of his sonnets Surrey introduces a variation – three quatrains and a concluding couplet – that was so attuned to the quality of the language that it became the standard "English" or Shakespearean form. Their poems were first published in 1557, the year before Elizabeth's accession, in an exceedingly popular miscellany entitled *Songs and Sonnets* (and now generally known from its publisher as *Tottel's Miscellany*). It is important in that we know from manuscript sources that its editor subjected the poems of Wyatt to a kind of niggling editing, regularizing lines that he felt showed metrical ineptitude but which some would argue exhibit a sensitivity to metrical variety. The logical assumption is that he did the same for Surrey and the uncertain writers for whom there are no manuscripts extant. As a result of the volume's popularity, readers became conditioned to a metronomic regularity and to certain kinds of subject matter for lyrical verse, including the dour and the moralizing. Other poetical miscellanies of composite authorship followed, none of literary importance exactly but well remembered by the later Elizabethans. *A Handfull of Pleasant Delights*, a collection of ballads (including "Greensleeves"), first published in 1566 and again in 1584, includes one that is a reply to a lost ballad beginning "Where is the life that late I led" which both Petruchio (*The Taming of the Shrew*, IV.i.143) and Pistol (*2 Henry IV*, V.iii.147) recall.

In the title of lyrical collections of midcentury – like Barnabe Googe's *Eclogues, Epitaphs, and Sonnets* and George Turbervile's *Epitaphs, Epigrams, Songs and Sonnets* – as much later with Donne's collection, the term "songs and sonnets" was applied to any collection of short lyrics; these writers do not generally adhere to the 14-line form of the sonnet proper, even as they do not exhibit the range of metrical variety typical of the more felicitous Elizabethans.

That remarkable vogue for sonnet sequences began with the pirated publication in 1591 of Sidney's *Astrophel and Stella* and in 1592 of 28 of Samuel Daniel's sonnets to Delia. Although the arrangement of Sidney's poems (as is somewhat true of Drayton's later collection) allows for a psychological progression, it is important to recognize that a sequence is a lyrical medley, most often projecting the emotional state of the poet-lover in an "anatomy of woes," but that state can also serve as a point of departure for the introduction of related topics. One of the more interesting of such departures is when the poet turns critic, commenting on current literary modes. Sidney, for example, mocks stylistic fashions – euphuistic, Petrarchan, alliterative, and allegorical (no. 3, 6, 15, 28) – or he derides the doctrine of inspiration (no. 55, 74), or he tells of the therapeutic value of writing and of the power of verse (no. 34, 45, 50, 57–8), or even adopts an anti-poetic vein (no. 70, 90): "In truth, I swear, I wish not there should be/Graved in mine epitaph a poet's name." Others follow suit, most notably Drayton and Shakespeare. Since many of the poets turned not only to the Italian but also to the French imitators of Petrarch (Ronsard, Du Bellay, and Desportes), the charge was made (by Sidney Lee) that the sonneteers were veritable plagiarists. Such a charge took little account of the doctrine of *imitatio*.

This doctrine, ably expounded by Ascham in the *Schoolmaster*, urges writers to follow the best models, not in servile imitation but in an attempt to re-create the admirable qualities of their models. Since the subject matter of the sonnet, when it is not simply an occasional piece, is invariably an aspect of love in one or several of its manifestations, the difficulty of being genuinely original is patent, particularly since more than a thousand of them, it is said, were written in England in the years between 1591 and 1600 – hence the attempt to find points of departure that can be related to the poet-lover's experience such as critical comment on current literary fashions. But, inevitably, the matter of these sonnets tends to be much the same, leaving only the manner of expression to be varied. Such motifs as that of the melancholic lover and his recalcitrant mistress, of time the destroyer (*tempus edax*) and of the consequent need to gather rosebuds while one may (*carpe diem*) tend to be endlessly repeated, but, surprisingly, distinct poetic voices emerge from the many examples. Sometimes it is by the dramatic projection of an Astrophel (Sidney), sometimes it is by the introduction of audaciously novel language (Drayton), sometimes it is by employing a wide range of emotional states and subtle melodic expression (Shakespeare), and sometimes it is by psychological intensity (Donne). As anthologies attest, almost any late Elizabethan could produce one or more striking examples. The question of the poet's personal involvement, or "sincerity" in 19th-century terms, is irrelevant, since it is measured only by the poet's artistic achievement.

Supplementing the sonnet vogue is the variety of literary genres that make their appearance in the 1590's. A relatively long-lived one was the epyllion or little epic where writers looked to the witty licentious Ovid as their model, ignoring any moral intent just as the sonneteers had ignored it. Delighting in verbal invention, in ornamenting their poems with lovely images, and in exploiting rhetorical devices by means of *sententiae*, oxymorons, and hyperboles, they produced artful short pieces to titillate the reading public. Marlowe's unfinished *Hero and Leander* is the most accomplished, but Cambridge undergraduates, it seems, kept Shakespeare's *Venus and Adonis* under their pillows. Minor 17th-century writers continued the vogue – all the way up to 1646 with James Shirley's *Narcissus; or, The Self-lover*, though it is perhaps an early work – and they tend to exploit the more shocking and risqué myths.

A counterpart genre also looking to Ovid was the tragical complaint. In presenting the fall of a protagonist, occasioned by love whether reciprocated or not, this genre looked to a compounding of Ovid's *Heroides* with the medieval *de casibus* tradition brought up to date by the substitution of figures from English history, the latter as exemplified in the many editions of the *Mirror for Magistrates* which recounts the fall of notable figures from Richard II on. It too was a highly rhetorical genre with verbal display substituting for the dramatic suspense inevitably lost through the *ex post facto* narration of the ghostly protagonist returning from hell to utter her complaint. But the form allowed for, even required, a moral, either admonitory or hortatory. Shakespeare's *Rape of Lucrece* offers a modification of this general pattern.

Satire also became popular, showing some influence of the conversational quality of Horace's *Sermones* but mostly following the harsh and crabbed style of Juvenal and Persius. Misunderstanding the etymology of the term (*satura* = a medley, in reference to the variety of subjects or of forms employed), the Elizabethans thought that it derived from *satyr* and therefore should be rough and bristling with syntactical and verbal difficulties. The medieval traditions of satire of estates and types (usurers, lawyers, etc.) and of fools were also tapped, and satiric elements were introduced into almost any genre (e.g., Daniel introduces passages on cosmetics in the *Complaint of Rosamund* even as Hamlet charges women in the person of Ophelia for their like affectation). Epigrammatists wrote satires in little which were often both scandalous and libellous. This practice resulted in the calling in of satires and epigrams by the authorities in 1599 and the restricting of future publications. Despite the ban, some 50 new collections were printed in the following 15 years.

The pastoral mode, whether in verse or prose, was also extremely popular. Spenser's *Shepheardes Calender* (1579) introduced a variety of classical and Renaissance forms (dirge, singing match, love complaint; allegory and beast fable), with the shepherd-*persona* taken to represent a poet, a lover, and a pastor-of-his-flock. Its experimental basis is patent in the variety of stanzaic forms employed, and it has a timely parallel in the prose experimentation that characterizes John Lyly's two "novels" (1578 and 1579), wherein he affects the highly mannered style of euphuism that has taken its name from his titular hero. The appeal of this mode rests on its juxtaposition of two realms – the real world (often of the court) and the, seemingly, idyllic green world to which characters retreat whether it be the forest of Arden (as in Thomas Lodge's pastoral romance *Rosalind* and in Shakespeare's appropriation of that story for *As You Like It*) or Arcadia (as in Sidney's prose epic which takes its title from the pastoral locale). In its wide confines the mode allowed for a range of genres – romantic epic (with Spenser), prose epic (with Sidney), prose romances (with Lodge and Robert Greene), and pastoral lyrics by a plethora of authors (*England's Helicon*). In their customary syncretic fashion the Elizabethans looked to classical writers like Theocritus and Vergil, to Italian writers like Sannazaro, Tasso, and Guarini, and to the Spanish Montemayor.

Offsetting the rural charms of the pastoral was a vogue for realism – tracts on roguery, which were climaxed by the cony-catching pamphlets of Robert Greene and Thomas Dekker or the picaresque novel with Thomas Nashe (*The Unfortunate Traveller*). Offsetting the concern with rhetoric in the popular euphuistic or Arcadian vein, or a combination of the two, was the exploitation of colloquial diction with its carry-over of the speaking voice, well exemplified in Sidney's sonnets which use dialogue (" 'What he?' say they of me, 'now I dare swear,/He cannot love: no, no, let him alone' ") or in Donne's *Songs and Sonnets* ("For God's sake, hold your tongue and let me love").

Translation, whether of the classics or of contemporary or near-contemporary works, was valuable on at least two counts. Either translators rendered the original in striking and vivid fashion so as to capture the flavour of the original even if somewhat transmogrified by prevailing attitudes or, if not, they made accessible important works that became the warp and woof of the Elizabethan ideational carpet. Examples of the first would include Sir Thomas North's noble translation of Plutarch's *Lives of the Noble Grecians and Romans*; Sir John Harington's sprightly translation of Ariosto's romantic epic, the *Orlando Furioso*; Edward Fairfax's elegant translation of Tasso's *Gerusalemma Liberata*, and John Florio's racy translation of Montaigne's *Essays*; examples of the second would include George Chapman's rendering of all the works of Homer and Philemon Holland's many translations of the classics – Livy, Plutarch, Suetonius, etc. The long labours of the last two translators continued well into the 17th century.

A special place should be accorded the earlier translation (1561) by Sir Thomas Hoby of Castiglione's *Courtier*, which in place of the humanist-scholar established the courtly man of letters as a paradigm to be copied. A measure of the Renaissance concern for the ideal is indicated by Castiglione's admission (in his dedication) that although the perfect courtier does not exist, he is following the pattern of Plato in setting forth the perfect state, of Xenophon in setting forth the perfect ruler, and of Cicero in setting forth the perfect orator. It truly was a seminal work, going through at least a hundred editions before 1600 with translations into Spanish, French, German, and Latin as well as English. In contrast to Machiavelli's *Prince* (significantly not to be translated into English until the 17th century), which sets forth the political man, Castiglione in his dialogue sets forth the apotheosis of the social man, the courtier serving as a median link between the ruler and the ruled. Ophelia's description of Hamlet records the qualities of this ideal figure:

> The courtier's, scholar's, soldier's eye, tongue, sword.
> The expectancy and rose of the fair state,
> The glass of fashion and the mould of form,
> The observ'd of all observers....

A special place should also be accorded the great composite work of translation in King James's reign – the Authorized Version of the Bible – since nine-tenths of it goes back to the translations of Tyndale and Coverdale in the 1530's, supplemented by other 16th-century versions.

Closely related to translation are the philosophic poems, since these tend to sum up the received wisdom of the period and reflect current views on a range of topics – psychology, philosophy, and theology. Despite the promptings of the new science, writers (as with Milton later) sometimes opted for the tried and well-worn world view to provide their basic construct. An example is Sir John Davies, who in a poem exploring the social, musical, astronomical, and cosmological implications of order and movement chooses to follow the Ptolemaic scheme in place of the Copernican (stanza 51, *Orchestra*, 1594). Two French works, both translated in the period, were to have a long influence, La Primaudaye's *French Academy*, which expounds the moral, metaphysical, and physiological doctrine of the microcosm (man as a "little world" in contrast to the macrocosm), and the Huguenot poet Du Bartas whose encylopaedic account of the history of man from the creation on influenced innumerable writers, as well as readers, from Donne to Milton.

In a somewhat different vein, Samuel Daniel's *Musophilus* (1599) offers a rare historical perspective; although humanistically oriented, he does not, like most of his contemporaries, reject the Middle Ages out of hand nor does he emphasize the value of fame (the common immortality *topos*) but rather the conviction that poetry and, by extension, learning is its own reward, the "thing," as he says, "that I was born to do." Ending with a somewhat uncommon literary glance at the current geographic explorations, he envisions the time when worlds in the "yet unformèd Occident" may speak in the accents of his native land.

The steady development of English as a literary medium continued the quarrel among those who wished, on the one hand, to enrich it by foreign borrowings and neologisms and, on the other, by the use of doublets and triplets to express near synonymous meaning – the transference of Erasmian copiousness to the vernacular. The quarrel also extended to the matter of spelling reform; a phonetic basis had been advocated as early as Sir John Cheke, and the question of correct orthography and pronunciation continued to be debated (see *Love's Labour's Lost*, V.i.).

A further long-lasting quarrel had to do with the introduction of classical meters and the displacing of "rude beggarly riming," which, according to the humanists, had been introduced by the barbaric Goths and Huns. Though classical writers opposed rhyme in poetry, they used it in prose to a certain extent, a rhetorical trick which became fashionable among Tudor preachers: "Let us as we be talkers so likewise be walkers" (or, much later, with Donne: God "flings and slings and stings the soul of the sinner"). Such a practice accounts for the frequent critical charge of "rime without reason." Some of the best poets toyed with the notion of writing unrhymed verse – Sidney, Spenser, and especially, and surprisingly, Thomas Campion, who as a musician-poet handled rhyme as well as metrics with enormous skill. Motivation for such a departure from the native tradition stemmed partly from the humanists' opposition to anything medieval, partly from the desire on the part of poets to extend the range of the vernacular and raise it to the level of Greek and Latin. Milton's preface to the second edition of *Paradise Lost* (1674) wherein he terms rhyme the "invention of a barbarous age" is a late instance of this attitude.

In all this ferment one must not disregard the changing status of the aspiring writer vis-à-vis the technological advance of the printing press and the increasing consumer market it produced. The early tradition that obtained among the poets at Henry VIII's court was aristocratic since they looked to an audience of their peers. Living a tickle existence within a context, as Lear puts it, of "Who loses and who wins; who's in and who's out," they recognized that their skills might serve their personal advancement within that courtly context, but they disdained publication. This aristocratic disdain for the press characterizes a certain number of Elizabethan authors – all of Sidney's writings were published posthumously and Sir Walter Ralegh caused the cancelling of the initials S. W. R. added to two lyrics in *England's Helicon*. The same distaste for publication continued into the 17th century as is evident with Donne and Marvell.

But in the 1580's young graduates from Oxford and Cambridge were coming up to London, sometimes taking up residence in that "third" university – the inns of court – and these so-called "university wits" often tried to earn a living by their pen. It was a precarious existence. Authors surrendered all rights to their work upon receiving payment from the publisher (about 40 shillings for a pamphlet by a popular writer, with perhaps a pottle of wine thrown in). Hence they needed to write in haste, to be capable of "yarking up" a pamphlet in a day and a night, as Robert Greene was reputed to do, in order to sustain themselves even if it were only by a meal consisting of Rhenish wine and pickled herring. (Such was the "fatal banquet" that caused Greene's early demise.) Their alternative was to seek patronage from a nobleman or prosperous member of society, but this too was precarious since patrons were notoriously niggardly or vacillating, or so the writers complained. Many like Nashe and Dekker suffered imprisonment for debt; others like John Lyly could only bequeathe patience to their creditors, melancholy without measure to their friends, and beggary not without shame to their families.

In the course of a life which spanned most of the century (1520–1604), the hack poet Thomas Churchyard wrote innumerable occasional pieces in order to elicit rewards from potential patrons in all levels of society. He could well be speaking for many professional writers of his day when in a begging letter to the Lord Chancellor Christopher Hatton (who had already beggared himself by building a lavish palace to honour the queen), he wrote: "I know it is miserable to crave, servitude to receive, and beggarly to want." He could also be speaking for an even greater number of those who gravitated to the court to pay homage and seek favour when in a second letter to Hatton, he wrote: "I blush, being old, to beg and yet not ashamed to receive, being a courtier."

In the last years of the aging queen, new moods began to prevail and a certain disenchantment set in. The politically attuned looked to the north to James VI of Scotland, but in only a short time after his arrival in England, Elizabethan disenchantment yielded to Jacobean pessimism. The world, to some, was running down, nature was decaying, the end of the world was being forecast, and, as Donne put it, the "new philosophy" was calling all in doubt. In the course of the next 60 years, the cosmology of microcosm-macrocosm which had provided an ideological basis for political, social, moral, and aesthetic views surrendered to a mechanistic outlook, the accumulated result of the Baconian concern with science and the actual scientific achievements of Copernicus, Gilbert, Galileo, and Descartes.

For literary writers, however, there was no sharp break with the late Elizabethans in the early decades of the century. Three lines of development had their origins in writers who bridged the two periods either by literary impact or by chronology. There is, first, the

Spenserian tradition which continues in writers fusing Christian and mythological resources and employing mellifluous rhythms and lush (or grotesque) imagery. The result is religious or philosophic narrative. Giles Fletcher the Younger, for example, wrote a short devotional epic (*Christ's Victory and Triumph*) which blends Spenserian allegory with something of the spirit of Catholic baroque literature; it looks back to the Elizabethan poet Robert Southwell and ahead to the intensely flamboyant style of Richard Crashaw. His brother Phineas Fletcher was also in the tradition, writing a (very) long anatomical and allegorical poem *The Purple Island* which, in a sense, takes its point of departure from *Faerie Queene* II.9. He was sufficiently Spenserian so that his erotic narrative *Britain's Ida* could be palmed off in 1628 as by the Prince of Poets himself.

The Spenserian pastoral vogue also continued unabated: idealized landscapes (nymphs and dryads) frequently offset by the rustic (milkmaids and hock carts); in this vein Drayton, Nicholas Breton, William Browne, and George Wither were all skilful practitioners. In departing from the vogue of the shepherd, real or symbolic, employed as a focal point, Phineas Fletcher obtained a certain novelty in his *Piscatory Eclogues* (compare Sannazaro's *Eglogae piscatoriae*, 1526) just as Marvell was to do later with his substituting a mower (and his scythe) for the more usual shepherd to evoke suggestions of mortality.

Though a number of minor writers (and a major one like Milton) show something of the Spenserian quality, others found the style too diffuse, too soft, too feminine. These became the "sons of Ben," influenced by the classical restraint and tautness of Jonson's writing, and they represent a second line of literary development. In his *Timber; or, Discoveries*, a commonplace book with excerpts and notations from his readings in classical and Renaissance writers, Jonson reveals his humanistic orientation – concern for moral truth and artful presentation. In his non-dramatic writings, he follows Martial for his epigrams and Catullus for his songs. His many occasional pieces show that he learned the art of courtly compliment perhaps all too well.

Jonson's fondness for the couplet connects him with other 16th-century figures who were shaping their rhyming verses with point but not yet with the constriction of the narrative flow that was to mark the later closed couplet, with Marlowe, for example, in *Hero and Leander*, Drayton in the *Heroical Epistles*, and Fairfax in translating the final couplets of Tasso's *ottave*. By the time of Edmund Waller and John Denham this earlier kind of metrical suppleness is moving rapidly in the direction of the antitheses and end-stopped lines of the Augustans.

The country parson Robert Herrick is perhaps the most unmistakable follower of Jonson with his dainty and elegant handling of amatory themes in carefully articulated forms. Despite the surface gaiety of his poetry, he frequently sounds a contrasting note, underscoring the themes of mutability and death. These *topoi* from the Latin and Elizabethan poets – *tempus fugit, carpe diem* – along with a prompting to libertinism, provide a logic of persuasion for the cavalier poets – Thomas Carew, Richard Lovelace, and Sir John Suckling. Their amateur and aristocratic status is carefully nurtured, with the poems of Carew, for example, though widely circulated, not appearing in print until after his death.

The third line of development is provided by John Donne, whose "masculine" voice influenced some of the same poets influenced by Jonson, even as he himself was on occasion. Though late Elizabethan poets – Chapman, for instance, and Shakespeare – show elements of the so-called metaphysical style of poetry, it is Donne who is its exemplar. It is a style characterized by Dr. Johnson, and later critics, as one yoking heterogenous ideas and images together, straining after novelty, and exploiting arcane learning in witty and abstract images. Contrastingly, Carew (in "An Elegy upon the Death of ... Donne") sums up Donne's contribution in quite other terms:

> The muses' garden with pedantic weeds
> O'erspread, was purg'd by thee; the lazy seeds
> Of servile imitation thrown away;
> And fresh invention planted.

Donne's "fresh invention" – a rhetorical term – is stylistic since his subjects are amatory or religious; his means are equally rhetorical – the employing of irony, paradox, and hyperbole. The use of the conceit had been popular since the time of Petrarch; what Donne and his followers do is to seek for ever more striking and ingenious analogies. Donne also capitalizes on the Ramist appropriation of the first two parts of rhetoric (invention and arrangement) to the art of dialectic, which, historically, was often considered the adjunct of rhetoric: hence the argumentative cast of his poetry, as in the logic-chopping of "Lovers' Infiniteness." (For a later example, note the syllogistic basis of Marvell's "To His Coy Mistress.") The witty, casuistical Ovidian note sounded in some of his poems may be said to be brought up to date by the influence of casuistry – the mustering of arguments to defend a case of conscience – which was expounded by the Cambridge divine William Perkins (d. 1602) and much employed by religious dissenters of the 17th century. Like Sidney and Drayton, Donne conveys a sense of direct reaction to emotional experience (though the best sonneteers, inevitably, seem concerned with their own psychic response rather than that of the lady who triggered it), but, almost uniquely, he gives expression to a mutual love. To accord with the complexity of his feelings, he adopts a tortuous style, a difficult rhythmic movement, and an abrupt association of ideas. Other poets who capture something of the Donnean characteristics include the two Herberts, Henry Vaughan, Henry King, and Marvell; the last mentioned may be taken as the prime example of how poets, exposed to a wide range of styles, could amalgamate aspects from any line of development in making their own artful constructs.

Religious poetry, to which Donne contributed importantly, constitutes an essential part of the 17th-century legacy. In the 1590's it had served as a partial corrective (or a new subject) to the pre-eminence of the love sonnet. In 1595 Barnabe Barnes (author of a notoriously licentious sonnet) published *A Divine Century of Spiritual Sonnets* – his muse, the Holy Ghost; and mention has already been made of the Jesuit Southwell who wrote two volumes of religious lyrics and whose prose meditation *Mary Magdalen's Funeral Tears* (1591) contributed to the fashion for poems on weeping (Crashaw's "The Weeper"; Marvell's "Eyes and Tears").

One of the marked aspects of this poetry is its employment of erotic language, often disturbingly sexual. Apologists look to the medieval worship of the Virgin, the allegorization of the Song of Songs, or the raptures of the mystics for justification but seldom to the ease with which a writer of both secular and religious lyrics could adopt the idiom of the one for the other. The principle of decorum – suiting the style to the subject – has ceased to apply, and the straining after intensity, as in some of Crashaw's poems, becomes maudlin if not offensive. George Herbert, on the other hand, conveys a sense of religious fervor in a great variety of stanzaic forms by distilling his emotion and relying on a pared language. His search after novelty is perhaps represented by his geometrical or "shaped" poems (for example, "The Altar" represents its subject in form), a device, Puttenham had said, exhibiting brevity and subtlety.

Closely related to such shaped poems was the vogue for emblem books. These include an illustration (usually an engraving), a motto, and a poem, as did the eclogues of Spenser's *Shepheardes Calender*, but, unlike Spenser, they dilate on the moral or religious symbolism of the picture. In 1586 Geoffrey Whitney published the first emblem book in English, most of it translated from Italian sources; in 1635 George Wither published a collection and in the same year appeared the most popular of all, that of Francis Quarles. The attraction of this capsuled visual-poetic morality stems, as Quarles put it, from the recognition that the "heaven, the earth, nay every creature [are] but hieroglyphics and emblems of His Glory." Its importance, apart from its "plebeian" appeal to contemporaries, rests on the appropriation of the emblematic mode by poets of greater stature.

If the emblematic mode reflected the ancient cosmic view of analogies and correspondences between macrocosm and microcosm, the ancient physiology of the doctrine of the humours continued – the notion that the balance or imbalance of the four fluids of the body (black bile, phlegm, blood, and choler), corresponding to the four elements, dictated an individual's temperament: one's psychology depended on his physiology. Elizabethan and Jacobean medical and moral writers expounded the topic at tiresome length, and Jonson's two humour plays made literary capital of the theory. Increasingly, melancholy came to dominate the scene, perhaps because Aristotle had affirmed it signified superior intellectual ability. Like many of his contemporaries, Donne languished, "pressed with melancholy." Seriously ill with the "vapors" in 1623, he wrote a series of meditations on his infirmity (*Devotions upon Emergent Occasions*): "But what have I done either to breed or to breathe these vapors? They tell me it is my melancholy; did I infuse, did I drink in melancholy into myself? It is my thoughtfulness; was I not made to think? It is my study; did not my calling call for that? I have done nothing willfully, perversely toward it, yet must suffer in it, die by it." Poets wrote "pills" to purge it or lyrics to glorify it, with Milton adopting countering poetic views in "L'Allegro" and "Il Penseroso." But the most extensive treatment, prompted by the author's need to be busy in order to avoid its effects, is found in Robert Burton's *Anatomy of Melancholy*, a title like many earlier ones (*Euphues, The Anatomy of Wit*; *The Anatomy of Abuses*; *The Anatomy of Absurdity*) proposing a dissection of the subject. Concerned primarily with manifestations of melancholy in love and religion – the two literary poles of the period – Burton provides a wealth of speculation and information on the human condition. The same impulse characterizes the physician Sir Thomas Browne whether he is considering religious belief, burial customs, or common errors; a Baconian approach to science, "oracular observation," and a rationalistic prompting jostle with an encyclopaedic concern for ancient authorities.

A very popular, and novel, genre was that of the "character," a sharp portrayal of a social type (the courtier, the gull), or of a scene (a tavern, a bowling green), or of a virtue but, more often, of a vice. It was a form which could lend itself to wit, to realism, to satire, or to moral adumbration. Its immediate sources are composite – the realistic depiction of rogues in the mid-16th century, the development of satire and epigram in the 1590's, and perhaps the extended *dramatis personae* that Jonson offered the reader of *Every Man Out of His Humour*; since his characters, though depicted in action, are marked by an obsessional bias, there is a similarity to the static types depicted in the "character" sketches.

The first characters (1608) were those of Joseph Hall, who in 1597 had claimed to be the earliest of the satirists. Entitled *Characters of Virtues and Vices*, his volume tends toward abstractions in a pithy antithetical style. A particular fillip was given to the genre with the publication in 1614 of a collection by Sir Thomas Overbury and his gentlemanly friends, a publication appearing after Overbury's poisoning in the Tower of London which resulted in a cause célèbre. Other writers, among them John Stevens, Nicholas Breton, and Richard Braithwaite, picked up the formula; a departure is Geoffrey Minshull's *Essays and Characters of a Prison and Prisoners*, 1618, written "to banish melancholy" while inside the King's Bench prison and addressed to friends at the inns of court. In a ready appropriation of cosmology, he defines a prison as a "microcosmus, a little world of woe ... a little commonwealth, although little wealth be common there." In 1628 John Earle published his collection entitled *Microcosmography*, his double-barreled title proffering either the "little world of man" as microcosm or a "little description" of the world of man. Much admired for his ironic and genial observations, he moves easily into the epigrammatic: "A GALLANT is one that was born and shaped for his clothes; and, if Adam had not fallen, had lived to no purpose."

When related genres are taken into account, the increasing tendency to prose writing in the 17th century becomes clear. There is, first, the essay, which shows an affinity with the "character" of, say, resolution, or of gardens, or of the wise statesman, or of the traitor (as with Thomas Fuller), the difference being that the essay writer tends to personal moral statement without the witty play of ideas or of language. Second, it shows an affinity with biography which was given an impressive nudge by the translation of classical sources such as Plutarch's *Lives* and Suetonius. In contrast with such heroic (or unheroic) delineation, the native tradition developed out of the medieval saints' legends and issued in two impressive 16th-century works that, significantly, were not to receive publication until the next century.

William Roper's life of Sir Thomas More is a touching and artful example of the hagiographic tradition by More's son-in-law while the life of the haughty prelate Cardinal Wolsey by his gentleman-usher William Cavendish is very much in the *de casibus* tradition of the rise and fall of an important historical figure. As mentioned earlier, More's *Richard III* is too much of a rhetorical projection to be accounted biography even as Bacon's *Henry VII* is so much concerned with the political scene that it more aptly falls into the category of history. The most famous of 17th-century literary biographers is the "angler" Isaak Walton who wrote sympathetic accounts of his two friends Donne and Sir Henry Wotton (for the *Reliquiae Wottonianae* of 1651) and of George Herbert and the "judicious" Richard Hooker.

The third form with affinity to the "character" (and the essay) is the epistolary. It goes back to the medieval formulary or *ars dictaminis*, which had as its source the letters of Cicero, Seneca, and the younger Pliny. Consequently, it falls under the governing principles of rhetoric with the triple ends of teaching, delighting, and persuading. Erasmus had written a treatise on letter writing (1522) in which the various kinds were categorized (encomiastic, familiar, etc.) with examples taken from classical authors. In 1586 two works in the vernacular appeared, William Fulwood's *Enemy of Idleness*, which was directed to a middle-class audience and Angel Day's *The English Secretary*, intended for professional writers who could make profitable use of his section on tropes and figures – the sure index to its rhetorical connection.

Though once again Joseph Hall claimed originality in a "new fashion" with the publication (1608–11) of *Epistles in Six Decades*, by 1602 Nicholas Breton had already anticipated the shift from the earlier formulary to an entertaining and informal approach with his *Post with a Mad Packet of Letters* (presumably transposed from its later title *Post with a Packet of Mad Letters*) which went through more than a dozen enlarged editions before the end of the century. This approach appears to best advantage in the four volumes published by James Howell, *Epistolae Ho-Elianae*, 1645–51, a collection dealing with his travels abroad (the Alps seemed "uncouth huge monstrous excrescences of nature"), his later report from Spain of the English travellers Mr. John and Mr. Thomas Smith, who had metamorphosed themselves into the Duke of Buckingham and Prince Charles and had come to woo the Infanta, and his imaginative excursions from Fleet Prison where he spent eight years writing, or revising, his specimens. The easy and lucid style of the letters, which frequently shade into short essays, is in striking contrast with the wayward quality of a Burton or the sonorous effects of a Browne, conveying rather a sense of familiar communication: "You know also how the gaggling of geese did once preserve the Capitol.... But the goose quill doth greater things; it conserves empires (and the feathers of it get kingdoms; witness what exploits the English performed by it in France), the quill being the chiefest instrument of intelligence, and the ambassador's prime tool. Nay, the quill is the usefullest thing which preserves that noble vertue, friendship, [which] else would perish among men for want of practice." Such writing manifests another in the several steps leading toward simplified and utilitarian prose.

Though the notion is initially surprising, the way was prepared by the sometimes acrimonious debate about proper preaching style which began in the 16th century and continued with much increased vigor into the 17th. In the Renaissance, homiletics was accepted as another aspect of the rhetorical art, and the various manuals of schemes and tropes were advertised as useful for the preacher as for the fictive writer or the lawyer or statesman. But with the increasing fervor of the religious reformers, a division sharpened between the traditionalists who advocated the enlisting of humane learning to make their sermons effective and the "modernists," often identified as puritans, who spurned such profane helps, advocating, instead, the concealing of human wisdom or even the rejection of it in favour of plain elucidation of the Scriptures. Since both puritan and anglican, whether of the 16th or 17th century, had been subjected to the same rhetorical training (the curriculum remaining the same except for an expansion of subjects), the division of opinion did not reflect doctrinal differences so much as it reflected differences as to what was the most efficacious means of persuading the greatest number to endorse Christian doctrines. Thus it was the case of one kind of rhetoric replacing another.

The very erudite Lancelot Andrewes, who began preaching under Elizabeth and became a bishop under James, is generally called a "witty" or "metaphysical" preacher, though his terseness, coupled with a philological and exegetical concern for his text, meant that his wit was appreciated only by those with like interest and like training – those educated at the university rather than the general populace. The sermons of Donne as Dean of St. Paul's offer, in contrast, a "metaphysical" style that exploits something of the compelling immediacy and dramatic effect of his poetry, but in place of love his themes now are disease, decay, death, and eternity:

> How barren a thing is arithmetic (and yet arithmetic will tell you how many single grains of sand will fill this hollow vault to the firmament)! How empty a thing is rhetoric (and yet rhetoric will make absent and remote things present to your understanding)! How weak a thing is poetry (and yet poetry is a counterfeit creation and makes things that are not as though they were)! How infirm, how impotent are all assistances if they be put to express this eternity!

Although a puritan, Thomas Adams continues the humanistic approach to sermons, illustrating a close knowledge not only of classical but of contemporary authors. He refers on different occasions, for example, to Tamburlaine, to his coloured sails, and to Bajazet, and he tells of the Jew who took a bond of a "pound of his Christian debtor's living flesh." In recognition of current literary vogues, he introduces character sketches into a sermon of 1614, which perhaps accounts for Robert Southey's terming him (somewhat extravagantly) the "prose Shakespeare of puritan theologians." With the fashion for "characters," it is not surprising, then, that he published a collection of them in 1615 entitled *Mystical Bedlam; or, The World of Madmen*; and in 1616 he published *The Soul's Sickness* in which the causes, symptoms, and cures of physical maladies are correlated to spiritual ills. Though designed to bring about moral regeneration, the lively descriptions had a popular appeal as in this description of a rake's progress – lust correlated with inflammation of the liver:

> The delight of his wickedness is the indulgence of the present, for it endures but the doing. He never rests so contentedly as on a forbidden bed. He is a felonious picklock of virginities, and his language corrupts more innocent truth than a bad lawyer's. He is an almanac from eighteen to eight and twenty if he scapes the fire so long. He can never call his hairs and his sins equal, for as his sins increase his hairs fall. He buys admission of the chambermaid with his first fruits. He lives like a salamander in the flames of lust, and quencheth his heat with fire, and continues his days under *zona torrida....* When his life's sun is ready to set, he marries and is then knocked with his own weapon: his own disableness and his wife's youthfulness like bells, ringing all in.

Such diverting elements were to be cabined and confined with the increasing triumph of the plain sermon, with plain exegetical handling of the scriptural text and, in secular literature, with the triumph of utilitarian prose. The movement away from the rhetorical handling of sermons is made clear in George Herbert's manual for a country parson, *A Priest to the Temple* (1652); there he declares that the proper style is not to be witty or learned or eloquent but to be holy – a character, he comments, that the rhetorician Hermogenes (with his seven characters of style) never dreamed of and therefore could not describe.

Such a stylistic movement from artifice to plainness has its origins in part in a religion of personal experience as opposed to formalized or ritualistic expression. It is thus in accord with the increasing attention to science with its emphasis on experience and observation, an emphasis which culminates in the establishing of the Royal Society in 1662. Emphasis is to be on "things" not "words." Reason is to come into its own with the result that entirely different aesthetic and critical principles were to obtain from those which obtained in the Renaissance.

But the history of the 17th century, as with the 16th, allows for no neat systematic development. Even as Hobbes and Descartes were providing a basis for materialism and scientific advancement, a group of Cambridge Platonists (Nathaniel Culverwell, Ralph Cudworth, and Henry More) were fighting a rearguard action, stressing the spiritual nature of the universe in an effort to reconcile truth and morality, religion and reason. Even as the vernacular was triumphing in a wide range of genres, Campion, Owen, Herbert, Crashaw, and Milton continued to write poems in Latin just as John Barclay turned to Latin prose for his courtly romance *Argenis* (1621), which by virtue of its being in an international language achieved European acclaim. (Within seven years of publication, it was twice translated into English!)

Nowhere are the multiple and diverse strands of Renaissance thought more evident than in the writings of Milton even though *Paradise Lost*, *Paradise Regained*, and *Samson Agonistes* did not appear until after the Restoration. Milton looks back to humanistic doctrines and often to the "sensuous and passionate" beauty of the Elizabethans; yet like so many of his contemporaries he reflects the tension that vibrates through the period giving it an uncertain equilibrium but an enormous vitality. In the next century this vitality is to be channeled by cooler sensibilities into, paradoxically, an even more earth-centered universe than the one the Renaissance knew.

READING LIST

1. Bibliographies, handbooks, etc.

Pollard, A. W., and G. R. Redgrave, *A Short-Title Catalogue of Books Printed in England, Scotland, and Ireland, and of English Books Printed Abroad 1475–1640*, 2 vols., 1926; revised by K. Pantzer, 1973.

Case, A. E., *A Bibliography of English Poetical Miscellanies 1521–1750*, 1935.

Pinto, V. de Sola, *The English Renaissance 1510–1688*, 1938; revised edition, 1966.

Mish, C. C., *English Prose Fiction 1600–1700: A Chronological Checklist*, 1952; revised edition, 1967.

O'Dell, Sterg, *A Chronological List of Prose Fiction in English 1475–1640*, 1954.

Lievsay, J. L., *The Sixteenth Century: Skelton Through Hooker*, 1968.

Heninger, S. K., Jr., *English Prose, Prose Fiction, and Criticism to 1660: A Guide to Information Sources*, 1975.

Ruoff, James E., *Handbook of Elizabethan and Stuart Literature*, 1975.

2. General histories

Baker, E. A., *The History of the English Novel*, vol. 2: *The Elizabethan Age and After*, 1929.

Bush, Douglas, *English Literature in the Earlier Seventeenth Century 1600–1660*, 1945; revised edition, 1962.

Atkins, J. W. H., *English Literary Criticism: The Renascence*, 1947; *17th and 18th Centuries*, 1951.

Wedgwood, C. V., *Seventeenth-Century English Literature*, 1950; revised edition, 1970.

Lewis, C. S., *English Literature in the Sixteenth Century, Excluding Drama*, 1954.

Evans, M., *English Poetry in the 16th Century*, 1955; revised edition, 1967.

Morris, H., *Elizabethan Literature*, 1958.

Schlauch, Margaret, *Antecedents of the English Novel 1400–1600: From Chaucer to Deloney*, 1963.
Taylor, E., *Literary Criticism of 17th-Century England*, 1967.
Muir, Kenneth, *Introduction to Elizabethan Literature*, 1967.
Inglis, F., *The Elizabethan Poets: The Making of English Poetry from Wyatt to Jonson*, 1969.

3. Themes, topics, short periods, etc.
Pinto, V. de Sola, *Introduction to English Biography in the Seventeenth Century*, 1915.
Williamson, George, *The Donne Tradition: A Study in English Poetry from Donne to the Death of Cowley*, 1930.
Stauffer, D. A., *English Biography Before 1700*, 1930.
Bush, Douglas, *Mythology and the Renaissance Tradition in English Poetry*, 1932; revised edition, 1963.
Bennett, Joan, *Four Metaphysical Poets*, 1934; revised edition, 1953; as *Five Metaphysical Poets*, 1964.
Willey, Basil, *The Seventeenth-Century Background: Studies in the Thought of the Age in Relation to Poetry and Religion*, 1934.
Leishman, J. B., *The Metaphysical Poets*, 1934.
Baldwin, C. S., *Renaissance Literary Theory and Practice 1400–1600*, 1939.
Sharp, R. L., *From Donne to Dryden: The Revolt Against Metaphysical Poetry*, 1940.
Hall, V., *Renaissance Literary Criticism: A Study of Its Social Content*, 1945.
Wilson, F. P., *Elizabethan and Jacobean*, 1945.
Nearing, H., *English Historical Poetry 1599–1641*, 1945.
Knights, L. C., *Explorations: Essays in Criticism Mainly on the Literature of the 17th Century*, 1946; *Further Explorations*, 1967.
Tuve, Rosamond, *Elizabethan and Metaphysical Imagery: Renaissance Poetic and 20th-Century Critics*, 1947.
Freeman, R., *English Emblem Books*, 1948.
Brooke, Tucker, *Essays on Shakespeare and Other Elizabethans*, 1948.
Zocca, L. R., *Elizabethan Narrative Poetry*, 1950.
Williamson, George, *The Senecan Amble: A Study in Prose Form from Bacon to Collier*, 1951.
Kermode, Frank, editor, *English Pastoral Poetry, from the Beginnings to Marvell*, 1952.
Bush, Douglas, *Classical Influences in Renaissance Literature*, 1952.
Danby, J. F., *Poets on Fortune's Hill*, 1952; revised edition, as *Elizabethan and Jacobean Poets*, 1965.
Smith, Hallett, *Elizabethan Poetry: A Study in Conventions, Meaning, and Expression*, 1952.
Martz, Louis L., *The Poetry of Meditation: A Study in English Religious Literature of the 17th Century*, 1954; revised edition, 1962.
Tillyard, E. M. W., *The English Epic and Its Background*, 1954.
Cruttwell, Patrick, *The Shakespearean Moment and Its Place in the Poetry of the 17th Century*, 1954.
Sells, A. L., *The Italian Influence in English Poetry from Chaucer to Southwell*, 1955.
Walton, G., *Metaphysical to Augustan: Studies in Tone and Sensibility in the 17th Century*, 1955.
Peter, John, *Complaint and Satire in Early English Literature*, 1956.
Lever, J. W., *The Elizabethan Love Sonnet*, 1956.
Tillyard, E. M. W., *The Metaphysicals and Milton*, 1956.
Bottrall, Margaret, *Every Man a Phoenix: Studies in 17th-Century Autobiography*, 1958.
Bush, Douglas, *Themes and Variations in English Poetry of the Renaissance*, 1957.
Campbell, L. B., *Divine Poetry and Drama in 16th-Century England*, 1959.
Miller, E. H., *The Professional Writer in Elizabethan England: A Study of Nondramatic Literature*, 1959.
Watson, C. B., *Shakespeare and the Renaissance Concept of Honor*, 1960.
Wedgwood, C. V., *Poetry and Politics under the Stuarts*, 1960.

Williamson, George, *Seventeenth-Century Contexts,* 1960; revised edition, 1969.

Allen, Don Cameron, *Image and Meaning: Metaphoric Traditions in Renaissance Poetry,* 1960; revised edition, 1968.

Wilson, F. P., *Seventeenth-Century Prose,* 1960.

Sasek, L. A., *The Literary Temper of the English Puritans,* 1961.

Williamson, George, *The Proper Wit of Poetry,* 1961.

Alvarez, A., *The School of Donne,* 1961.

Hollander, John, *The Untuning of the Sky: Ideas of Music in English Poetry 1500–1700,* 1961.

Hardison, O. B., Jr., *The Enduring Monument: A Study of the Idea of Praise in Renaissance Literary Theory and Practice,* 1962.

Keast, W. R., editor, *Seventeenth-Century English Poetry: Modern Essays in Criticism,* 1962.

Kerman, J., *The Elizabethan Madrigal: A Comparative Study,* 1962.

Hamilton, K. G., *The Two Harmonies: Poetry and Prose in the 17th Century,* 1963.

Lewis, C. S., *The Discarded Image: An Introduction to Medieval and Renaissance Literature,* 1964.

Richmond, H. M., *The School of Love: The Evolution of the Stuart Love Lyric,* 1964.

Scoular, K. W., *Natural Magic: Studies in the Presentation of Nature in English Poetry from Spenser to Marvell,* 1965.

Williamson, George, *Milton and Others,* 1965.

Bush, Douglas, *Prefaces to Renaissance Literature,* 1965.

Colie, Rosalie, *Paradoxia Epidemica: The Renaissance Tradition of Paradox,* 1966.

Lewis, C. S., *Studies in Medieval and Renaissance Literature,* 1966.

Simpson, C. M., *The British Broadside Ballad and Its Music,* 1966.

Williamson, George, *Six Metaphysical Poets: A Reader's Guide,* 1967; as *A Reader's Guide to the Metaphysical Poets,* 1968.

Peterson, D. L., *The English Lyric from Wyatt to Donne: A History of the Plain and Eloquent Styles,* 1967.

Thomson, P., *Elizabethan Lyrical Poets,* 1967.

Levin, Harry, *The Myth of the Golden Age in the Renaissance,* 1969.

Delany, P., *British Autobiography in the 17th Century,* 1969.

Martz, Louis L., *The Wit of Love: Donne, Carew, Crashaw, Marvell,* 1969.

Grundy, Joan, *The Spenserian Poets: A Study in Elizabethan and Jacobean Poetry,* 1969.

Miner, Earl, *The Metaphysical Mode from Donne to Cowley,* 1969.

Davis, W. R., *Idea and Act in Elizabethan Fiction,* 1969.

Ricks, Christopher, editor, *Poetry and Prose 1540–1674,* 1970.

Summers, Joseph H., *The Heirs of Donne and Jonson,* 1970.

Gransden, K. W., *Tudor Verse Satire,* 1970.

Bradbury, Malcolm, and David Palmer, editors, *Metaphysical Poetry,* 1970.

Halwood, W. H., *The Poetry of Grace: Reformation Themes and Structures in English 17th-Century Poetry,* 1970.

Miner, Earl, editor, *Seventeenth-Century Imagery: Essays,* 1971.

Ebner, Dean, *Autobiography in Seventeenth-Century England,* 1971.

Fish, Stanley E., editor, *Seventeenth-Century Prose: Modern Essays in Criticism,* 1971.

Miner, Earl, *The Cavalier Mode from Jonson to Cotton,* 1971.

Rivers, Isabel, *The Poetry of Conservatism 1600–1745,* 1972.

Fish, Stanley E., *Self-Consuming Artifacts: The Experience of Seventeenth-Century Literature,* 1972.

Knights, L. C., *Public Voices: Literature and Politics, with Special Reference to the Seventeenth Century,* 1972.

Patrides, C. A., *The Language of Renaissance Poetry,* 1972.

Johnson, Paula, *Form and Transformation in Music and Poetry of the English Renaissance,* 1972.

Cole, Howard C., *A Quest of Inquirie: Some Contexts of Tudor Literature,* 1973.

Nelson, William, *Fact or Fiction: The Dilemma of the Renaissance Story-Teller,* 1973.

Southall, Raymond, *Literature and the Rise of Capitalism,* 1973.

Sloan, Thomas O., and Raymond B. Waddington, editors, *The Rhetoric of Renaissance Poetry from Wyatt to Milton,* 1974.

Webster, Charles, editor, *The Intellectual Revolution of the Seventeenth Century,* 1974.

Grant, Patrick, *The Transformation of Sin: Studies in Donne, Herbert, Vaughan, and Traherne,* 1974.

Hammond, Gerald, editor, *The Metaphysical Poets: A Casebook,* 1974.

Miner, Earl, editor, *Illustrious Evidence: Approaches to English Literature of the Early Seventeenth Century,* 1975.

Yates, Frances A., *Astraea: The Imperial Theme in the Sixteenth Century,* 1975.

Galdon, John A., *Typology and Seventeenth-Century Literature,* 1975.

Wanamaker, Melissa C., *Discordia Concors: The Wit of Metaphysical Poetry,* 1975.

Ferry, Anne, *All in War with Time: Love Poetry of Shakespeare, Donne, Jonson, Marvell,* 1975.

Fowler, Alastair, *Conceitful Thought: The Interpretation of English Renaissance Poems,* 1976.

Herlgerson, Richard, *The Elizabethan Prodigals,* 1976.

Keach, William, *Elizabethan Erotic Narratives: Irony and Pathos in the Ovidian Poetry of Shakespeare, Marlowe, and Their Contemporaries,* 1977.

4. Anthologies of primary material

Saintsbury, G., editor, *Minor Poets of the Caroline Period,* 3 vols., 1905–21.

Spingarn, J. E., editor, *Critical Essays of the 17th Century,* 3 vols., 1908–09.

Fellowes, E. H., editor, *English Madrigal Verse, 1588–1632,* 1920; revised edition, 1929; revised edition, edited by F. W. Sternfeld and D. Greer, 1967.

Chambers, E. K., editor, *The Oxford Book of Sixteenth-Century Verse,* 1929.

Hebel, J. W., and H. H. Hudson, editors, *Poetry* [and *Prose*] *of the English Renaissance 1509–1660,* 2 vols., 1929–52; as *Tudor Poetry and Prose,* 1953.

Judges, A. V., editor, *The Elizabethan Underworld: A Collection of Tudor and Early Stuart Tracts and Ballads of Vagabonds,* 1930.

Grierson, H. J. C., and Geoffrey Bullough, editors, *The Oxford Book of Seventeenth-Century Verse,* 1934.

Boas, F. S., editor, *Songs and Lyrics from the English Play Books,* 1945; *Songs and Lyrics from English Masques and Light Operas,* 1949.

Southern, A. C., editor, *English Recusant Prose 1559–82,* 1950.

Wallerstein, Ruth, and Ricardo Quintana, editors, *Seventeenth-Century Verse and Prose,* 2 vols., 1951.

Ashley, R., and E. H. Moseley, editors, *Elizabethan Fiction,* 1953.

Rollins, H. E., and H. Baker, editors, *The Renaissance in England: Non-Dramatic Prose and Verse of the 16th Century,* 1954.

McClure, N. E., editor, *Sixteenth-Century English Poetry,* 1954.

Holzknecht, K. J., editor, *Sixteenth-Century Prose,* 1954.

Bowman, I., editor, *A Theatre of Natures: Some 17th-Century Character Writings,* 1955.

Winny, J., editor, *The Descent of Euphues: Three Elizabethan Romance Stories,* 1957.

Gardner, Helen, editor, *The Metaphysical Poets,* 1957; revised edition, 1961, 1972.

Sabol, A. J., editor, *Songs and Dances from the Stuart Masque,* 1959.

Peterson, S., editor, *The Counterfeit Lady Unveiled and Other Criminal Fiction of Seventeenth-Century England,* 1961.

Mish, C. C., editor, *Short Fiction of the Seventeenth Century,* 1963.

Martz, Louis L., editor, *The Meditative Poem: An Anthology of Seventeenth-Century Verse,* 1963.

Donno, Elizabeth Story, editor, *Minor Elizabethan Epics,* 1963.

Hardison, O. B., Jr., editor, *English Literary Criticism: The Renaissance,* 1963.

Kenner, Hugh, editor, *Seventeenth-Century Poetry: The Schools of Donne and Jonson,* 1964.

Partridge, A. C., editor, *The Tribe of Ben: Pre-Augustan Verse in English,* 1966.

Starkman, M. K., editor, *Seventeenth-Century Poetry,* 2 vols., 1967.

Miller, P. S., editor, *Seven Minor Epics, 1596–1624,* 1967.

Lawlis, M., editor, *Elizabethan Prose Fiction,* 1968.

Martz, Louis L., and R. S. Sylvester, editors, *The Anchor Anthology of Seventeenth-Century Verse,* 2 vols., 1969.

Doughtie, E., editor, *Lyrics from English Airs 1595–1622,* 1970.

Zall, P. M., editor, *A Nest of Ninnies and Other English Jestbooks of the Seventeenth Century,* 1970.

Willy, Margaret, editor, *The Metaphysical Poets,* 1971.

Lever, J. W., editor, *Sonnets of the English Renaissance,* 1974.

Seymour-Smith, Martin, editor, *The English Sermon,* vol. 1: *1550–1650,* 1976.

Salgādo, Gāmini, editor, *The Elizabethan Underworld,* 1977.

ALABASTER, William. English. Born in Hadleigh, Suffolk, 27 January 1568. Educated at Westminster School, London; Trinity College, Cambridge (Queen's Scholar), 1584, Fellow, 1589, M.A., 1591; ordained Anglican priest. Married Katherine Fludd in 1618. Chaplain to Robert Devereux, Earl of Essex, 1596–97. Converted to Roman Catholicism, 1597, and arrested and deprived of Anglican orders, 1598; broke parole, went to Rome and enrolled in the English College; returned to England in 1599 and was imprisoned in the Tower of London and later in Framlingham Castle, Suffolk; pardoned on the accession of James I, but was imprisoned again in 1606; travelled in the Low Countries in 1606; at the English College, Rome, 1609; imprisoned by the Inquisition, 1609, declared heretical and fled to England, where he recanted of Catholicism, then recanted his recantation, then recanted again; created Doctor of Divinity at Cambridge in 1614, and given the rich living of Therfield, Hertfordshire; later a chaplain to James I. *Died 28 April 1640.*

PUBLICATIONS

Verse

   The Sonnets, edited by G. M. Story and Helen Gardner. 1959.

Play

   Roxana (in Latin), from a play by Luigi Groto. 1632.

Other

   Apparatus in Revelationem Jesu Christi. 1607.
   De Bestia Apocalyptica. 1621.
   Ecce Sponsus Venit. 1633.
   Spiraculum Tubarum. 1633(?).
   Lexicon Pentaglotton (Hebrew, Chaldean, Syriac, Talmudic-Rabbinic, Arabic; an abridgement of a work by V. Schindler). 1635.

Reading List: *Recusant Poets* by Louise Imogen Guiney, 1938.

*   *   *

During a decade flooded by amorous sonnet sequences, Alabaster, in prison or in hiding after his first conversion to the Roman Catholic Church, wrote some seventy religious sonnets which his modern editors place "among the earliest metaphysical poems of devotion that we have." Composed around 1594–1598 and circulated in manuscripts of which six survive, the sonnets were not printed in full until 1959, edited by G. M. Story and Helen Gardner.

His early, unfinished Latin epic *Eliaeis* and his Latin play *Roxana* were praised by Spenser and Dr. Johnson respectively; his contemporary reputation rested primarily on Latin essays in mystical theology and scriptural interpretation, such as the *Apparatus in Revelationem Jesu Christi,* which, though written in one of his Catholic periods, caused him trouble with the Inquisition. In his calmer later years, reconciled to the Anglican Church, married, made a

Doctor of Divinity at Cambridge (in the same year as Donne), he continued to write learned prose, but produced no more poetry.

Like Donne in his fondness for compression, ingenious working out of imagery, colloquial vigour, and even in occasional punning on his own name (as in "This alabaster box" which he presents in "A New Year's Gift to my Saviour"), he often celebrates paradox, especially in the fifteen sonnets on that paradoxical subject, the Incarnation. At some points, in combining Biblical phrasing and homely imagery, he may suggest Herbert, or, in a sonnet uniting a survey of contemporary religious problems with anxiety about personal commitment, Milton: Sonnet 40, "To Christ (2)" rings with vigorous vocabulary as it portrays angels charged "to break the heads of heresy/Or scatter them in their apostasy,/Or against the Turkish swads to make a stand," before concluding quietly, "Lo here I am lord, whither wilt thou send me?" A recent article compares Alabaster's sonnets with those of La Ceppède, and, indeed, the associations called up by his poems may suggest whatever range of sixteenth and seventeenth century poetry one knows – on the continent or in England – and thus underline the community of devotional and aesthetic traditions of the period.

—Kay Stevenson

AYTON, Sir Robert. Scottish. Born in Kinaldie, Fife, c. 1569. Educated at St. Leonard's College, University of St. Andrews, 1584–88, M.A. 1588. In Paris, 1603; thereafter a courtier of James I: served as Groom of the Privy Chamber, 1608, and Secretary and Master of Requests to Queen Anne; also went on diplomatic mission to Germany, 1609; Secretary and Master of Requests to Queen Henrietta Maria, 1626; Master of the Royal Hospital of St. Katherine, 1636. Knighted, 1612. Granted royal pension, 1611, additional pension, 1620. *Died 25 February 1638.*

PUBLICATIONS

Collections

A Choice of Poems and Songs, edited by Helena Mennie Shire. 1961.
The English and Latin Poems (includes letters), edited by Charles B. Gullans. 1963.

Verse

De Foelici et Semper Augusto Jacobi. 1603.
Basia. 1605.
In Obitum Thomae Rhaedi, Epicidium. 1624.
Lessus in Funere Raphaelis Thorii. 1626.

Reading List: *Song, Dance, and Poetry of the Court of Scotland under King James VI* by Helena Mennie Shire, 1969.

*   *   *

Robert Ayton was born of gentlefolk at Kinaldie in Fife, and graduated from St. Andrew's University. He was already writing verses, not only in the literary Scots of the poets under King James VI of Scotland but also in the neo-Latin of European renaissance style (Latin poems of his were included in the distinguished collection *Delitiae Poetarum Scotorum,* 1637), when he hailed King James's accession to the English throne by a Latin panegyric, printed in Paris in 1603.

The new court of King James in Westminster was hospitable to poets from the north and Ayton soon made his way there. He was knighted in 1612 and served as Secretary to Queen Anne and later to Queen Henrietta Maria. Court service was his life. A gracious and well-loved personality (Ben Jonson was happy to say that Ayton was his friend), the Scots poet composed, now in English, witty, graceful, and dignified pieces to celebrate royal occasions, glad or sorrowful. And from his "jocund muse" flowed many delightful songs of love's pleasures or pains. Tender or teasing, simply but subtly phrased, they were always finely articulate. Some were written to match tunes or songs already known, for instance an air by Campion; more were set in different song-styles by musicians such as Henry Lawes, William Blagrave, and John Wilson.

Sir Robert did not cherish his muse. His vernacular lyrics remained in manuscript, the favourites widely known and sonetimes printed in miscellany or song-book. Watson's *Choice Collection* (1706) featured a number, in tribute to a poet of Scotland. Ayton was the last of King James' "Castalian poets" of the north.

—Helena Mennie Shire

BACON, Francis; Baron Verulam; Viscount St. Albans. English. Born in London, 22 January 1561; elder brother of the diplomatist Anthony Bacon. Educated at Trinity College, Cambridge, 1573–76; Gray's Inn, London, 1576, 1579–82; called to the Bar, 1582. Married Alice Barnham in 1606. Accompanied Sir Amyas Paulet, as Ambassador to France, 1576–79; Member of Parliament for Melcombe Regis, Dorset, 1584, Taunton, 1586, Liverpool, 1589, Middlesex, 1593, Southampton, 1597, Ipswich, 1604, and Cambridge University, 1614; enjoyed the patronage of the Earl of Essex from 1591, and advised him to undertake suppression of Tyrone's rebellion in Ireland, 1598, but later took part in the trial for treason against him, 1601; one of the Queen's learned Counsel, 1595–1603, and King's Counsel from 1604; commissioner for the union of Scotland and England, 1603; Solicitor-General, 1607–13; Attorney-General, 1613–17; Privy Councillor, 1616; Lord Keeper, 1617–18, and Lord Chancellor, 1618; accused of bribery, confessed to general guilt, and stripped of offices, 1621; later pardoned by the king. Knighted, 1603; created Baron Verulam, 1618, and Viscount St. Albans, 1621. *Died 9 April 1626.*

PUBLICATIONS

Collections

Works (including life and letters), edited by James Spedding, R. L. Ellis, and D. D. Heath. 14 vols., 1857–74.

Essays, Advancement of Learning, New Atlantis, and Other Pieces, edited by R. F.
    Jones.   1937.
The New Organon and Related Writings, edited by F. H. Anderson.   1960.

Prose

Essays.   1597; revised edition, 1612, 1625.
A Declaration of the Treasons Committed by Essex.   1601.
A Brief Discourse Touching the Happy Union of the Kingdoms of England and
    Scotland.   1603.
His Apology in Certain Imputations Concerning Essex.   1604.
Certain Considerations Touching the Church of England.   1604.
Of the Proficience and Advancement of Learning, Divine and Humane.   1605; translated
    into Latin as De Augmentis Scientiarum, 1623; as The Advancement of Learning,
    1640.
De Sapientia Veterum.   1609.
The Charge Touching Duels.   1614.
Novum Organum: Summi Angliae Cancellarii Instauratio Magna.   1620.
The History of the Reign of Henry VII.   1622.
Historia Naturalis et Experimentalis: [Historia Ventorum].   1622.
Historia Vitae et Mortis.   1623.
Sylva Sylvarum; or, A Natural History in Ten Centuries (includes The New Atlantis: A
    Work Unfinished).   1626.
Considerations Touching a War with Spain.   1629.
Certain Miscellany Works.   1629.
The Lawyer's Light; or, A Due Direction for the Study of the Law.   1629.
The Elements of the Common Laws of England.   1630.
Cases of Treason.   1641.
The Confession of Faith.   1641.
Three Speeches.   1641.
The Learned Reading upon the Statute of Uses.   1642.
Remains.   1648; as The Mirror of State and Eloquence, 1656.
Scripta in Naturali et Universali Philosophia.   1653.
Resuscitatio; or, Bringing into Public Light Several Pieces of the Works Hitherto
    Sleeping, edited by William Rawley.   2 vols., 1657–70.
Opuscula Varia Posthuma, edited by William Rawley.   1658.
Baconiana; or, Certain Genuine Remains.   1679.

Editor, Apothegms New and Old.   1625.

Translator, Certain Psalms (verse).   1625.

Bibliography: Bacon: A Bibliography of His Works and of Baconiana to the Year 1750 by R.
W. Gibson, 1950.

Reading List: Bacon on Communication and Rhetoric, 1943, and Bacon on the Nature of Man,
1967, both by Karl R. Wallace; Bacon: His Life and Thought by F. H. Anderson, 1962;
Bacon and Renaissance Prose by B. Vickers, 1968; Peace among the Willows: The Political
Philosophy of Bacon by H. B. White, 1968; Bacon: Discovery and the Art of Discourse by Lisa
Jardine, 1975; Bacon and the Style of Science by James Stephens, 1975; Bacon: A Political
Biography by Joel J. Epstein, 1977.

*   *   *

Francis Bacon's main interest lay in matters of interpretation, interpretation of nature in his scientific works, of human constructs in his work on myth and history, of human experience in his essays. *The Advancement of Learning* was devoted to an inventory of human learning in order to discover the deficiencies in history (a result of the faculty of memory), poetry (imagination), and philosophy (reason), and the main hindrances to its advancement, chief among which were the tendencies of his time to create circular fictions (by means of final causation, analogy, the syllogism, and systems) which reduced a mysterious nature to the ordered forms of the mind itself. And so, later in *The New Organon*, when he had narrowed his scope to natural philosophy Bacon had come to realize that the hindrances to the interpretation of nature lay in the human mind itself, which tends to impose order on phenomena (Idols of the Tribe) and does so by its selection of operations and interests (Cave), its use of words (Marketplace), and its construction of philosophical systems (Theater); this tendency he intended to counteract by the inductive method, in which human reason was restrained by strict method, the chief element of which was the use of negative instances which deliberately frustrated the mind's rage for order, in the service of accurate interpretation. What Bacon was after in *The Great Instauration* (of which *The New Organon* formed the second of its six parts, a greatly expanded version of the *Advancement* the first) was the invention of "new models to understand new things," or the discovery of "a new myth for thought," which must now be seen as the reproduction of nature in the human mind instead of the mind proliferating itself outward (Elizabeth Sewell, *The Orphic Voice*). Such a "new model" was created by translating the "common logic" of words into a new logic of things, so that invention or finding arguments became finding experiments (Part 3), judgment or constructing arguments and refuting sophisms became the operating of scientific method and restricting the human mind (*New Organon*, Part 2), memory became the setting out of discoveries in tables (Part 4), and so on.

The *Instauration* was never pushed to completion, but scattered images throughout suggest that it was informed by the grand vision of repairing the Fall, which had caused a divorce between the human mind and nature and had caused the mind to turn in on itself; Bacon's method would rectify the senses by experiment, would "re-marry" the purged senses to the mind, rectify the mind by the inductive method, then "re-marry" the mind to nature and hence lead man to the Adamic state in which his investigations would be like playing with the God of created nature. *The New Atlantis* is Bacon's visionary myth of the completion of the *Instauration*; in it, the pious and charitable actions of Bensalem proceed from a model of the mind (Salomon's House) rectified by the inductive method so as to become an accurate mirror of God's Creation. For Bacon, myth and image prescinded the logic of words in a way different from the inductive method but complementary to it; hence in his book of myth interpretation, *The Wisdom of the Ancients*, he presented pagan myth as the pathway to things, closer to experience and the true interpretation of political, moral, and natural matters than philosophy, both in its focus and in its imitative method (see Sewell). Of considerable importance to the understanding of Bacon's science of interpretation is *The History of the Reign of King Henry VII*, long admired for its vigorous prose style and its relentless drive to discover the true causes of human events.

Bacon's *Essays* exhibit an informal operation of the inductive method as applied to the interpretation of human experience. They exist in three versions. The slim volume of 1597 contains ten essays in the aphoristic form recommended by the *Advancement* whereby, in order to lead readers to discover things for themselves, only direct observations are admitted and such things as illustrations, examples, and transitions are excluded. Their style is curt or Senecan (in reaction to the Ciceronian periodic style which Bacon considered one of the diseases of learning), sparing of modifiers and connectives, pulling concepts into juxtaposition by parallelism and antithesis. In their insistence on the empirical basis of experience, they teach the usefulness and limits of interpretation, and their aphoristic manner mirrors their matter. The edition of 1612 was much expanded: it contained revisions of the original essays and twenty-eight new ones, and expanded the scope of subjects treated beyond mere civil issues to morality and the life of man in general (love, death, fortune); the style is now less curt, more antithetical, imagistic, and suggestive; and the essays are more fully formed, either by symmetry (the revised "Of Studies") or by contrast, as when two parts revolve around a large contrast in subject or point of view ("Of Nobility"). The final edition of 1625 contains fifty-eight essays; its range of subjects is expanded still more to include manners as well as civil and moral matters; its style is more relaxed, full of images, illustrations, examples, even personal reminiscences; and the essays show a greater fulness and coherence of structure, often made explicit by formal subdivisions ("Of Friendship"). This is a fully unified volume, containing cross-references and paired essays ("Of Building" and "Of Gardens," "Of Beauty" and "Of Deformity," "Of Envy" and "Of Love").

Bacon's *Essays* are designed to make the reader examine rather than accept ideas, and most precepts therein are therefore provisional and occasionally disturbing. Their keynote is tonal complexity – the usefulness of a practice as well as its corruptions ("Of Usury"), moral judgment offered then blocked ("Of Negotiating"), contempt for a habit changing to precepts for using it ("Of Cunning"), full entrance into an amoral point of view ending with sudden moral judgment ("Of Simulation"). As an essay proceeds it tends to offer constant re-evaluation of its subject, whether it be in the form of a series of associative links, as in "Of Delays," or a two-part structure balancing excessive and moderate views of a subject in the high and middle styles respectively ("Of Adversity"). "Of Truth" is one of the finest examples of such subtle re-evaluation; it starts with a consideration of the difficulty of seeking truth but then shifts to the divine imperative to follow truth no matter what the consequences; the shift is accomplished imagistically by moving from man-made half-lights to the full light of Creation, syntactically from a loose style to a series of tight tripartite sentences, and allusively from our life as it now seems to us (after Pilate's denial) to our life as God sees it from Creation to Fall to the Second Coming evoked by its last sentence.

—Walter R. Davis

BARNES, Barnabe. English. Born in Yorkshire c. 1569. Educated at Brasenose College, Oxford, 1586. A volunteer in the expedition led by the Earl of Essex to Dieppe, to assist Henry IV, 1591. *Died in December 1609.*

PUBLICATIONS

Collections

Poems, edited by Alexander B. Grosart. 1875.

Verse

Parthenophil and Parthenophe: Sonnets, Madrigals, Elegies, and Odes. 1593; edited by Victor A. Doyno, 1971.
A Divine Century of Spiritual Sonnets. 1595.

Play

The Devil's Charter (produced 1607).   1607; edited by J. H. Farmer, 1913.

Other

Four Books of Offices Enabling Private Persons for the Service of Princes.   1606.

Reading List: *Lyric Forms in the Sonnet Sequences of Barnes* by Philip E. Blank, Jr., 1974.

*   *   *

The unifying characteristics of Barnabe Barnes's life and work are consistent extravagance and artfulness. His earliest publication, *Parthenophil and Parthenophe* (Virgin-Lover and Virgin), was intended to be anonymous, but the sole surviving copy has an insertion which identifies the author. The volume presents a wide variety of types of poems: sonnets, elegies, odes, madrigals, and sestinas. The volume narrates a love affair; several poems, such as Sonnet 66 and Elegies 4 and 5, have a pleasing combination of a life-like tone and a clever wit. The story sequence has an unusual solution to the conventional woes of the Petrarchan lover: in the last major poem the lover casts a magical spell upon the mistress and rapes her. This extraordinary conclusion is rendered in a triple sestina which is, in part, a translation and transformation of poems by Theocritus and Virgil. The volume represents the Renaissance ability to emphasize the human while absorbing and transforming earlier culture; the poems include translations from many Classical and Renaissance poets. The discriminating reader will find this major work of a minor writer to be both an example of growth of prosodic control and a significantly different treatment of a tradition, combining Petrarchan idealism and classical eroticism.

The wit and rhetorical flourish of the secular love poems are duplicated, but the object of adoration is different, in *A Divine Centurie of Spiritual Sonnets*, Barnes's collection of devotional verse. The volume offers a combination of the rhetorical method of poetic development with the meditative habit of mind. The tone of worship is effectively rendered.

Barnes's achievement also includes several non-poetic pieces. *Four Bookes of Offices* is a conduct book. The text is developed in terms of the classical virtues. It includes extensive translations or paraphrases and personal remarks, such as Barnes's complimentary thoughts about the executed rebel Essex. Barnes's final work is in yet another genre. *The Divils Charter* is a melodramatic complicated revenge play. Barnes represents, in a minor key, the variety of achievement which typifies an Elizabethan man of letters.

—Victor A. Doyno

BARNFIELD, Richard.   English.   Born in Norbury, Shropshire, baptized 13 June 1574. Educated at Brasenose College, Oxford, 1589–92, B.A. 1592. Country gentleman: settled at Darlaston, Staffordshire. *Died 6 March 1627.*

PUBLICATIONS

Collections

Poems 1594–1598, edited by Edward Arber.   1882.
Poems, edited by Montague Summers.   1936.

Verse

The Affectionate Shepherd, Containing the Complaint of Daphnis for the Love of Ganymede.   1594.
Cynthia, with Certain Sonnets and The Legend of Cassandra.   1595.
The Encomium of Lady Pecunia, The Complaint of Poetry for the Death of Liberality, The Combat Between Conscience and Covetousness, Poems in Divers Humours.   1598; revised edition, 1605.

Reading List: *Barnfield, Colin's Child* by Harry Morris, 1963.

*   *   *

Richard Barnfield demonstrated at an early age that he was capable of emulating the styles of England's most skillful poets, but the curious variety in his three slim volumes attests to the difficulty he encountered in developing his art. About a year after he came to London with a B.A. from Oxford he published his first volume, *The Affectionate Shepherd*. Its most ambitious piece is its title poem, a two-part complaint in which an aging Daphnis bemoans the absence of his youthful Ganymede (a situation derived from Virgil's second Eclogue). Possibly the poet hoped to exploit the popularity of Shakespeare's *Venus and Adonis* (1593) or to invite comparison with it, for Barnfield's poem is cast in the same stanza form and imitates its diction and imagery:

> His Ivory-white and Alabaster skin
> Is staind throughout with rare Vermillion red,
> Whose twinckling starrie lights do never blin
> To shine on lovely Venus (Beauties bed:)
> But as the Lillie and the blushing Rose,
> So white and red on him in order growes.

Despite Barnfield's success with Shakespeare's style, the poem is encumbered with narrative inconsistencies, a recurring fault in Barnfield's longer poems. The remainder of the volume is made up of diverse matter indeed: a pastoral poem celebrating the contentment of rustic life; a sonnet which attempts to be an envoy to the first two pieces; a confusing harangue entitled "The Complaint of Chastity"; and "Helen's Rape," an amusing piece of nonsense, sometimes brilliant, satirizing by implication the hexameters it is written in:

> Happie Helen, Woman's most woonder, beautiful Helen.
> Oh would God (quod he) with a flattering tongue he repeated:
> Oh would God (quod he) that I might deserve to be husband
> To such a happy huswife, to such a beautiful Helen.

Although there are some happy moments in *The Affectionate Shepherd*, one senses the truth of Harry Morris's observation: Barnfield pasted poems together to complete a first volume.

In a preface to his second volume, *Cynthia, with Certain Sonnets and The Legend of Cassandra*, Barnfield announces that his title poem, a paean to Elizabeth, is "the first imitation of the verse of that excellent Poet, Maister Spenser, in his Faerie Queene." Since the poem's situation is taken from Peele's *The Arraignment of Paris*, little room exists for originality; nonetheless the narrative is well-structured, the verses highly accomplished. Following "Cynthia" Ganymede returns as the object of praise in twenty sonnets, most of which are better than competent. In the most imposing work in this volume, "The Legend of Cassandra," Barnfield takes up the Ovidian-Mythological genre, elements of which had informed his earlier pastoral laments, but, as in those pastorals, Barnfield's inability or lack of concern to keep his narrative free from extraneous elements (such as several stanzas late in the poem in praise of Cassandra's chastity when initially she is portrayed as treacherous) mars his characterization and muddles the poem's effect.

In his third volume Barnfield tries his hand at lightly ironic verse satire ("The Encomium to Lady Pecunia"), a pastoral elegy for an unusual "personage" ("The Complaint of Poetry, for the Death of Liberality"), and a debate poem ("The Combat Between Conscience and Covetessnesse"). Included in the volume are eight "Poems: in Divers Humors," two of which were printed in *The Passionate Pilgrim* and attributed to Shakespeare ("If music and sweet poetry agree"; "As it fell upon a day/In the merry month of May"). It is a workmanlike volume, the longer poems showing none of the structural deficiencies of those in his earlier volumes, but lacking their occasional brilliance. Some of the "Poems: in Divers Humors," as do the sonnets to Ganymede, suggest that the abilities of this talented young poet, whose literary career lasted only four years, were best employed upon the short forms.

—Frank Fabry

BEAUMONT, Sir John.   English.   Born, probably at Grace-Dieu, Leicestershire, in 1582; brother of the dramatist Francis Beaumont. Educated at Oxford University, 1596–98; Inner Temple, London. Married a lady of the Fortescue family; four sons. Succeeded to his father's estates, 1605; court career under the patronage of his relative, the Duke of Buckingham. Associated with Edmund Bolton in plans for a Royal Academy. Created Baronet, 1626. *Died 19 April 1627.*

PUBLICATIONS

Collections

Poems, edited by Alexander B. Grosart.   1869.
The Shorter Poems, edited by Roger D. Sell.   1974.

Verse

The Metamorphosis of Tobacco.   1602.
Bosworth Field, with a Taste of the Variety of Other Poems.   1629.

Play

The Theatre of Apollo (produced 1625).   Edited by W. W. Greg, 1926.

Reading List: "Beaumont's 'The Crowne of Thornes': A Report" by Ruth Wallerstein in *Journal of English and Germanic Philology,* 1954.

*   *   *

Sir John Beaumont recommends, and himself illustrates, a style which Hobbes must later have admired: neither too prosaic, nor "dancing"; avoiding ostentatious roughness and Metaphysical obscurities; favouring the couplet, as involving little padding; emulating the Greeks and Romans only in

> Pure phrase, fit Epithets, a sober care
> Of Metaphors, descriptions cleare, yet rare,
> Similitudes contracted smooth and round,
> Not vext by learning, but with Nature crown'd;

and otherwise using normal contemporary English, with exactly referential statement rather than figurative elaboration. This style contributes a steady tempo and a certain matter-of-factness to, say, "Bosworth Field."

Less soberly, Beaumont can anticipate Waller. Many pieces addressed to James I, Charles I, and Buckingham are patently sycophantic and ornately artificial, recalling the imagery and paraphernalia of a court masque. And in "Bosworth Field" Henry VII, idealized as a forerunner of James I both in pedigree and as unifier of the realm, dreams a tableau-vision of his glorious descendant.

Again, whereas Ben Jonson reproved "Womens-*Poets*" who "write a verse, as smooth, as soft, as creame;/In which there is no torrent, nor scarce streame," Beaumont can envisage a milky smoothness redeemed by torrential force: "When verses like a milky torrent flow,/ they equall temper in the Poet show." His stream metaphor, and the *media via* proposed, anticipate the qualities for which Denham, in a famous passage, emulated the Thames. Hardly less than "Cooper's Hill," "Bosworth Field," where Beaumont's balanced smoothness can be seen at large, became a touchstone of Augustan literary taste, though what was then an asset has since become something of a liability.

To Beaumont's contemporaries, however, including Ben Jonson, he was primarily a Renaissance Christian Humanist. He himself stresses that poetry has a religious and ethical role; its true themes are "brave examples, sage instructions" and "celestiall things," its aim to "knit chaines of vertue in the hearers mind." His translations from Latin and Greek are of poems which recommend the ancient rural simplicities and self-examination, Stoicism and Christianity. His funeral elegies, besides expressing affectionate grief, trumpet the fame of the dead for the moral enlightenment of posterity. His Christian-Stoic didactic poems declaim an Augustinian view of man and traditional concept of right reason, with an occasional anti-Petrarchanism and a certain neo-Platonism. And, despite its sycophancy, "Bosworth Field" shares with Edmund Bolton's proposed Royal Academy the aim of presenting the great men of British history in an effort to raise the tone of the Stuart court. Writing from these interests, Beaumont sometimes achieves considerable force.

His most distinctive work is his more purely religious poetry, which is again not forward-looking. Sometimes he conceives his state in powerfully Ignatian terms, fluctuating between a black desolation conscious of Hell's gaping jaws and a joy so ecstatic as to be fearful. The best writing in "Bosworth Field," the portrayal of Richard III, is actually a study of damnation. And his "sacerdotal" writing, extensively in the unpublished "The Crowne of Thornes" and more pithily in some shorter poems, encourages his fellow-religionists to vicarious participation in biblical events with a sometimes sharply Metaphysical wit and an ability to spiritualize the physical. Despite his successful court career, Beaumont, a recusant, is the voice of the persecuted Old Religion.

Sometimes there is conflict between his new-style acquiescing conformity and his old-fashioned religious and ethical concerns. But his best work has a unique interest in its fusion of the neo-classical and Augustan stylistic impulses with the themes of an earlier age.

—Roger D. Sell

BEAUMONT, Joseph. English. Born in Hadleigh, Suffolk, 13 March 1616. Educated at Hadleigh Grammar School; Peterhouse, Cambridge, 1631–38, B.A. 1634, M.A. 1638. Married Miss Brownrigg in 1650; six children. Fellow, Peterhouse, 1636 until expelled by the Puritans, 1644; returned to his home at Hadleigh; Non-Resident Rector of Kelshall, Hertfordshire, 1643; appointed Prebend, Ely Cathedral, 1651, installed 1660; lived at his wife's home at Tatingston Place, Suffolk, 1650–60; appointed a king's chaplain, 1660; Master of Jesus College, Cambridge, 1662–63; appointed Master of Peterhouse, 1663, and Professor of Divinity, Cambridge University, 1674. *Died 25 September 1699.*

PUBLICATIONS

Collections

Complete Poems, edited by Alexander B. Grosart.   2 vols., 1877–80.
Minor Poems, edited by Eloise Robinson.   1914.

Verse

Psyche; or, Love's Mystery, Displaying the Intercourse Betwixt Christ and the Soul.   1648; revised edition, edited by Charles Beaumont, 1702.
Original Poems in English and Latin, edited by John Gee.   1749.

Other

Some Observations upon the Apology of Henry More for His Mystery of Godliness.   1665.

Reading List: "St. Teresa in Beaumont's *Psyche,*" in *Journal of English and Germanic Philology,* 1963, and "A Portrait of Stuart Orthodoxy," in *Church Quarterly Review,* 1964, both by P. G. Stanwood.

*   *   *

Joseph Beaumont composed nearly two hundred brief lyrics, mostly devotional, in the manner of Herbert and Crashaw, but his chief distinction is to have written the longest narrative poem in the English language. His *Psyche; Or, Love's Mystery* consists of 38,670 lines in *Venus and Adonis* stanzas. Although the narrative is chiefly concerned with the attempts of Satan to seduce the young woman, Psyche, who is protected and instructed by her guardian angel, Phylax, nearly half the poem is devoted to a retelling of the life of Jesus. Psyche is tested by lust, heresy, persecution, and dereliction; with the help of Phylax she passes all these tests and, in the last lines of the poem, dies with the assurance that her heavenly yearnings will be fulfilled.

The narrative interest is very slight and Beaumont is relentlessly didactic. All his characters are allegorical except for Satan, whose energy and proud defiance remind one of Milton's fallen archangel. Both the length of the poem and the allegorical method invite comparison with *The Faerie Queene*. Beaumont had reservations about Spenser: "Right fairly dress'd were his welfeatur'd *Queen,*/Did not her Mask too much her beauties screen." Nevertheless his allegorical figures frequently resemble Spenser's, and the Palace of Ecclesia episode reminds one of the House of Alma. The other obvious comparison is with Bunyan. But Spenser and Bunyan, both committed to a narrative, use their allegorical characters in the action, while Beaumont's figures are, with few exceptions, quite inactive. The quest, which gives strength and unity to Spenser's and Bunyan's narratives, is lacking in *Psyche*.

Beaumont's verse flows smoothly but without power. He pays the highest praise to Crashaw, Herbert, Marino, and Tasso. And his allegorical figures frequently recall Virgil. But his verse is too lacking in character to suggest a pedigree. It is simply competent English verse, seldom distinguished by qualities of sound, meter, or metaphor. The following stanza, spoken by Satan, is unusually vigorous.

> I yield not yet; Defiance *Heav'n*, said He,
> And though I cannot reach thee with my fire,
> Yet my unconquer'd Brain shall able be
> To grapple with thee; nor canst thou be higher
> Than my *brave Spight*: Know, though below I dwell,
> Heav'n has no stouter Hearts than strut in Hell.

A careful poet would not have allowed such a combination as "Know, though below," and *strut* is the wrong word in Satan's mouth. But the lines do suggest energy and strength.

Beaumont's besetting vice is prolixity. To tell the reader that virtue is active, he uses eleven stanzas of analogies and thirteen stanzas of general statement – 144 lines in all. Ecclesia, described in 24 stanzas, has 22 handmaidens, described in 45 stanzas. There are fine passages in *Psyche*, but Beaumont's work is not likely to appeal to the general reader. Scholars, however, will be interested in it as an excellent example of English baroque sensibility.

—Thomas Wheeler

BENLOWES, Edward. English. Born at Brent Hall, Finchingfield, Essex, 12 July 1602; eldest son of a recusant family. Educated as a Protestant at St. John's College, Cambridge, 1620–22; Lincoln's Inn, London, 1622–23. Inherited Brent Hall in 1613, and lived as a country gentleman, except for a grand tour of Europe, 1627–30; abandoned Catholicism by 1630. Captain of a troop of horse in Essex Militia by 1636; took no part in the Civil War until 1648, when he was commissioned in Royalist army. After destruction of Brent Hall by fire in 1653, lived in London; sold estate, 1657, and involved in litigation, 1657–65; lived with niece at Mapledurham, Oxfordshire, 1665–67; briefly imprisoned for debt in Oxford Castle, 1667; lived in poverty in Oxford after 1667. *Died 18 December 1676.*

Reading List: *Benlowes: Biography of a Minor Poet* by Harold Jenkins, 1952 (includes bibliography); "Benlowes' Borrowings from Herbert" by E. E. Duncan-Jones, in *Review of English Studies*, 1955.

*   *   *

Edward Benlowes is one of those unfortunate authors whose chief claim to fame consists of having been derided by a greater writer. He was pilloried for the extravagance and eccentricity of his style in Samuel Butler's "Character of a Small Poet," yet his verse is not without life and a certain quaint attractiveness.

Discussion of Benlowes may be confined to his spiritual epic, *Theophila*, since his handful of shorter English poems shows similar characteristics. The subject of *Theophila* is the spiritual warfare and victory of the soul, celebrated in thirteen cantos. Most of the poem is in English, but parts are in Latin, while some English sections, for no discernible reason, reappear in Latin later. For the most part Benlowes uses a strange stanza composed of a decasyllable, an octosyllable and an alexandrine rhyming together, but verses in other forms are inserted from time to time. The argument is as incomprehensible as the construction, for in Benlowes the witty, strong-lined style was carried to such an extreme that it is hard to gain any sense of connection between one stanza and the next. *Theophila* provides an experience more like solving a puzzle than reading a poem. This effect is increased by Benlowes' fondness for borrowing from his contemporaries: lines from Milton, Jonson, Herbert, and others, only slightly altered, are woven into his text throughout, providing all the pleasures of a literary quiz.

Benlowes' frequent coinages contribute to his obscurity and oddity. He is fond of learned or technical expressions ("ovant," "angelence," "collyrium," "Danaize") and compounds ("Sodom-storms," "dwarf-words," "woolly-curdled"). These are jumbled together with colloquialisms and abbreviations, just as the poem mixes mystical ardours with political satire and natural description. One mixed metaphor treads upon another's heels, while startling epithets, far-fetched conceits, and word-play of every kind are brought in at any opportunity. Adam "yielding to a wo[e]man, made man yeild to woe"; Theophila "fears want of fears ... depraved by vice, deprived by grace"; drunkards are warned "healths, health deprive"; blood is "luke-warm claret," men, "our wormships." Distortion of syntax and omission of connecting words produce packed lines whose difficulty is reminiscent of Hopkins, and titles for the cantos like "Prelibation" and "Disincantation" hardly make the course of the poem any clearer.

Yet that same lack of discrimination and judgement which makes *Theophila* an example of the metaphysical style at its worst also contributes to its disarming zest. Exhausting though the poem is, it is seldom boring; and the glittering heap contains real gems among the curious baubles and coloured glass. The poet who could write "th'icy mantle of a wrinkled skin/ Candies the bristles of thy chin" could also produce the strangely beautiful line "No planet seen to sail through that dead ebb of night." Benlowes' imagination is fired by genuine ardour, and though the results are usually odd and not infrequently comic, they are far from being the work of a seventeenth-century William McGonagall. *Theophila* is not bad verse; it is poetry run mad.

—Margaret Forey

BRETON, Nicholas. English. Born in London c. 1545; stepson of George Gascoigne, *q.v.* Possibly educated at Oriel College, Oxford. Married Ann Sutton in 1592; two sons, one daughter. Mary, Countess of Pembroke, was an early patron – little else is known of his life. *Died c. 1626.*

PUBLICATIONS

Collections

A *The Works in Verse and Prose,* edited by Alexander B. Grosart. 2 vols., 1879.
A Mad World My Masters and Other Prose Works, edited by Ursula Kentish-Wright. 2 vols., 1929.

Verse

A Small Handful of Fragrant Flowers. 1575.
A Flourish upon Fancy. 1577; revised edition, 1582.
Breton's Bower of Delights. 1591; edited by Hyder E. Rollins, 1933.
The Pilgrimage to Paradise. 1592.
Mary Magdalen's Love, A Solemn Passion. 1595.
The Passions of the Spirit. 1599.
Pasquil's Mad-Cap and Mad-Cap's Message. 1600.
The Second Part of Pasquil's Mad-Cap, The Fool's-Cap. 1600.
Pasquil's Mistress. 1600.
Pasquil's Pass and Passeth Not. 1600.
Melancholic Humours. 1600; edited by G. B. Harrison, 1929.
No Whipping nor Ripping, But a Kind Friendly Snipping. 1601; edited by A. Davenport, 1951.
A Divine Poem: The Ravished Soul and the Blessed Weeper. 1601.
An Excellent Poem upon the Longing of a Blessed Heart to Be with Christ. 1601.
The Soul's Heavenly Exercise. 1601.
Mary Magdalen's Lamentations. 1601.
The Mother's Blessing. 1602; revised edition, 1621.

A True Description of Unthankfulness.   1602.
Old Mad-Cap's New Gallimaufry.   1602.
The Passion of a Discontented Mind.   1602.
The Soul's Harmony.   1602.
The Passionate Shepherd.   1604.
Honest Counsel.   1605.
The Soul's Immortal Crown.   1605.
The Honour of Valour.   1605.
I Would and Would Not.   1614.
The Hate of Treason.   1616.
Machiavel's Dog.   1617.
Poems Not Hitherto Reprinted, edited by Jean Robertson.   1952.

Fiction

The Miseries of Mavillia.   1597.
The Strange Fortunes of Two Excellent Princes.   1600.
Grimello's Fortunes.   1604; edited by E. G. Morice, in *Two Pamphlets,* 1936.

Other

The Works of a Young Wit.   1577.
A Discourse in Commendation of Francis Drake.   1581.
The History of Don Federigo de Terra Nuova.   1590.
The Will of Wit, Wit's Will or Will's Wit.   1597.
Auspicante Jehova.   1597.
Wit's Trenchmour.   1597.
A Post with a Mad Packet of Letters.   1602; revised edition, 1603; part 2, 1605; revised
   edition, 1607, 1609.
Wonders Worth the Hearing.   1602.
A Dialogue Full of Pith and Pleasure Between Three Philosophers.   1603.
A Merry Dialogue Betwixt the Taker and the Mistaker.   1603; as *A Mad World My
   Masters,* 1635.
A Piece of Friar Bacon's Brazen-Head's Prophecy.   1604.
An Old Man's Lesson and a Young Man's Love.   1605; edited by E. G. Morice, in *Two
   Pamphlets,* 1936.
I Pray You Be Not Angry.   1605.
Choice, Chance, and Change; or, Conceits in Their Colours.   1606.
A Murmurer.   1607.
Wit's Private Wealth.   1607.
The Uncasing of Machiavel's Instructions to His Son.   1613; as *Machiavel's Advice,*
   1681.
Characters upon Essays Moral and Divine.   1615.
*The Good and the Bad; or, Descriptions of the Worthies and Unworthies of This
   Age.*   1616; abridged edition, as *England's Selected Characters,* 1643.
Crossing of Proverbs: Cross-Answers and Cross-Humours.   2 vols, 1616; revised
   edition, 1676(?).
The Court and the Country.   1618; edited by S. Pargellis and W. H. Dunham, Jr., in
   Complaint and Reform in England 1436–1714, 1938.
Conceited Letters Newly Laid Open.   1618.
Strange News Out of Divers Countries.   1622.
Soothing of Proverbs.   1626.

Fantastics, Serving for a Perpetual Prognostication.   1626; selection edited by Brian
   Rhys, as *The Twelve Moneths*, 1927.
The Figure of Four; or, A Handful of Sweet Flowers.   2 vols., 1626–31.

Bibliography: *Breton: A Concise Bibliography* by S. A. and D. R. Tannenbaum, 1947; *Breton*
by T. R. Howlett, 1975.

Reading List: *Breton und Seine Prosaschriften* by T. F. C. Kuskop, 1902; *Breton as a
Pamphleteer* by Nellie E. Monroe, 1929.

*   *   *

Except for a period of eight years when he may have been on the Continent (1582–1590),
Nicholas Breton steadily published poetry and prose in nearly equal quantity for almost 50
years. The variety in his extensive canon gives proof of one who was obliged to write for a
living. We find love lyrics and "pastorals"; meditative, moral, and religious poems; satires in
prose and verse; pamphlets, letters, dialogues, character sketches, and essays. Although
Grosart, the first editor of Breton's collected works, praised the prose for its economy of
expression and attention to specific detail (and in his enthusiasm recommended its style to his
contemporaries as a corrective to their rhetorical excesses), Breton's prose is of little literary
worth nor was it influential in his own time, though some was popular. While his prose is
interesting as an index of popular taste, its study belongs more to the realm of sociology than
to literature.

Breton's poetry is somewhat more significant: he published just before and throughout
England's most important period of poetic development, and early in his career he is
recognized by Puttenham to be among that "crew of courtly makers, noblemen and
gentlemen ... who have written exceedingly well" (*The Arte of English Poesie*, 1589). His
early poems show the influence of his stepfather, George Gascoigne, in their metrical
heaviness and their dependence upon alliteration (characteristics which, except in his few
pastoral poems, his later poetry never entirely lost). They place the poet squarely in the native
tradition of versifying, separating him from the later English Petrarchans like Watson,
Sidney, and Drayton – even when his subject is love, as "The Toyes of an Idle Head":

> If I had skill to frame a cunning Vearse
> Wherein I mought my loathsome life lament,
> Or able were in rimes for to rehearse
> The gryping griefes, that now my haeart have hent:
>   Such privie panges of love I could descrie,
>   As never any lover felt but I.

Yet, despite his provincialism he would later learn from the new poets to handle gracefully
the content of the imported pastoral, as in this simple but charming trochaic passage
reminiscent of Campion from *The Passionate Shepherd*:

> Pretty twinckling starry eyes,
> How did nature first devise,
> Such a sparkling in your sight,
> As to give love such delight,
> As to make him like a flye,
> Play with looks untill he die?

Although his pastoral lyrics comprise a very small fraction of his poems, Breton's name
remained alive to posterity through those which first appeared in *Britton's Bowre of Delights*

and, subsequently, in *England's Helicon*, an anthology still admired in the nineteenth century when it was reissued.

More characteristic of the bulk of Breton's work are those long poems in six-line or rhyme royal stanzas affirming the received values of his time – in successive poems he is against "unthankfulness," for honor, against treason, for constancy, humility, patience, and wisdom. An extension of this moralizing attitude is found in the satires of his "Pasquil" series, four lengthy verse tracts all published in 1600, attacking in catalogue fashion the general abuses of his (or any) time or decrying such unwholesome types as the proud courtier, the lady quean, and the wealthy beggar. These poems bear the stamp of a poet in search of a patron and a market, variously dedicated as they are to members of the nobility and the wealthy middle-class alike and attempting overtly to appeal to the widest possible readership.

At the end of his career Breton was apparently reduced to doing hack-work for booksellers; nonetheless his name will endure because of those well wrought pastoral lyrics which found their way into *England's Helicon*, where they are displayed to advantage among lyrics by Sidney, Lodge, Drayton, Marlowe, Ralegh, and Shakespeare.

—Frank Fabry

BROWNE, Sir Thomas.   English.   Born in London, 19 October 1605. Educated at Winchester College, 1616–23; Broadgates Hall, now Pembroke College, Oxford, matriculated 1623, B.A. 1626, M.A. 1629; studied medicine at the University of Leyden, M.D. 1633; granted Oxford M.D. 1637. Married Dorothy Mileham in 1641; twelve children. Practised medicine in Norwich, 1637 until the end of his life. Knighted, 1671. *Died 19 October 1682.*

PUBLICATIONS

Collections

> *Works,* edited by Geoffrey Keynes.   6 vols., 1928–31; revised edition, 4 vols., 1964.
> *The Major Works,* edited by C. A. Patrides.   1977.

Prose

> *Religio Medici.*   1642; revised edition, 1643.
> *Pseudodoxia Epidemica; or, Enquiries into Very Many Received Tenets and Commonly Presumed Truths.*   1646; revised edition, 1650, 1658, 1669, 1669, 1672.
> *Hydriotaphia, Urn-Burial; or, A Discourse of the Sepulchral Urns Lately Found in Norfolk, Together with The Garden of Cyrus; or, The Quincuncial Lozenge, or Network Plantations of the Ancients, Artificially, Naturally, Mystically Considered.*   1658.
> *Certain Miscellany Tracts,* edited by Archbishop Tenison.   1683.

Posthumous Works. 1712.
Christian Morals, edited by John Jeffery. 1716.
Notes and Letters on the Natural History of Norfolk, edited by Thomas Southwell. 1902.

Bibliography: *A Bibliography of Browne* by Geoffrey Keynes, 1924; revised edition, 1968.

Reading List: *Science and Imagination in Browne* by Egon S. Merton, 1949; *Browne: A Doctor's Life of Science and Faith* by J. S. Finch, 1950; *Browne: A Biographical and Critical Study* by Frank L. Huntley, 1962; *Browne: A Man of Achievement in Literature* by Joan Bennett, 1962; *Studies in Browne* by Robert Ralston Cawley and Gen Yost, 1965; *The Strategy of Truth: A Study of Browne* by Leonard Nathanson, 1967.

*   *   *

The narrator in Sir Thomas Browne's *Religio Medici* describes his life as "a miracle of thirty yeares, which to relate, were not a History, but a peece of Poetry, and would sound to common eares like a fable." But Browne's own life was certainly not a poem, much less a miracle. The fable must instead be sought in the works of his fertile imagination.

Browne's style depends on the generalisation he ventures in *Religio Medici* ("The Religion of a Physician") that man is "naturally inclined unto Rhythme." Such rhythm implied for Browne the existence of an ultimate order which, emanating from the One, is diversified into the Many – witness in the first instance the diverse yet harmonious aspects of the created universe, and in the second the variable yet unified tonal range of the given work of art. In this respect Browne's characteristic "doublets" – his sequentially arranged synonymous words or parallel phrases – may not be considered in isolation since they form part of his intention to create effects which, cumulatively, assert the all-pervasive presence of order. The basic principle he articulated in the penultimate paragraph of *The Garden of Cyrus* applies as much to style as to the theme delineated: "All things began in order, so shall they end, and so shall they begin again; according to the ordainer of order and mysticall Mathematicks of the City of Heaven." For Browne no less than for many of his contemporaries such as Herbert, language is sacramental in that its several units inclusive of words are sufficiently emblematic or allusive to intimate the divine through the profane. The attitude is characteristic not of Christians generally but of Christian Platonists in particular.

Browne wore his Platonism with casual abandon, it is true. But as *Religio Medici* confirms explicitly enough, Platonism had in any case been adapted in the symbolic form it had assumed ever since the advent of the legendary Hermes Trismegistus, the supposed Egyptian author of widely venerated works believed to have predated Plato although actually written in the second century A.D. The fundamental Hermetic concept of "hieroglyphics" led Browne to accept, in *Religio Medici*, that "this visible world is but a picture of the invisible," itself but a different way of affirming the presence of a transcendent principle as stated in *Christian Morals*: "The Hand of Providence writes often by Abbreviatures, Hieroglyphicks or short Characters." Confirmation of this principle in *Religio Medici* is ample, and may most evidently be discerned in the assertion of the vertical order inherent in the Scale of Nature and the horizontal order of history that extends from the creation through the Last Judgement.

Pseudodoxia Epidemica ("Vulgar Errors") demonstrates through its several amendments Browne's unfailing commitment to the latest developments in various disciplines. The method is vital; the constant appeal to the triad of experience, reason, and authority, proclaims that Browne had, like Bacon, intended to suggest the best possible ways to journey through the labyrinthine routes that lead to truth. Even while annihilating "vulgar errors," however, he was responding to them through the rhythms of his prose. His major scientific treatise is, all too obviously, articulated in aesthetic terms.

The connexion between the jointly published *Hydriotaphia* and *The Garden of Cyrus* has been described as "nexus through contrast": the two works are related in that "the obsession of death in one, is balanced by the celebration of life in the other," even as "accident is opposed to design, body to soul, time to space, ignorance to knowledge, substance to form, darkness to light, mutability to immutabilty" (see Huntley, *Browne*). *Hydriotaphia* poses the problem of the incomprehensible physical evil of death, to resolve it at last through the haunting rhythms of its final paragraphs where death is subsumed within the larger vision of immortality. *The Garden of Cyrus* extends the awareness of the other work, save that here the tonal range tends constantly toward a joyous whimsey. The underlying purpose remains serious in the extreme, however. It coincides with Browne's sustained concern to establish "how nature Geometrizeth, and observeth order in all things." His ultimate aspiration was clearly the attainment of harmony: the rhythm within the universe as within art.

—C. A. Patrides

———————

BROWNE, William.   English.   Born in Tavistock, Devon, in 1591. Educated at Tavistock Grammar School; Exeter College, Oxford, M.A. 1625; Inner Temple, London, 1611. Married the daughter of Sir Thomas Eversfield; two sons. Tutor at Oxford to Robert Dormer, Earl of Carnarvon, 1624; subsequently in the service of the Earls of Pembroke at Wilton. *Died in 1643*.

PUBLICATIONS

Collections

> *Whole Works*, edited by W. C. Hazlitt.   2 vols., 1868.
> *Poems*, edited by Gordon Goodwin.   2 vols., 1894.

Verse

> *Two Elegies*, with Fulke Greville.   1613.
> *Britannia's Pastorals*.   2 vols., 1613–16; book 3 edited by T. C. Croker, 1852.
> *The Shepherd's Pipe*, with George Wither.   1614.
> *Original Poems*, edited by Egerton Brydges.   1816.

Play

> *The Inner Temple Masque* (produced 1614; as *Ulysses and Circe*, produced 1615).   Edited by Thomas Davies, in *Works*, 1772; edited by R. F. Hill, in *A Book of Masques in Honour of Allardyce Nicoll*, 1967.

Other

Translator, *The History of Polexander,* by Marin Le Roy.   1647.

Reading List: *Browne* by F. W. Moorman, 1897; "Browne as Satirist" by J. McLennan, in *Papers of the Michigan Academy 33,* 1949.

*   *   *

Little is known of William Browne's early life. His circle of friends included Michael Drayton, George Wither and John Davies of Hereford. Browne, Drayton, and Wither, especially, shared a close literary association, inspired by a common allegiance to the poetry of Spenser. All three were professional poets, conscious of a vocation, and they firmly resisted the literary developments after 1600 – an antipathy largely directed at the metaphysical school, but also towards the progress of the drama.

Browne was, first and foremost, a pastoralist. In *Britannia's Pastorals* the poet superimposes classical borrowings on an English landscape drawn largely from Spenser. The stories are typical pastoral accounts of love-lorn swains, suicidal nymphs, lustful satyrs, and Ovidian metamorphoses. Fletcher, Tasso, and Guarini as well as Spenser are plundered for stories. For a great undertaking, the rewards are rare. There are passages and lyrical interludes where poetic skill is evident, but a rambling narrative and a great deal of allegory, satire, and didacticism too often produce dullness and prolixity.

In *The Shepheards Pipe,* a series of seven eclogues, something of the closeness of the Browne-Wither-Drayton group can be seen. In the first eclogue, Willie (Browne) tries to cheer up Roget (Wither), who has suffered from ill reports of his piping. Then in the second eclogue their insular, pastoral world is invaded by a troublesome swineherd. A sullen, hostile mood such as this often surfaces in Browne's work. We find it again in the third book of *Britannia's Pastorals* and in his odes and sonnets. The poet, however, is not simply disgruntled at a dearth of artistic integrity, but he relates this to a wider decline in morality, politics, and religion which he sees as having set in at the end of the Elizabethan Golden Age.

The inability of Browne, Drayton, and Wither to heed changes in literary taste meant that neglect inevitably fell upon their work. Browne, therefore, largely uses the shepherd persona to air personal grievances about what he regards as a malaise in society and to celebrate the poetic commitment of himself and his associates – when reasons for celebration are often conspicuously absent. The result of this self-centred stance is frequently an unhealthy one: Browne's tedious longwindedness is the direct result of his determination to play the role of the poet as saviour, usually to the detriment of the poetry.

Though Browne's work is thus sometimes marred by self-indulgence, yet he remains one of the few successful imitators of Spenser. The influence of Spenser as a model is of course strongly felt in the multitude of poets who dragged the tradition into the middle of the seventeenth century. In most, however, the matter is merely borrowed with slavish emulation, and is not developed or individualised. Browne, Wither, and Drayton, on the other hand, responded to specific elements in *The Shepheardes Calender*, such as the role of the shepherd persona, the archaic language and the realistic landscape, and made them their own.

In Browne it is primarily the closely detailed and affectionate treatment of nature and the countryside that we can value today. In typically native manner, he tells us in *Britannia's Pastorals* of his intention to eschew the artifice and unreality of the Arcadian landscape: "My Muse for lofty pitches shall not rome/But homely pipen of her native home." And, despite moments of rather stilted rhetoric, he provides us with some agreeably down-to-earth vignettes of, for example, the local blacksmith who "spits in his Buckthorne fist,/And bids his Man bring out the five-fold twist,/His shackles, shacklocks, hampers, gyves and chains,/His linked bolts." It is the influence of Shakespeare, perhaps, rather than Spenser that is present in his description of winter "when hardly fed the flocks/And Isicles hung dangling on the Rocks.... When every Barne rung with the threshing Flailes,/And Shepherds Boyes for cold gan blow their nailes."

In *Britannia's Pastorals*, the background is one of homely English activities, farming, hunting, fishing; buxom milkmaids replace the elegant shepherdesses of Arcadia, and conventional Classical myth frequently gives way to native fairy lore. Of course this semi-realistic backdrop often clashes incongruously with the Ovidian narrative material, and it would be futile to pretend that the pastorals of Browne of Tavistock can lay any claim to being considered as coherent works of art. Neither, however, do they merit the almost total oblivion they enjoy at present – a far cry from the days when, according to George Eliot (in *Daniel Deronda*), "the welfare of our Indian Empire [might] be somehow connected with a quotable knowledge of Browne's Pastorals."

—B. W. Lyle

BURTON, Robert.   English.   Born in Lindley, Leicestershire, 8 February 1577. Educated at Sutton Coldfield School, Warwickshire; Nuneaton Grammar School, Warwickshire; Brasenose College, Oxford, 1593–99; elected student of Christ Church, Oxford, 1599, and took the degree of B.D. 1614. Presented to the Christ Church living of St. Thomas, Oxford, 1616, also served as Rector of Seagrave, Leicestershire, 1630–40. *Died 25 January 1640.*

PUBLICATIONS

Prose

   The Anatomy of Melancholy, What It Is.   1621; revised edition, 1624, 1628, 1632, 1638, 1651(?); edited by Holbrook Jackson, 1932.

Play

   Philosophaster (produced 1618).   In *Philosophaster, Poemata,* 1862; translated by Paul Jordan-Smith, 1931.

Other

   Philosophaster, Poemata, edited by W. E. Buckley.   1862.
   Philosophaster, with an English Translation, and Minor Writings in Prose and Verse, edited by Paul Jordan-Smith.   1931.

Reading List: *Bibliographia Burtoniana: A Study of Burton's Anatomy of Melancholy* by Paul Jordan-Smith, 1931 (includes bibliography); *Burton's Knowledge of English Poetry* by H. J.

Gottlieb, 1937; *The Anatomy of Burton's England* by W. R. Mueller, 1952; *Sanity in Bedlam: A Study of Burton's Anatomy of Melancholy* by Lawrence Babb, 1959; *Burton et l'Anatomie de la Melancholie* by J. R. Simon, 1964.

*   *   *

In 1621 Robert Burton published *The Anatomy of Melancholy*, in a thick quarto format. With a brief, uncluttered preface and a short postscript it is a rather unpretentious volume, not at all reminiscent of the carefully outlined, elaborately prefaced book with which we usually associate Burton. Ostensibly a medical treatise which purported to examine fully the causes, symptoms, and cures of the dreaded disease – melancholy – his work was an immediate success and according to legend its publisher Henry Cripps "got an estate by it." A minister by profession, a physician by inclination, and thought by many to be a prose stylist by accident, Burton revised and expanded the *Anatomy* five times. From the first through the sixth editions the *Anatomy* grew from approximately 300,000 to 480,000 words. Although he deleted some words and phrases, and revised some sentences, the most important change is the additions, especially those made between the first and second editions. It is clear that in the process of expanding, Burton very early lost interest in the purely medical aspects of his subject and became increasingly fascinated with the ramifications of melancholy, especially as applied to love and religion. In addition, the short postscript of the first edition is incorporated into a greatly expanded preface, entitled "Democritus Junior to the Reader," in which Burton reveals the purpose of his volume, together with the development of a major persona of the book. The use of Democritus is a key to understanding the tone and meaning of the *Anatomy*. To Burton's seventeenth-century audience Democritus was known as the "laughing philosopher," a satiric, witty observer of the foibles of human nature. But Burton is not consistent in his use of the persona. Frequently, he simply drops the mask and speaks straightforwardly and autobiographically. Occasionally, his persona in no way resembles Democritus.

On first reading the *Anatomy*, one has the impression that Burton has read everything that he could get his hands on and then commented on it in his volume. The margins fairly bristle with references to authorities, and his offhand, casual remarks about his own prose style suggest the idea that he gave little serious thought to the organization and method of the *Anatomy*. Consequently, until the twentieth century Burton was thought to have written a brilliant compendium of digressions, a hodge-podge of interesting but unrelated comments, ranging from the creation of a utopia to a detailed listing of the miseries of scholars, from a delightful discussion of the pleasures of travel and sightseeing – "A Digression of Air" – to a sermon on the most serious form of seventeenth-century melancholy – religious despair. A rich mine of anecdotes and strange tales, the *Anatomy* was deservedly popular during the seventeenth, eighteenth, and nineteenth centuries, exerting an important influence on such diverse authors as John Ford, Swift, Johnson, Sterne, Lamb, Keats, Thackeray, and Melville. Although an important source for numerous writers he was not taken seriously as a thinker or prose stylist. Considered an interesting eccentric, he was best characterized in Lamb's words as the "fantasticke, old great man."

In our century, criticism has focused on the artistry and unity of the *Anatomy*. Critics have discovered that Burton (despite his open disclaimers) was a much more careful prose stylist than once was thought to be the case. They have seen that, like any artist, Burton subtly varies his style to suit his purposes. There is a clearly defined "medical style" which contrasts markedly with the exuberant rhetoric of "Love Melancholy," and the eloquent pulpit strains of "Religious Melancholy."

Scholars have rightly noted that what may appear at first glance haphazard and ill-organized possesses a unity which binds the work together. They have observed (according to their inclinations) Burton's clear indebtedness to several satirical traditions, all of which suggest a unity of tone which was earlier overlooked. But the most fruitful approach to studying the unity of the *Anatomy* has been the belated recognition that Renaissance concepts of aesthetic unity allow for a much greater diversity of parts than do modern concepts of unity; in short, the Renaissance concept of unity is encyclopedic rather than "organic."

At the moment, there is much critical interest in Burton. His considerable position as a prose stylist is secure; his reputation as a thinker is growing. The Anglican minister and amateur physician remains an important seventeenth-century literary figure.

—Dennis G. Donovan

CAMPION, Thomas. English. Born in Witham, Essex, 12 February 1567. Educated at Peterhouse, Cambridge (gentleman pensioner), 1581–84; admitted to Gray's Inn, London, 1586; studied medicine, probably at the University of Caen, qualified c. 1605. A volunteer in the expedition led by the Earl of Essex to Dieppe, to assist Henry IV, 1591. Composer and physician: practised as a physician, 1606 until his death. *Died 1 March 1620.*

PUBLICATIONS

Collections

Works, edited by P. S. Vivian. 1909.
Works: Complete Songs, Masques, and Treatises, edited by Walter R. Davis. 1967.
Selected Poems, edited by Joan Hart. 1976.

Verse

Poemata: Ad Thamesin, Fragmentum Umbrae, Liber Elegiarum, Liber Epigrammatum. 1595.
A Book of Airs to Be Sung to the Lute, Orpherian, and Bass Viol, by P. Rosseter (part 1 by Campion). 1601.
The First Book of Airs. 1613(?).
Two Books of Airs. 1613(?).
Songs of Mourning Bewailing the Death of Prince Henry. 1613.
The Third and Fourth Book of Airs. 1617(?).
Epigrammatum Libri II, Umbra, Elegiarum Liber Unus. 1619.
A Friend's Advice in a Ditty Concerning the Variable Changes in the World. 1625(?).

Plays

The Description of a Mask at Whitehall in Honour of the Lord Hayes and His Bride; Other Small Poems (produced 1607). 1607.
The Description of a Mask at the Marriage of the Earl of Somerset and Frances Howard (produced 1613). 1614.

A Relation of the Late Royal Entertainment Given by Lord Knowles on the Marriage Night of the Count Palatine and the Lady Elizabeth (produced 1613). 1613.
The Lords' Masque (produced 1613). With *A Relation …*, 1613.

Other

Observations in the Art of English Poesie. 1602.
A New Way of Making Four Parts in Counterpoint. 1613.

Reading List: *England's Musical Poet, Campion* by Miles M. Kastendieck, 1938; *Campion, Poet, Composer, Physician* by Edward Lowbury, Timothy Slater, and Alison Young, 1970; *Campion: His Poetry and Music 1567–1620* by Muriel T. Eldridge, 1971.

*　　*　　*

Thomas Campion's artistic reputation was much enhanced by the vogue for Elizabethan music and poetry which began in the 1920's. E. H. Fellowes's editorial work prompted a younger generation of critics to counter misconceptions surviving from the days of earlier "revivals." A typical view, adopted by such enthusiasts as Cecil Gray and Peter Warlock, was that Campion, though an interesting song-writer, was a better poet than musician. "He may be conceded to possess a fertile vein of pleasant, but rather undistinguished melody," wrote Gray (*History of Music*, 1928), "and that is about all." Warlock also finds the music less engaging than "the superlative excellence of the poems" (*The English Ayre*, 1926). To Bruce Pattison Campion was "the finest lyric poet of his age" (*Music and Poetry of the English Renaissance*, 1948).

The somewhat derogatory attitude towards Campion the musician may have been due to an unconscious preference for Dowland, whose idiom largely rules out the possibility of those "complacent four-square songs of the conventional hymn-tune pattern to be found in Campion's song-books …" (Warlock). Few, however, would now deny that at his best Campion is a composer of real genius. The term "lyric" has several connotations, and in Campion's work more than one of these apply. In his shorter pieces he evolved word-patterns which fall naturally into acceptable melodic shapes; yet when considered independently of their music, these poems evoke emotional situations which are of interest for their own sake. Thus in "Breake now my heart and dye" (*Third Book of Ayres*) we have a miniature essay in self-questioning which avoids the customary clichés of amatory experience; sung to a melodic line supported by adventurous modulations, it achieves a striking poignancy. Many similar examples could be given; but in the light of this sort of accomplishment we can appreciate why Campion stressed the "epigrammatic" nature of the solo song as he conceived it.

Campion's ingenuity in this field, indeed, is such that we must revise our notions of him as an "amateur." His penchant for experimenting with classical metres was seldom an excuse for elegant trifling since he believed that the Greek and Latin poets were the "first inventers of Ayres." Yet, paradoxically, although the much-quoted "Rose-cheekt *Lawra*, come" (Chapter 8 of Campion's *Observations*) is a successful application of quantitative measure to English poetry, the musical setting of "Come, let us sound with melody" (a paraphrase of Psalm 19 in Sapphics from *A Book of Ayres*) is less than congenial. In fact, Campion's plea for a reversion to older metrical forms was something he could not fully live up to, and his objections to rhyme are, as Daniel's *Defence* suggests, slightly misplaced. In his masques he uses rhyme extensively, interspersing it with lyrical stanzas and racy prose dialogue. The masque form, in fact, suited Campion's versatility admirably. As a song-writer he was rivalled by John Danyel, Robert Jones, and others; yet in some respects he was slightly in advance of his time. His *New Way of Making Fowre Parts in Counter-point* advocates a system of musical composition in which the bass rather than the tenor is the starting-point for the harmonic structure. In both poetry and music, however, Campion's attitude to his art reveals a searching mind and creative powers of uncommon inventiveness.

—E. D. Mackerness

CAREW, Thomas.   English.   Born in West Wickham, Kent, c. 1595. Educated at Merton College, Oxford, 1608–11, B.A. 1611; Middle Temple, London, 1612. Secretary to the English Ambassador to Venice, Sir Dudley Carleton, c. 1612–16; accompanied Lord Herbert of Cherbury to France, 1619; Gentleman of Charles I's Privy Chamber, 1630, and Sewer in Ordinary, c. 1630. With the King's forces in First Bishops' War, 1639. *Died 21 March 1640.*

PUBLICATIONS

Collections

Poems, with His Masque Coelum Britannicum, edited by Rhodes Dunlap.   1949.
Cavalier Poets, edited by Thomas Clayton.   1978.

Verse

Poems.   1640; revised edition, 1642, 1651.

Play

Coelum Britannicum: A Masque at Whitehall (produced 1634).   1634.

Reading List: *The Flourishing Wreath: A Study of Carew's Poetry* by E. I. Selig, 1958.

*   *   *

The slapdash Suckling, in "A Sessions of the Poets," good-naturedly chides his friend Tom Carew for being so slow and painstaking a writer. Such a reproach could hardly have disturbed Carew, whose poetic address "To Ben Jonson" emphasises the high value he set on the Jonsonian (and Horatian) ideal of hard-won perfection:

> Repine not at the Taper's thrifty waste
> That sleeks thy terser Poems; nor is haste
> Praise, but excuse.

The result of Carew's careful writing was a set of lyrics – probably the finest poetry produced at the court of Charles I – which seem almost effortless.

Most of his work circulated only in manuscript; unlike Jonson, whose "itch of praise" he deplored, he troubled himself little about any wider audience or more lasting fame than might be found in his own select world. He read widely, though, and his poems contain images and ideas borrowed from French and Italian writers such as Ronsard and Marino. His longest poem, "A Rapture," was apparently one of the first by which he attracted serious attention; its eighty-three pentameter couplets, which summon his mistress Celia to a paradise of love, achieve a powerful intensity which derives not merely from an accumulation of boldly sensuous images but from the precision with which these images take form within a framework of logically expounded libertinism. Carew's shorter lyrics, mostly stanzaic, achieve similar control through a strong pattern of thought which guides and reinforces the flow of feeling. Skilfully versified, many of these lyrics were set to music by Henry Lawes and other contemporary composers.

His single masque, *Coelum Britannicum*, was written to order for performance by the King and his gentlemen at Whitehall, and it carries the Jonsonian pattern of the masque to an elaborate extreme, with no less than eight anti-masques. The central idea derives from philosophic dialogues by Giordano Bruno, and perhaps in response to this source some of the speeches achieve a striking degree of grave eloquence. But whereas it had been the object of Bruno's speakers to decide what virtues are worthy of a place among the stars, Carew solves the question more simply by elevating his King and Queen to that symbolic eminence.

He contributed perceptive commendatory poems to the publications of his friends, and wrote the best of the Elegies which accompanied the posthumous publication of Donne's poems in 1633. Here, in an extended analysis of Donne's distinctive achievement, he shows critical insights which go far beyond his own poetical practice, which only occasionally allowed itself a touch of the metaphysical. In another poem, prefixed to George Sandys' translated *Psalms* in 1638, he professes a desire to turn from earthly beauties to the love of God. But his own translated Psalms seem to have been youthful exercises rather than the product of any important spiritual urge, early or late.

—Rhodes Dunlap

CHAPMAN, George.   English.   Born near Hitchin, Hertfordshire, c. 1560. Educated possibly at Cambridge University and Oxford University. Lived on the Continent, 1585–91, and served with the forces of Sir Francis Vere in the Low Countries; returned to London and wrote for Philip Henslowe until 1599, then for the Children of St. Paul's Chapel (later known as the Children of the Queen's Revels) until 1608, and thereafter devoted himself mainly to his translations; Sewer-in-Ordinary to Prince Henry, 1603–12; imprisoned in the Tower of London for satirical references to James I, 1605; in later life enjoyed patronage of the Earl of Somerset. *Died 12 May 1634.*

PUBLICATIONS

Collections

   Tragedies, Comedies, edited by T. M. Parrott.   2 vols., 1910–14.
   Poems, edited by Phyllis Brooks Bartlett.   1941.
   Plays: The Comedies. edited by Allan Holaday.   1970.

Verse

The Shadow of Night, Containing Two Poetical Hymns.   1594.

Ovid's Banquet of Sense, A Coronet for His Mistress Philosophy, and His Amorous Zodiac.   1595; edited by Elizabeth Story Donno, in *Elizabethan Minor Epics*, 1963.

Seven Books of the Iliad of Homer.   1598; *Achilles' Shield,* 1598; *Twelve Books,* 1609(?); complete work, 1611.

Hero and Leander, Begun by Marlowe, Finished by Chapman.   1598; edited by Louis L. Martz, 1972.

Euthymiae Raptus; or, The Tears of Peace, with Interlocutions.   1609.

An Epicede or Funeral Song on the Death of Henry Prince of Wales.   1612.

Petrarch's Seven Penitential Psalms, Paraphrastically Translated with Other Philosophical Poems and a Hymn to Christ upon the Cross.   1612.

Andromeda Liberata; or, The Nuptials of Perseus and Andromeda.   1614.

Eugenia; or, True Nobility's Trance for the Death of William Lord Russell.   1614.

Homer's Odyssey, 12 books.   1614(?); complete work, 1615(?).

The Divine Poem of Musaeus.   1616; edited by Elizabeth Story Donno, in *Elizabethan Minor Epics*, 1963.

The Georgics of Hesiod.   1618.

Pro Vere Autumni Lachrymae, Inscribed to the Memory of Sir Horatio Vere.   1622.

The Crown of All Homer's Works, Batrachomyomachia, or, The Battle of Frogs and Mice, His Hymns and Epigrams.   1624(?).

A Justification of a Strange Action of Nero, Being the Fifth Satire of Juvenal Translated.   1629.

Chapman's Homer: The Iliad, The Odyssey, and the Lesser Homerica, edited by Allardyce Nicoll.   2 vols., 1956.

Plays

Fedele and Fortunio: The Deceits in Love, with Munday and Stephen Gosson (produced 1584?).   1585; edited by P. Simpson, 1909.

The Blind Beggar of Alexandria (produced 1596).   1598; edited by Lloyd E. Berry, in *Plays,* 1970.

An Humorous Day's Mirth (produced 1597).   1599; edited by Allan Holaday, in *Plays.* 1970.

The Gentleman Usher (produced 1602?).   1606; edited by Robert Ornstein, in *Plays,* 1970.

All Fools (produced 1604).   1605; edited by G. Blakemore Evans, in *Plays,* 1970.

Monsieur D'Olive (produced 1604).   1606; edited by Allan Holaday, in *Plays,* 1970.

Bussy D'Ambois (produced 1604).   1607; edited by M. Evans, 1965.

Eastward Ho, with Jonson and Marston (produced 1605).   1605; edited by C. G. Petter, 1973.

Sir Giles Goosecap, Knight (produced?).   1606; edited by W. Bang and R. Brotanek, 1909.

The Conspiracy and Tragedy of Charles, Duke of Byron, Marshal of France (produced 1608).   1608; edited by W. L. Phelps, 1895.

May Day (produced 1609).   1611; edited by Robert F. Welsh, in *Plays,* 1970.

The Widow's Tears (produced before 1609).   1612; edited by Robert Ornstein, in *Plays,* 1970.

The Revenge of Bussy D'Ambois (produced 1610?).   1613; edited by F. S. Boas, 1905. ·

The Memorable Masque of the Middle Temple and Lincoln's Inn (produced 1613).   1613; edited by G. Blakemore Evans, in *Plays,* 1970.

The Wars of Caesar and Pompey (produced 1613?).   1631.

Chabot, Admiral of France (produced 1613?).   Version revised by Shirley, published 1639; edited by Ezra Lehman, 1906.

Other

A Free and Offenceless Justification of Andromeda Liberata.   1614.

Bibliography: *Chapman: A Concise Bibliography* by S. A. Tannenbaum, 1938; supplement, 1946.

Reading List: *Chapman: The Effect of Stoicism upon His Tragedies* by John W. Weiler, 1949; *Chapman: Sa Vie, Sa Poésie, Son Théâtre, Sa Pensée* by Jean Jacquot, 1951; *The Tragedies of Chapman: Renaissance Ethics in Action* by Ennis Rees, 1954; *Homeric Renaissance: The Odyssey of Chapman* by George de F. Lord, 1956; *Chapman: A Critical Study* by Millar MacLure, 1966; *Chapman* by C. Spivak, 1967; *An Index to the Figurative Language of Chapman's Tragedies* by L. C. Stagg, 1970; *The Mind's Empire: Myth and Form in Chapman's Narrative Poems* by Raymond B. Waddington, 1974; *Chapman: Action and Contemplation in His Tragedies* by Peter Bement, 1974.

*   *   *

Chapman's activities as poet, dramatist, and translator place him second only to his friend and sometimes collaborator Ben Jonson as a man of letters. While the two men shared a devotion to learning and a sense of vocation as professional writers, in other respects the differences are large. To the clarity which is Jonson's stylistic ideal, Chapman retorts that oratorically plain poetry "were the plaine way to barbarisme." His own style is so notoriously difficult that – mistakenly – he has been associated with the Metaphysicals. Instead, Chapman wrote as a Platonic mystagogue, using meaningful obscurity to conceal his truth from the many and reveal it to the worthy few. He should be seen as one in the line of visionary poets extending from Spenser through Milton and Blake.

Chapman was influenced heavily by Marsilio Ficino; and Chapman's Platonism supplies the key to his thought and poetics, as his various theoretical statements make clear. Poetry is an epiphany of Truth, always associated with wisdom and learning, attained through divine inspiration. The vatic poet accommodates this Truth to human understanding through symbolic images, fables, and myths. Although few men will undertake the intellectual and spiritual discipline necessary to comprehend such poetry, for the "understanders" it will "turne blood to soule" and "heighten [man's] transition into God." Central to Chapman's poetics is his conception of *form:* this includes conventional literary form (genre) by which the poet announces his general intentions; the inner form of the myth, fable, or story (understood via the traditions of allegorical commentary); and the indwelling form or "soul" of the Truth, a notion deriving from the Platonic Idea.

Chapman's most important poems were those published at the beginning of his career. *The Shadow of Night* consists of two hymns addressed to Night and to Cynthia, both revealed by the Orphic poet as religious mysteries, which anatomize man's condition and prescribe remedies. In the second, around the triune identity of the goddess as Cynthia-Diana-Hecate, Chapman interweaves a complex, three-level allegory – philosophical, political, and poetic. *Ovids Banquet of Sence*, an oblique riposte to the fashion of Ovidian erotic narratives, ironically presents Ovid as seducer, glibly misusing Platonic doctrine to achieve his end; deliberately ambiguous, the entire poem – as the title-page emblem suggests – is a *trompe l'oeil*, warning us not to trust our senses. Chapman's continuation of *Hero and Leander* "corrects" Marlowe's incomplete narrative (as does his editing of the Marlowe), restoring the moral balance and high seriousness in an Ovidian epic, written from the perspective of the allegorical commentaries upon *The Metamorphoses*. Of the Jacobean poems, two deserve mention: *The Teares of Peace*, oddly combining medieval dream-vision and Hermetic revelation, is Chapman's most sustained defense of learning; and *Andromeda Liberata* projects political allegory through mythological narrative in a manner reflecting the influence of court masques.

By 1598 Francis Meres could list Chapman among "the best Poets" for both comedy and tragedy; and theatrical writing in several dramatic genres dominated his activities for the next decade. M. C. Bradbrook credits *An Humorous Day's Mirth* with initiating the comedy of humours; and Jackson Cope has demonstrated that *The Gentleman Usher* and *The Widow's Tears* − tragi-comic romance and satiric comedy, respectively − are philosophic dramas, using mythic frameworks to explore positive and negative versions of the Platonic quest for absolute knowledge. In the tragedies Chapman obsessively rewrites the script of a flawed Titan, greater by far than the surrounding society, yet contaminated and eventually destroyed by his compromises with that society and by his own hubris. It is conventional to mark the shift from the Achillean active heroes, Bussy and Byron, to the passive, Stoic virtue of Clermont, Cato, and Chabot. But, just as Platonism always informs his poetics, so Stoicism is the foundation of his ethics throughout, a personal and eclectic Stoicism that is flexible enough to encompass both Achilles's justified wrath and the encomium of Clermont as "this Senecal man." *Bussy D'Ambois* "inwardly" measures its hero's greatness and failure against the myths of Hercules, Prometheus, and Christ; "outwardly" it is heroic tragedy and sensational melodrama. This combination of dimensions has earned its modern status as the single "anthology piece" among the tragedies. An age as receptive as ours to the drama of ideas, however, might well give more attention to the interiorized tragedies of *Byron* and *The Revenge of Bussy D'Ambois*. Although only *The Memorable Maske* survives as evidence of Chapman's skill at this new form, we have Jonson's testimony "That next himself only Fletcher and Chapman could make a Mask."

Chapman launched his Homer translation with *Seaven Bookes of the Iliades* and *Achilles Shield* (1598); *The Teares of Peace* (1609) announces his visionary inspiration by Homer and his renewed dedication to the task. *The Iliads* was finished in 1611, the complete *Odyssey* in 1615, the two published together as *The Whole Works* the next year, and the lesser Homerica followed later. Despite his unfulfilled promise to present "my Poeme of the mysteries/ Reveal'd in Homer," Chapman does not encumber the epics with Platonic exegesis; rather, he sees "naked *Vlysses* clad in eternall Fiction" as totally mythic. Disdaining "word-for-word traductions," he regarded his job as *translation*, making the universal values of Homer comprehensible and therefore relevant to his own time and culture. His English systematically renders explicit the ethical and philosophical attitudes which he perceived as implicit in the text. Chapman's famous statement that the "Proposition" of each epic is contracted in the first word (*wrath* and *man*) itself epitomizes his approach to translation: "in one, the Bodie's fervour and fashion of outward Fortitude to all possible height of Heroicall Action; in the other, the Mind's inward, constant and unconquered Empire...." The adequacy of Chapman's Greek and the degree of fidelity to the original are much mooted questions which can distract attention from his very considerable achievement. Despite the hiatus in composition, Chapman's *Iliads* is generally viewed as more successful than his *Odyssey* in its consonance to the meaning of the Homer and in its unity. Certainly Chapman's *Iliads* is a splendid poem. His other literary accomplishments notwithstanding, his description of the Homer translations as "The Worke that I was borne to doe" is one to which most readers give assent.

—Raymond B. Waddington

CHURCHYARD, Thomas. English. Born in Shrewsbury, Shropshire, in 1520. Married. Served as a page to the Earl of Surrey; lived a wandering life, partly as a soldier and partly as a hanger-on of the court and nobility, hoping, unsuccessfully, for preferment: served under Sir William Drury in Scotland, and thereafter in Ireland, the Low Countries, and France; served under Lord Grey for eight years. Granted a pension by Queen Elizabeth I, 1592. *Died 4 April 1604.*

PUBLICATIONS

Verse

A Mirror for Man. 1552; revised edition, 1594.
The Contention Betwixt Churchyard and Camell upon David Dycer's Dream (flyting pamphlets). 1560.
Shore's Wife, in *A Mirror for Magistrates.* 1563; *Thomas Wolsey,* in 1587 edition; edited by Lily B. Campbell, 1938.
A Farewell Called Churchyard's Round. 1566.
A Greater Thanks for Churchyard's Welcome Home. 1566.
Churchyard's Lamentation of Friendship. 1566.
Churchyard's Farewell. 1566.
The Epitaph of the Earl of Pembroke. 1570.
The First Three Books of Ovid's De Tristibus Translated. 1572.
Churchyard's Chips, part 1. 1575.
A Pleasant Labyrinth Called Churchyard's Chance. 1580.
The Epitaph of Sir Philip Sidney. 1587.
A Light Bundle of Lively Discourses Called Churchyard's Charge. 1580; edited by John Payne Collier, 1870.
A Reviving of the Dead. 1591.
A Handful of Gladsome Verses Given to the Queen's Majesty at Woodstock. 1592.
A Feast Full of Sad Cheer. 1592.
Churchyard's Challenge. 1593.
The Mirror of Man, and Manners of Men. 1594; edited by A. Boswell, in *Frondes Caducae,* 1816.
The Honour of the Law. 1596.
A Sad Funeral of Sir F. Knowles. 1596; edited by A. Boswell, in *Frondes Caducae,* 1816.
A Pleasant Discourse of Court and Wars Called His Cherishing. 1596; edited by A. Boswell, in *Frondes Caducae,* 1816.
The Fortunate Farewell to the Earl of Essex. 1599; edited by J. Nichols, in *Progresses of Queen Elizabeth,* 1788–1823.
The Wonders of the Air, The Trembling of the Earth. 1602.
Sorrowful Verses on the Death of Queen Elizabeth. 1604; edited by Hyder E. Rollins and H. Baker, in *The Renaissance in England,* 1954.
Churchyard's Good Will: An Epitaph for the Archbishop of Canterbury. 1604; edited by H. Huth, in *Fugitive Tracts 2,* 1875.

Plays

The Whole Order How Queen Elizabeth Was Received into the City of Bristol (produced 1574). 1575.

A Discourse of the Queen's Majesty's Entertainment in Suffolk and Norfolk, A Welcome Home to M. Frobisher, A Commendation of Sir H. Gilbert's Venturous Journey. 1578.
A Pleasant Conceit Presented to the Queen's Majesty. 1593; edited by J. Nichols, in *Progresses of Queen Elizabeth,* 1788–1823.
A Musical Consort Called Churchyard's Charity; A Praise of Poetry Out of Sir Philip Sidney. 1595; edited by A. Boswell, in *Frondes Caducae,* 1816.

Other

Come Bring in May with Me: A Discourse of Rebellion 1570.
A Praise and Report of Master Martin Frobisher's Voyage to Meta Incognita. 1578.
A Lamentable and Pitiful Description of the Woeful Wars in Flanders. 1578.
The Misery of Flanders, Calamity of France, Misfortune of Portugal. 1579.
The Most True Report of James Fitz Morrice' Death. 1579(?).
A Warning for the Wise of the Late Earthquake. 1580.
A Plain Report of the Taking of Macklin. 1580.
A Scourge for Rebels. 1584.
The Worthiness of Wales. 1587; edited by C. E. Simms, 1876.
A Spark of Friendship and Warm Good Will; A Description of a Paper-Mill Built by M. Spilman. 1588; edited by J. Nichols, in *Progresses of Queen Elizabeth,* 1788–1823.
A Wished Reformation of Wicked Rebellion. 1598.

Editor, *The Censure of a Loyal Subject,* by George Whetstone. 1587.
Editor, *Giacomo di Grassi His True Art of Defence Englished by I. G.* 1594.

Translator, with R. Robinson, *A True Discourse of the Succeeding Governors in the Netherlands and the Civil Wars There,* by E. van Meteren. 1602.

Reading List: *Churchyard* by H. W. Adnitt, 1880 (includes bibliography).

* * *

Thomas Churchyard wrote a score of narrative and descriptive poems, most of them black-letter broadsides, with alliterative titles like *Churchyard's Chips* and *Churchyard's Challenge.* He began his poetic career in the early 1550's with a collection of wooden, didactic verses, *A Mirror for Man,* and was still writing in the same drab, early Tudor style into the reign of James I. His longevity is alluded to by Spenser in *Colin Clout,* wherein Churchyard is "Old Palaemon" who "sung so long until quite hoarse he grew." Most of his poems are descriptive or narrative, and reflect his experiences as a minor courtier and professional soldier. His *Woeful Wars in Flanders* is rich in autobiographical reminiscences, and *The Worthiness of Wales* is still worth reading for its occasional descriptive power. Churchyard wrote numerous elegies on Elizabethan worthies such as his early patron, the Earl of Surrey, and contributed poems to the first edition of Tottel's Miscellany. His best poem is "Shore's Wife," the narrative he contributed to the second edition of William Baldwin's *A Mirror for Magistrates.* Churchyard's concluding observation on the sad fate of Jane Shore, Edward IV's much-abused mistress ("And bent the wand that might have grown full straight") was picked up by Marlowe to form his famous epilogue to *Doctor Faustus:* "Cut is the brancht have grown full straight."

—James E. Ruoff

CLEVELAND, John. English. Born in Loughborough, Leicestershire, baptized 20 June 1613. Educated by Reverend Richard Vynes in Hinckley, Leicestershire; Christ's College, Cambridge, 1627–34, B.A. 1631, M.A. 1635; Rhetoric Reader, 1636, and possibly M.A., 1637, Oxford University. Joined the King at Oxford, 1643; Fellow, St. John's College, Cambridge, 1643–45; served as Judge-Advocate at the garrison at Newark, 1645–46; after defeat of Royalists, subsequent activities unknown until he arrived in Norwich to take up position as tutor, arrested by the Puritan forces, imprisoned at Yarmouth, 1655; released by Cromwell, and lived in various places, probably finally at Gray's Inn, London. *Died 29 April 1658.*

PUBLICATIONS

Collections

Poems, edited by Brian Morris and Eleanor Withington.   1967.

Verse

The Character of a London Diurnal, with Several Select Poems (includes prose).   1645; revised edition, as *Poems,* 1651; revised edition, as *Poems, Characters, and Letters,* 1658.
The Scots' Apostacy.   1646.
The Character of a Moderate Intelligencer, with Some Select Poems (includes prose).   1647.
The King's Disguise.   1647.
The Hue and Cry after Sir John Presbyter.   1649.
Cleveland Revived.   1659.
On the Most Renowned Prince Rupert.   N.d.

Other

Majestas Intemerata; or, The Immortality of the King.   1649.
Character of a Country Committee-Man.   1649.
Character of a Diurnal-Maker.   1653.
The Idol of the Clowns; or, The Insurrection of Wat the Tyler.   1654; as *The Rustic Rampant,* 1658; as *The Rebellion of the Rude Multitude,* 1658.
Petition to the Lord Protector.   1657.
Clevelandi Vindiciae; or, Cleveland's Genuine Poems, Orations, Epistles, etc.   1677.

Bibliography: *Cleveland: A Bibliography of His Poems* by Brian Morris,   1967.

Reading List: *Cleveland* by Lee A. Jacobus, 1975.

*   *   *

With John Cleveland the metaphysical mode of John Donne and his school becomes an academic style in which inventiveness and ingenuity are the sole concerns. A coterie poet with many admirers in his day who, like the editors of *Clevelandi Vindiciae,* extolled the intellectual brilliance of his wit, he yet found a detractor in John Dryden, who dubbed catechresis (the compressed conceit) a wretched "Clevelandism"; and the detractors have since, by and large, won the day.

His most frequently attacked poem is the elegy on Edward King (the subject of Milton's *Lycidas*), whose beginning illustrates catechresis:

> I like not tears in tune; nor will I prise
> His artificiall grief, that scannes his eyes....
> I am no Poet here: my penne's the spout
> Where the rain-water of my eyes runs out.

The elegy is little more than a series of loosely related ingenious conceits, each of which achieves point and closure, like an epigram, and hence does little more than make a witty "clench" which is then left for another one. Yet, there is a kind of decorum to this elegy, for its disjointed manner illustrates well the mind of the poet disjointed by grief which its opening stresses; Lee A. Jacobus further suggests that his academic audience would see that "in the extremes of his invention are embedded the extremes of his grief." "Fuscara; or, The Bee Errant" and "Upon Phillis Walking in a Morning Before Sun-Rising" are more successful poems; while they lack sequential development, they do have thematic unity that pulls all the conceits together – Fuscara is sweeter than anything, Phillis is like the sun – and the hyperbolic conceits become purposeful in the service of a playful tone. In them, we see the metaphysical poem becoming a display of wit, deflating all assumptions of seriousness by over-inflation; the deliberate seeking of conceits that pull together as unlikely images as possible becomes a comic gambit. His most successful poem is "The Hecatomb to His Mistresse," in which the reader's attention is deliberately drawn to the playful poet's ability to outdo others' praise of their mistresses (even Donne's, line 4) in one hundred lines of extreme conceits, in so doing demonstrating how his mistress excels all thought; as he proceeds through a series of "shifts in gear" (to use a modern catechresis), he takes her first beyond all previous love poetry, then beyond all sensation, finally beyond all imagining.

It is no surprise that Cleveland excels as a satirist, for in satire deliberate hyperbole appears as grotesque humor. In "The Rebell Scot," for instance, deliberate disparity carries the theme of the overturn of natural order by the Scots, and the poet's self-display (as in "The Hecatomb") serves the action of the poem, which is incantation, rhyming the Scots out of existence. Cleveland at his worst is full of tactless self-display; at his best he uses poetry as a kind of incantation, and harnesses the deliberate ingenuity of fancy and far-fetched conceits to the purposes of playful poetic ritual.

—Walter R. Davis

CONSTABLE, Henry. English. Born in Newark in 1562. Educated at St. John's College, Cambridge, B.A. 1580. After conversion to Roman Catholicism, settled in Paris; possibly a spy for the English government, 1584–85, afterwards served the French government: employed in confidential missions to England; Papal Envoy to Edinburgh, 1599–1603; received a pension from the French king, 1603, and returned to London, 1604; imprisoned, released, and probably returned to the Continent: nothing is known of his later life. *Died 9 October 1613.*

PUBLICATIONS

Collections

Poems, edited by Joan Grundy. 1960.

Verse

Diana, The Praises of His Mistress. 1592; revised edition, 1594.

Other

Examen Pacifique de la Doctrine des Huguenots. 1589.

Reading List: in *Biographical Studies* vol. 2, by George A. Wickes, 1954.

* * *

Henry Constable was known to his contemporaries and later readers as the author of the sonnet sequence *Diana*. We know him also from the much larger collection of secular sonnets left in manuscript, as well as from the seventeen *Spiritual Sonnets*, also existing only in manuscript.

By his contemporaries, including fellow poets such as Drayton and Jonson, he was highly esteemed, and, although we may not altogether endorse their estimate, we can understand it. His love sonnets (some of them, like Sidney's, addressed to Penelope Rich) came at the very start of the great Petrarchan explosion of the 1590's, and provided a strikingly pure example of the form. The "sweet conceits" from which they were fashioned were the stock-in-trade of the Petrarchan tradition: his lady is an object of adoration, far above him – a queen, a sun, a goddess; her beauty is the source of beauty in Nature; her hair is a golden net which entraps the lover like a bird; her hand wounds him with its "ivory arrows," and so on. Yet, though typical, the conceits are not hackneyed, for Constable handles them freshly, giving to the thought a graceful turn which makes it legitimately his own. Since the essence of Petrarchan discipleship was the production of variations on a theme, this makes him an almost model examplar. A modern reader misses the richness of texture, the sensuous warmth, and the elegiac note he finds in other practitioners, such as Shakespeare or Daniel, to say nothing of the "true voice of feeling," which, whenever it occurs in such sequences, is to be regarded as a bonus. The virtues of these sonnets are, rather, their neatness, elegance, order, delicacy, and control. Their very artificiality is their charm. Seldom producing a memorable phrase, they are to be enjoyed like a song or an Elizabethan air, as, on the whole, trifles, but agreeable ones. Nor perhaps was personal feeling entirely lacking in them: distanced very far, Constable's "busyness" (he was described on one occasion as "a busie yong man"), his ambition, and his anxiety, may have found both an outlet and a sedative in them.

Not all his secular sonnets were love sonnets. Some were poems of compliment, addressed to various influential people, including Queen Elizabeth I and King James. The interest of these sonnets is slight.

Much more rewarding are the Spiritual Sonnets, written after Constable's conversion to Roman Catholicism. These, addressed to "God and His Saints," have a fervour, and with it a poetic density, both intellectual and emotional, lacking in the secular sonnets. They are among the finest religious sonnets produced in English before Donne. Their style approaches the Metaphysical: it has a certain intellectual toughness and energy, and thought and emotion are fused in a compelling way which makes the conceits more than merely decorative. The completeness of Constable's conversion is clear: most of the saints addressed are women, and, as in much Counter-Reformation literature, the feeling expressed turns the poems into sacred love-poems, considerably more passionate than the love-sonnets themselves.

—Joan Grundy

CORBETT, Richard. English. Born in Ewell, Surrey, in 1582. Educated at Westminster School, London; Broadgates Hall, now Pembroke College, Oxford, 1598; Christ Church, Oxford, 1599–1612, B.A. 1602, M.A. 1605, B.D. 1617; Proctor, 1612; took holy orders, 1613. Married Alice Hutten (died, 1628). Vicar of Cassington, near Oxford; Chaplain to James I; Dean of Christ Church, Oxford, 1620–28; Prebendary of Salisbury, 1620–31; Vicar of Stewkley, Berkshire, 1620–35; Bishop of Oxford, 1628–32; Bishop of Norwich, 1632–35. *Died 28 July 1635.*

PUBLICATIONS

Collections

   Poems, edited by J. A. W. Bennett and H. R. Trevor-Roper.   1955.

Verse

   Certain Elegant Poems.   1647.
   Poetica Stromata; or, A Collection of Sundry Pieces.   1648.
   The Times' Whistle; or, A New Dance of Seven Satires and Other Poems, edited by J. M.
      Cowper.   1871.

*   *   *

Poetry had for Richard Corbett essentially a social function. It was therefore naturally incorporated in his place-seeking activities, which account for several tasteless pieces whose forced wit contrasts with the simplicity and restraint (enhanced by the use of octosyllabics) found in poems on his father, mother, and son. These give the impression of genuine feeling and achieve a dignity unusual in Corbett.

But most of Corbett's better pieces are the result of his conviviality and the literary interchange of Caroline Oxford. His longest poem "Iter Boreale," a lively account in his favourite decasyllabic couplet of a tour made with friends, was popular and influential in its day. It remains the best example of Corbett's characteristic virtues: pace, gusto, humour (generally in the form of ludicrous exaggeration), and delighted awareness of the teeming life of inns and market-places, kitchens and conventicles. He transports us to the world of Dogberry and Bottom the weaver; we savour the authentic life of Jacobean England in the energy of his colloquial speech larded with proverbs and allusions, and in the people with whom his poems are crammed: waiters at a banquet purloining tarts and pies, an "old

Popish-Lady" fasting on gingerbread, tapsters fiddling accounts, a Puritan distracted from prayer by the sight of girls dancing round a maypole. Humour touches everything, from the broken crosses now making "stools for horsemen that have feeble knees" to the chucker-out who hurls Corbett repeatedly for an hour, while onlookers measure the record throw. Corbett's solid world bustles with activity; in a Vice-Chancellor's preparations before a royal visit ("Both morn and even he cleansed the way,/The streets he gravelled thrice a day"), in the nation's excitement over a new comet ("The mason's rule, the tailor's yard alike/Take altitudes"), or in the anguish of dons biting their finger-nails as they struggle to compose verses for their aristocratic pupils to publish as their own, we sense vigorous involvement which is partly Corbett's own, partly that of the society he portrays.

Mentally, Corbett's world looks back, not forwards. His enjoyment of popular culture (shown particularly in his love of ballads, which he both sang and wrote) enables him to recreate for us an intellectual climate in which Puck and Bevis of Hampton are realities, men still talk of the days of the abbeys and the old religion, sing of Arthur or Chevy Chase, and dance at Whitsun Ales. Had Corbett sensed how much his Merrie England was threatened by his constant butts, the Puritans, his mockery of them might have been less good-humoured. Appropriately, he is best remembered today by "Farewell, Rewards and Faeries," the charming lament for the passing of the old order which he wrote to be sung as a ballad by learned and unlearned alike.

Extroverted and morally insensitive, Corbett lived exuberantly on the surface of his age. His humorous delight in the everyday, the unsophisticated, and the traditional aspects of his society is what chiefly endures in his verse.

—Margaret Forey

COWLEY, Abraham.   English.   Born in London, 24 July 1618. Educated at Westminster School, London (King's Scholar), 1628–35; Trinity College, Cambridge (Scholar), 1637–42, B.A. 1639, M.A. 1642; Oxford University, 1656–57, M.D. 1657. Fellow, Trinity College, Cambridge, 1640–44 (ejected by Parliament because of Royalist sympathies); lived at St. John's College, Oxford, 1644–45; Secretary to Lord Jermyn (Queen's Chamberlain), from 1645, and lived in the exiled court in France, 1646–56: employed in various diplomatic missions, also a cipher secretary to Queen Henrietta Maria; returned to London, possibly as a spy, imprisoned briefly by mistake, and released on bail, 1656; returned to France, 1658; restored to fellowship at Trinity College, 1661; associated with Davenant's Duke Theatre from 1661. Retired to Chertsey, Surrey. *Died 28 July 1667.*

PUBLICATIONS

Collections

Prose Works, edited by J. R. Lumby, 1887; revised by Arthur Tilley, 1923.
English Writings, edited by A. R. Waller.   2 vols., 1905–06.
Poetry and Prose, edited by L. C. Martin.   1949.

Verse

> *Poetical Blossoms.*   1633; revised edition, 1636.
> *A Satire: The Puritan and the Papist.*   1643.
> *The Mistress; or, Several Copies of Love-Verses.*   1647.
> *Poems.*   1656.
> *Ode upon the Blessed Restoration and Return of His Sacred Majesty Charles the Second.*   1660.
> *Plantarum Libri Duo.*   1662; revised edition, edited by Thomas Sprat, as *Angli Poemata Latina,* 1668.
> *Verses Lately Written upon Several Occasions.*   1663.
> *A Poem on the Late Civil War.*   1679; edited by Allan Pritchard, as *The Civil War,* 1973.

Plays

> *Love's Riddle* (produced ?).   1638.
> *Naufragium Joculare* (in Latin) (produced 1638).   1638.
> *The Guardian* (produced 1641).   1650; revised version, as *Cutter of Coleman Street* (produced 1661), 1663.

Other

> *A Proposition for the Advancement of Experimental Philosophy.*   1661.
> *Visions and Prophecies.*   1661; as *Definition of a Tyrant,* 1668.
> *Works.*   3 vols., 1668–89.

Bibliography: *Cowley: A Bibliography* by M. R. Perkin, 1977.

Reading List: *Cowley, The Muse's Hannibal* by Arthur H. Nethercot, 1931; *Cowley's World of Order* by Robert B. Hinman, 1960; *Cowley* by James G. Taaffe, 1972.

*   *   *

Often described as the last of the seventeenth-century metaphysical poets, Abraham Cowley actually wrote in a variety of styles, and his intellect and temperament incline as much toward the Age of Enlightenment as to the Renaissance. His *Poetical Blossoms,* written at fifteen while still at Cambridge, reflects the influences of Spenser and the Latin pastoralists, and his comedy of manners *The Guardian,* also done at Cambridge, shows him to be an admirer of Jonson's London comedies. The metaphysical strains in his work are not sounded until *The Mistress; or, Several Copies of Love Verses,* a conscious imitation of Donne's *Songs and Sonnets.* Of the nearly one hundred poems in *The Mistress,* some are philosophical reflections and eulogies of rural life; others are loosely connected to suggest the story of Cowley's unrequited passion for a beautiful woman of superior social position. *The Mistress* is in a medley of styles, combining echoes of Donne and the cavalier "sons of Ben," coupling archly obscure metaphysical conceits and lucid, polished rhetoric; but the affinities to Donne are most salient. Several poems, such as "The Exstasie," Cowley composed expressly to contrast with Donne's. Like Donne, he often begins a love lyric with a dramatic exclamation reminiscent of "For God's sake, hold your tongue and let me love," and many of Donne's images, only slightly modified, reappear in *The Mistress;* "Resolve to Be Beloved," for example, offers a magnetic needle to do somewhat the same work as Donne's two twin compasses. Most of the poems reverberate with what Ben Jonson called "strong lines" – elegantly complex metaphors designed to wring the last drop of intellectual speculation out of cunningly constructed paradoxes. In reaction to these calculated incongruities, Samuel Johnson in his famous life of Cowley (1779) described him as a writer of *discordia concors* perversely enamored of obscure paradoxes, forced wit, and absurd quibbles. Johnson's essay remains the most perceptive analysis ever written of Cowley's poetry, but Johnson, in his effort to discredit the "metaphysicals," may have exaggerated Cowley's similarities to Donne. In reality, Cowley is an imitator of Donne's poetic devices; totally lacking in Donne's intellectual passion, he copies the form but not the substance. He depends upon rhetorical precision rather than complexity of metaphors, and his versification is as smoothly regular as Jonson's.

The Mistress provides only a glimpse of Cowley's variegated style, which is more apparent in his *Poems*, containing his Pindaric odes, elegies, Anacreonics, and the incomplete Biblical epic "Davideis." The fifteen Pindaric odes, or "pseudo-Pindaric" odes, as they were called, were widely imitated in the eighteenth century. Only two follow Pindar closely; the rest are constructed in a dozen or more stanzas of very irregular, rhymed free verse of ingenious prosody and on a variety of philosophical and religious subjects. One ode is a stately tribute to Thomas Hobbes. A somewhat similar tribute, but in elegiac form, is his lengthy poem commemorating his Cambridge friend William Hervey, a magnificent elegy which, if Milton had not composed *Lycidas*, might well stand as the best of the century. Of equally high quality are Cowley's witty and joyous imitations of Anacreon which exhibit a classical compression comparable to Pope's. Taken as a whole, Cowley's poetry suggests poetic instincts that were essentially classical; occasional conceits notwithstanding, his verse is characterized by economy, lucidity, and precision. His "Davideis" was a project he wisely abandoned as alien to his temperament. Written in monotonous decasyllabic couplets, it may have inspired Milton's invectives against rhyme in his preface to *Paradise Lost*. By the time he came to write "Davideis," Cowley's heart was more stirred by the literary beauties of Virgil than the spiritual revelations of the Old Testament. Johnson condemned the poem for its plethora of conceits, but its real flaw is simply absence of inspiration. Exhausted by the religious turbulence of his times, and looking toward the cool rationalism of Bacon and Hobbes and the new science as guides, Cowley could summon only token enthusiasm for angels, miracles, and prophecies.

His retirement to Chertsey after the Restoration enabled him to continue his botanical studies, write tracts for the Royal Society (e.g., *The Advancement of Experimental Philosophy*), and compose his collection of brilliant personal essays. Like Bacon's, Cowley's essays are on abstract subjects such as ambition, solitude, and procrastination, but Cowley avoids Bacon's aloofness of tone and tautness of style. Instead, he writes in the flowing, digressive, and intimate style of his other master, Montaigne. One of his finest essays, the autobiographical "Of My Life," sets a landmark in that genre for its freshness and candor. The most "modern " prose stylist before Dryden, Cowley writes in the lucid, concrete, and direct manner advocated by Bacon and the founders of the Royal Society. Thus, at the conclusion of his life the precocious imitator of the fiery and visionary Donne found his emotional and intellectual resting place in the Age of Reason.

—James E. Ruoff

CRASHAW, Richard. English. Born in London c. 1613. Educated at Charterhouse, London; Pembroke Hall, Cambridge (exhibitioner), 1631–37, B.A. 1634. Fellow, Peterhouse,

Cambridge, 1635–43 (deprived of Fellowship because of his religious beliefs); Curate, Little St. Mary's, Cambridge, 1639; went to Paris, and by 1645 had embraced Roman Catholicism; through intervention of Cowley was introduced to Queen Henrietta Maria who recommended him to Cardinal Palotto: given a post in Palotto's entourage, 1647; appointed a sub-canon at the Cathedral of Santa Casa, Loreto, 1649. *Died 21 August 1649.*

PUBLICATIONS

Collections

Complete Works, edited by Alexander B. Grosart.   2 vols., 1872–73; *Supplement,* 1887–88.
Poems English, Latin, and Greek, edited by L. C. Martin.   1927; revised edition, 1957.
Complete Poetry, edited by George Walton Williams.   1970.

Verse

Epigrammatum Sacrorum Liber.   1634; as *Poemata et Epigrammata,* 1670.
Steps to the Temple: Sacred Poems, with Other Delights of the Muses.   1646; revised edition, 1648, 1670.
Carmen Deo Nostro, Te Decet Hymnus, Sacred Poems, edited by Miles Pinckney.   1652.

Other

Translator, *The Suspicion of Herod,* by Giovanni Battista Marini.   1834.

Reading List: *Crashaw: A Study in Style and Poetic Development* by Ruth Wallerstein, 1935; *Crashaw: A Study in Baroque Sensibility* by Austin Warren, 1939; *Crashaw* by Mario Praz, 1945; *Three Metaphysical Poets: Crashaw, Traherne, Vaughan* by Margaret Willy, 1961; *Rhyme and Meaning in Crashaw* by Mary E. Rickey, 1961; *Image and Symbol in the Sacred Poetry of Crashaw* by George Walton Williams, 1963; *The Art of Ecstasy: St. Teresa, Bernini, and Crashaw* by Robert T. Petersson, 1970.

*   *   *

Richard Crashaw is the odd man out among 17th-century English devotional poets, and it is difficult for a 20th-century reader to do justice to his poetry without a well-developed historical imagination. Some knowledge of the Counter-Reformation and of the consequent upsurge of religious fervour in Catholic countries, especially in Spain, enables us to put Crashaw's ardent devotion to the saints, the blessed sacrament, and the holy name of Jesus into perspective. Some familiarity with Baroque architecture, sculpture, and painting helps to illuminate Crashaw's poetic techniques. "Un-English" is an epithet frequently applied to him. He is accused of sensationalism, affectation, errors of taste. Whereas Palladian restraint appealed to English connoisseurs, the Baroque never became acclimatised. Yet the Rome which Milton visited before the Civil War, and to which Crashaw migrated after his conversion, was a city which embodied a new vision of splendour. Baroque is essentially an assertive style, rhetorical, often theatrical. It arouses amazement and impresses by sheer sumptuousness. As a term of literary criticism, Baroque is often misused, but it does apply to Richard Crashaw.

Possibly the current vogue for Baroque music may herald a new appreciation of Crashaw's flamboyant poems. He described his version of the "Stabat Mater" as "A Patheticall Descant upon the devout plainsong"; and "The Weeper" might be viewed as the verbal equivalent of virtuoso variations on a theme. Nevertheless, words and phrases are capable of conveying such mundane associations that poetical and musical compositions produce very different impressions and reactions. One of Crashaw's dominant topics was religious ecstasy. The vocabulary he used to describe it was of course not peculiar to himself. Many writers in the western mystical tradition, notably St. John of the Cross and St. Teresa, employ the metaphors of sexual love and of eating and drinking to express the closeness of the union between the soul and God. Unfortunately it is all too easy for post-Freudian readers to interpret such language as the utterance of sexual frustration. There are indeed morbidities in some of Crashaw's image-clusters which are hard to explain in any other way, no matter how much account is taken of the prevalence of bleeding hearts, milky or panting breasts, and fiery darts in the devotional manuals and emblem-books with which the poet was familiar. Nowadays, too, when the Church of Rome itself is abandoning the cult of the saints, it is more than ever difficult to respond to Crashaw's passionate devotion to swooning and weeping holy women. Yet he is a poet of great enterprise and accomplishment, whose strength of feeling is allied with considerable intellectual force.

In the preface to his *Steps to the Temple*, published after he had quitted England, Crashaw is described as "Herbert's second but equal." In tenderness of tone and sometimes in purity of diction, Crashaw does resemble his predecessor; but he differs from him radically in a total absence of self-analysis. The texture of his verse is less sinewy, his wit less compact. He has strong poetic affinities with Cowley. They were friends at Cambridge, and engaged in a famous poetic dialogue on Hope. Milton, too, four years Crashaw's senior, overlapped with him at Cambridge. There are a good many stylistic and thematic parallels between Milton's 1645 *Poems* and Crashaw's *Steps to the Temple*, printed in 1646. Unlike Herbert, Crashaw produced some good secular verse. Like both Herbert and Milton, he was a precocious scholar and an exceptionally fine Latinist. He resembles Milton in being a literary poet, drawing his inspiration from books, pictures, and music rather than from the life of his fellow-men. Like him, he was an extremely careful craftsman, tireless in revision. He experimented with odes of a Pindaric type, and was master of many lyric and narrative measures. Crashaw's verse is rhythmically varied and never discordant. There is more intellectual vigour in his poems than their sensuous imagery and mellifluous fluency might at first suggest. A fine example of ardour controlled by brainwork is his "Hymn to the Name of Jesus."

If Crashaw's poems are considered in the context of Caroline culture, they do not appear particularly exotic. The King's taste in art and entertainment was refined and cosmopolitan. His piety was profound, and he was as anxious as Archbishop Laud to emphasise the Catholic heritage of the Anglican church. Dignity of ritual and beauty of ornament were not lacking in the places of worship frequented by Crashaw at Cambridge. The chapels of Pembroke College and Peterhouse had recently been embellished, as had Little St. Mary's, of which Crashaw became a curate. The Master of Peterhouse was Dr. John Cosin, an eminent liturgical scholar, interested in church music, whose *Collections of Private Devotions in the Practice of the Ancient Church* may well have been "the little volume but large book" which Crashaw sent to "Mrs M. R." The community at Little Gidding, visited in time of tribulation by King Charles himself, was very dear to Crashaw, who shared in the devotional life and became an intimate friend of the Ferrar family -- another link, incidentally, with Herbert. The young cleric was famed for the ravishing eloquence of his sermons and the intensity of his prayer-life. He was in no sense a misfit in Cambridge during the 1630's.

Many of his ardently devout poems were composed while he was still a member of the Church of England. Those published posthumously, in *Carmen Deo Nostro*, are on the whole rather more subdued in tone, more disciplined in feeling, than the earlier pieces. They include his variants on some of the great Latin hymns. These celebrate, perhaps, his sense of home-coming. For it cannot be denied that Crashaw's was an *anima naturaliter cattolica*, as Mario Praz observed. The zeal of Parliament and its Commissioners against Laudian Anglicanism eventually drove Crashaw into exile, and into the arms of Mother Church. The Rome of St. Filippo Neri, the Rome of Bernini, offered him marvels beyond the scope of Cambridge; and in the fulness of Catholic doctrine, ritual, and piety his spirit found unbounded satisfaction. The elegy by his friend Cowley opens with the lines: "Poet and Saint! to thee alone are given/The two most sacred names of earth and heaven." A very different poet from "holy Mr. Herbert," who was esteemed "little less than sainted"; but one who in his most exalted moments far outsoared him.

—Margaret Bottrall

DANIEL, Samuel. English. Born near Taunton, Somerset, c. 1562. Educated at Magdalen Hall, Oxford, 1581–84. Served with the English Ambassador to Paris, Lord Stafford, 1586; with Sir Edward Dymoke, the Queen's Champion, in Italy, c. 1590–91, at Lincoln, 1592; with the Countess of Pembroke, c. 1592–94; with Lord Mountjoy, c. 1595; Tutor to the Countess of Cumberland's daughter, Lady Anne Clifford, c. 1599; Licenser to the Children of the Queen's Revels, 1604–05; served with the Earl of Hertford, c. 1605–08; Groom of the Queen's Privy Chamber, 1607–12, and Gentleman Extraordinary of the Queen's Privy Chamber, 1613–19; also Manager of the Youths of Her Majesty's Royal Chamber of Bristol, 1615–18. Lived in Beckington, Somerset, after 1611. *Buried 14 October 1619.*

PUBLICATIONS

Collections

Complete Works in Verse and Prose, edited by Alexander B. Grosart.   5 vols., 1885–96.
Poems, and A Defence of Rhyme, edited by Arthur Colby Sprague.   1930.

Verse

Delia, An Ode, The Complaint of Rosamond.   1592; revised edition, 1592; as Delia and Rosamond Augmented, Cleopatra, 1594; revised edition of Delia, in Works, 1601; Delia edited by A. Esdaile, with Idea by Michael Drayton, 1908; The Complaint of Rosamond edited by N. Alexander, in Elizabethan Narrative Verse, 1967.
The Civil Wars, books 1–5.   1595; books 1–6, in Works, 1601; books 1–8, 1609; edited by Laurence Michel, 1958.
Poetical Essays.   1599; Musophilus edited by Raymond Himelick, 1965.
Works.   1601.
A Panegyric Congratulatory to the King's Majesty, Certain Epistles.   1603.
Certain Small Poems, Philotas.   1605; revised edition, as Certain Small Works, 1607, 1611.

A Funeral Poem upon the Earl of Devonshire. 1606.
The Whole Works in Poetry. 1623.

Plays

Cleopatra (produced 1593?). In Delia and Rosamond Augmented, Cleopatra, 1594;
edited by Geoffrey Bullough, in Narrative and Dramatic Sources of Shakespeare 5,
1964.
The True Description of a Royal Masque (produced 1604). 1604; as The Vision of the
12 Goddesses, 1604; edited by Joan Rees, in A Book of Masques in Honour of
Allardyce Nicoll, 1967.
Philotas (produced 1604). In Certain Small Poems, Philotas, 1605; edited by Laurence
Michel, 1949.
The Queen's Arcadia (produced 1605). 1606.
Tethys' Festival (produced 1610). In The Creation of Prince Henry, Prince of Wales,
1610; edited by J. Nichols, in Progresses of James I, 1828.
Hymen's Triumph (produced 1614). 1615.

Other

A Defence of Rhyme, in A Panegyric Congratulatory to the King's Majesty. 1603; edited
by G. B. Harrison, with Observations in the Art of English Poesie by Thomas
Campion, 1925.
The First Part of the History of England. 1612; revised edition, as The Collection of the
History of England, 1618.

Translator, The Worthy Tract of Paulus Jovius Containing a Discourse of
Imprese. 1585.

Bibliography: Daniel: A Concise Bibliography by S. A. Tannenbaum, 1942; supplement by
G. R. Guffey, 1967.

Reading List: Daniel: A Critical and Biographical Study by Joan Rees, 1964; Daniel by Cecil
Seronsy, 1967; Daniel: Sa Vie, Son Oeuvre by Pierre Spriet, 1968.

*   *   *

Samuel Daniel's literary career is of a kind and quality which have always brought him the
attention and admiration of the discriminating. The range of his work includes lyric, Ovidian
narrative, plays (both closet drama and works intended for performance), masques, an
historical poem of epic character, and a prose history. He also wrote a critical essay of
unusual breadth and penetration, verse epistles of distinction, and an admirable verse treatise
embodying a "general defence of all learning." His sonnet sequence, Delia, one of the earliest
and best of the time, using, predominantly, the English or Shakespearian form, lacks the
drama and variety found in some others but compensates for this by its skilful patterns of
imagery and subtle use of assonance, alliteration, and balance. The lyric impulse is fortified
by an intelligence which controls the verse patterns and penetrates to some depth the
situation of the frustrated lover.
    As Daniel grew older, a vein of mature reflectiveness became one of his most striking
characteristics. Beautiful and powerful passages may occur anywhere in his work but the
distinctive tone is one of sober, thoughtful eloquence. He is among the most humane of the

Elizabethans and his commentaries on people and events, in all the modes which he employed, are marked by a firm sense of moral values coupled with a sympathetic and imaginative understanding of human predicaments. This is as true when he deals with the life of Cleopatra in a play as when he writes a fine funeral elegy for his friend and patron, Charles Blount, Duke of Devonshire. He was keenly aware of the many-sidedness of experience and may have learnt to treat this with special insight and feeling because of the degree of conflict in his own personality, between his lyric gifts on the one hand and his critical and scholarly intelligence on the other. The duality sometimes weakens his work but often enriches it, for the range and intelligence of his sensitivity and responsiveness constitute a large part of his attractiveness as a writer. Those readers who allow his quiet voice to speak to them understand why his contemporaries (including Shakespeare) found him worth imitating and why Wordsworth and Coleridge, among many others, singled him out for praise.

—Joan Rees

DAVIES, Sir John. English. Born in Tisbury, Wiltshire, baptized 16 April 1569. Educated at Winchester School; Queen's College, Oxford, 1586–90, B.A. 1590; Middle Temple, London, 1588–94; called to the Bar, 1595; disbarred, 1597; reinstated, 1601. Married Eleanor Touchet in 1609; two children. Member of Parliament for Corfe Castle, 1601, and for Newcastle under Lyme, 1615, 1621; also, Member of the Irish Parliament: Solicitor-General for Ireland, 1603–06, Attorney-General for Ireland, 1606–19, and Speaker of the Irish Parliament, 1613; King's Sergeant after 1609; named Lord Chief Justice of the King's Bench, 1626. A Founder, Society of Antiquaries, c. 1615. Knighted, 1609. *Died 8 December 1626.*

PUBLICATIONS

Collections

Works in Verse and Prose, edited by Alexander B. Grosart.   2 vols., 1869–76.
Poems, edited by Clare Howard.   1941.

Verse

Epigrams and Elegies of Ovid, with Christopher Marlowe.   1595(?); as *Epigrams,* with *All Ovid's Elegies: 3 Books,* 1598(?).
Orchestra; or, A Poem of Dancing.   1596; revised edition, 1622; edited by E. M. W. Tillyard, 1945.
Hymns of Astraea in Acrostic Verse.   1599.
Nosce Teipsum: This Oracle Expounded in Two Elegies: Of Humane Knowledge, Of the Soul of Man and the Immortality Thereof.   1599.
A Poetical Rhapsody, edited by F. Davidson.   1602.
Gulling Sonnets, edited by Alexander B. Grosart.   1873.

Other

A Discovery of the True Causes Why Ireland Was Never Entirely Subdued until His Majesty's Reign. 1612; as *A Discovery of the State of Ireland,* 1613; edited by Henry Morley, in *Ireland under Elizabeth and James I,* 1890.

Le Primer Report des Cases Resolves en les Courts del Roy en Ireland. 1615.

The Question Concerning Impositions, Tonnage, Poundage, Prizage, Customs, etc. 1656.

Editor, *A Perfect Abridgement of the Eleven Books of Reports,* by Sir Edward Coke. 1651.

Reading List: *Philosophy in Poetry: A Study of Nosce Teipsum* by E. N. Sneath, 1903; *The Poet as Philosopher: A Study of Nosce Teipsum* by Mabel D. Holmes, 1921; *Five Poems* by E. M. W. Tillyard, 1948.

*   *   *

Written primarily during the 1590's, when expulsion from the Middle Temple threatened the great public career as a jurist he ultimately achieved, Sir John Davies's poetry, with the notable exception of *Orchestra,* stays gracefully within the technical and intellectual range of the gifted amateur and divides neatly into either serious or comic verse.

Nosce Teipsum, his best known and, until recently, most admired work, enjoins man to "Use all thy powers that blessed power to praise/Which gives thee power to *be,* and *use the same.*" The optimistic tone derives not only from Davies's manipulation of his sources in classical and Christian thought but also from the order and balance of the over 1900 lines, however apparently somber their theme:

> The wits that div'd most deepe, and soar'd most hie;
> Seeking Mans powers, have found his weaknes such:
> "Skill comes so slow, and life so fast doth flie,
> We learne so litle, and forget so much."

The mood of this representative stanza prefigures much 18th-century elegiac verse and explains Davies's popularity and influence in that period. The positive reactions of a wider range of readers from James I to T. S. Eliot presumably derive from Davies's embodying of complex philosophical ideas in concrete images.

But this apparent clarity is merely a soothing over-simplification with little emotional coloration, an effect making the poem's reputation puzzling. Further, Davies's explications of Renaissance psychology sometimes sink to a monosyllabic textbook style which flattens even his attempts at paradox: "Though *will* do oft, when *wit* false formes doth show,/Take *ill* for *good,* and *good* for *ill* refuse." Yet his technique is often subtle, and his analogy between the soul and a river demonstrates that elegant clarity the style can attain:

> Yet *nature* so her streames doth leade and carry,
> As that her course doth make no finall stay,
> Till she her selfe unto the *Ocean* marry,
> Within whose watery bosome first she lay.

The same technical skill informs *Hymnes of Astraea,* 26 16-line acrostics with initial letters spelling ELISABETHA REGINA. Hymnes XXI, XXII, and XXIV are especially felicitous. His *Epigrammes* earned him much contemporary praise as a comic writer (Guilpin's epithet of "English Martiall") and some condemnation (ecclesiastical authorities ordered the public burning of the volume containing the *Epigrammes* and Marlowe's *Elegies* in 1599). Like his serious verse, Davies's *Epigrammes* are competent, and he was apparently serious enough about his role as innovator to define for his audience the function of the epigram: "Which taxeth under a particular name,/A generall vice that merits publique blame" ("Ad Musam 1"). Davies is, however, often repetitive and unsubtle, as he condescendingly mocks the pretentions and excesses, primarily sexual, of his contemporaries. Perhaps familiarity with the actual victims would give needed substance to the humor, which only rarely, as in the climax to the satiric catalogue of tobacco's virtues, wittily illuminates the reality threatening Elizabethan fashionable life: "I would but say, that it the pox wil cure:/This were inough, without discoursing more,/All our brave gallants in the towne t'alure" ("Of Tobacco 36").

Davies's other major comic venture, the *Gullinge Sonnets* (composed 1594?), displays similar competence as he mocks excesses of Elizabethan imagery and implies the contrasting ideal of a utilitarian style like that of *Nosce Teipsum.* Perhaps the best is Sonnet 8, which celebrates a passion for Zepheria in an elaborate metaphor built from legal jargon like "distrein'de," "impounds," "highe Shreife," "esloynde," and "withername," imagery that threatens with ridicule even Shakespeare's powerful "sessions of sweet silent thought."

Davies wrote many occasional verses, including some recently accepted into his canon, but none approaches the brilliant fusion of philosophy and parody that characterizes *Orchestra Or a Poeme of Dauncing,* a gloss on the *Odyssey* in which a very un-Homeric Antinous uses all the charms of "courtly love" to persuade Penelope to dance, an activity combining cosmic significance with sexual innuendo. His speech of persuasion lovingly traces the concept of the universe as a dance to its genesis:

> *Dauncing* (bright lady) then began to be,
> When the first seedes whereof the world did spring,
> The Fire, Ayre, Earth and Water did agree,
> By Loves perswasion, Natures mighty King,
> To leave their first disordred combating;
> And in a daunce such measure to observe,
> As all the world their motion should preserve.

This sempiternal equation of dancing and order pervades all levels of cosmic and earthly activity, from planetary motions to military exercises. Although most of *Orchestra* focuses on Antinous's exposition of this argument (like Sidney's painstaking amplification of the antiquity and power of poetry in the *Defense*), Penelope's interruptions illuminate the delicate situation within which he discourses. Antinous carries his translation of even sexual myth into the dance metaphor so far that the process tends ironically to reverse itself, undercutting the professed motive of his invitation to the dance. Like a moralizer of Ovid obsessed by dance, he retells the stories of Mars and Venus, Caenus, and Tiresias as dance allegories; the puns in the portrait of Tiresias show that play of wit for its own sake overshadows the serious theme: "He tooke more pleasure in a womans part."

That Davies revised the ending of the 1622 version of *Orchestra* and added the phrase "not finished" raises further questions about the poem's tone. He may have wished to remove all reference to the original dedicatee, Richard Martin, with whom he had quarrelled, or to sharpen the satiric thrust of the poem with the added stanzas on Elizabeth. Antinous's gift of a magic mirror with a vision of Elizabeth and her court dancing seems about to cause Penelope's capitulation, a curious effect for one Elizabethan archetype of chastity to have on another, when the poem abruptly ends. Though Penelope's fascination with the mirror seems to satirize the effect of similar admonitory gifts in the popular Elizabethan complaint genre, and other elements mock the equally popular Ovidian mythological poetry, *Orchestra* has no consistent satiric pattern.

Irony and parody everywhere flank straightforward, though exuberant, exposition of the dance metaphor. Davies seems secure enough in his view of the universe to be playful with one of its key images, and to glance wittily at a number of Elizabethan excesses. His most distinctive poem, a dazzling catchall of Renaissance wit and cosmology, occasionally fuses, sometimes confuses the serious and comic elements that inform his other verse.

—Burton Kendle

DELONEY, Thomas.   English.   Born c. 1543. Very little is known about his life: worked as a silk-weaver, possibly in Norwich; member of the London Clothiers Guild; popular balladeer, especially after the death of William Elderton, c. 1585. *Died c. 1600*

PUBLICATIONS

Collections

> *Works,* edited by F. O. Mann.   1912.
> *Novels,* edited by Merritt E. Lawlis.   1961.

Fiction

> *The Gentle Craft: A Discourse Showing What Famous Men Have Been Shoemakers in Time Past.*   1598(?); part 1, 1627; complete version, 1635(?).
> *Thomas of Reading; or, The Six Worthy Yeomen of the West.*   1612 (12th edition).
> *The Pleasant History of John Winchcomb, Called Jack of Newbery.*   1619 (8th edition).

Verse

> *Three Old Ballads,* edited by J. O. Halliwell.   1860.

Other

> Editor, *Strange Histories of Kings, Princes, Dukes, etc.*   1600; revised edition, 1612, 1631; as *The Royal Garland of Love and Delight,* 1674.
> Editor, *The Garland of Good Will.*   1628; edited by J. H. Dixon, 1851.

> Translator, *A Declaration Made by the Archbishop of Cologne upon the Deed of His Marriage.*   1583.
> Translator, *The Mirror of Mirth and Pleasant Conceits,* by J. B. Des Periers, edited by James Woodrow Hassell.   1959.

Reading List: *An Inquiry into Aspects of the Language of Deloney* by T. Dahl, 1951; *Two Elizabethan Writers of Fiction: Thomas Nashe and Deloney* by R. G. Howarth, 1956; *Apology for the Middle Class: The Dramatic Novels of Deloney* by Merritt E. Lawlis, 1960; *Historischer Roman und Realismus: Das Erzählwerk Deloneys* by K. M. Paetzold, 1972.

*   *   *

Though he was England's most popular balladeer in the 1590's, Thomas Deloney's major accomplishment was to articulate in his fiction the dignity and power of hard work, a power reinforced by the blessings of a Protestant Providence. The disappearance or doubtful attribution of many of his ballads makes an assessment of his work in this genre difficult. Ironically, the tradition that Deloney provoked the authorities with a ballad on the scarcity of grain that depicted the Queen in a dialogue of a "very fond and indecent sort" is more interesting than any of his extant ballads, whether versified episodes from Holinshed (*Strange Histories*), or lurid journalistic treatments of contemporary scandals ("The Lamentation of Mr. Pages Wife – of Plimouth, who, being forc'd to wed him, consented to his Murder, for the love of G. Strangwidge; for which they suffered at Barnstable in Devonshire.") Deloney does little to raise the Elizabethan ballad to the level of its medieval ancestor, but his characteristic voice sounds occasionally, as in "A pleasant Dialogue betweene plaine *Truth* and blind *Ignorance*," when a Catholic Ignorance defends his faith in the rustic dialect Deloney was to use brilliantly in his fiction: "Ich care not for this Bible Booke,/tis too big to be true./Our blessed Ladies Psalter,/zhall for my mony go."

Whatever their provenance in the oral tradition that fed these ballads, in Renaissance jest-books, and in his observation of Elizabethan manners, Deloney's four prose narratives published during his last four years constitute his distinctive contribution to English literature and foreshadow the work of later novelists like Defoe. Deloney's embryonic novels, all celebrating the rise to success and the ethics of both individual clothiers and shoemakers and of the crafts collectively, were very popular in his day and were frequently reprinted in the 17th and 18th centuries as the English middle class increased in numbers and influence. Significantly, Deloney addressed *Jack of Newbery* and *The Gentle Craft* to the clothiers and "cordwayners" who are the heroes of these books, rather than to the aristocratic patrons who subsidized and presumably inspired many Renaissance works. He embodies his core myth in the career of Jack, a dedicated weaver who indulges in decorous amusement only on Sundays, and who learns never to carry more than 12 pence to lend to improvident fellow workers. Jack becomes head of the business by marrying his boss's widow, who appreciates his youthful comeliness less than his hard work and leadership potentiality; he creates a world of happy singing workers, and he arms soldiers to defeat cowardly Scottish invaders (foreigners are invariably unattractive in Deloney's xenophobic world). Crowning these achievements, Jack skillfully defends his class against the wily Cardinal Wolsey in a dispute over unfair trade restrictions. He ultimately patronizes many aristocrats and dresses his own retainers in livery, but refuses a title, preferring to "rest in my russet coat, a poore clothier to my dying day." Deloney is ambivalent about aristocrats: they are necessary symbols of traditional order, but their unearned privilege makes more attractive the cheerful and persistent labors of rising workers.

The Gentle Craft (2 parts) teaches that princes have worked proudly at shoemaking since ancient times, a tradition justifying the adjective "gentle," and explaining the comforting adage that "a shoemaker's son is said to be a prince born." The strongest exemplar of the financial and civic success that rewards honest industry is Simon Eyre (part 1), a Dick Whittington variant who rises from country apprentice to Lord Mayor of London. Eyre's pride in his ascent generates an elevated concept of responsibility toward workers, fellow entrepreneurs, and the economic health of the nation.

Thomas of Reading, which traces the careers of several clothiers in the time of Henry I, shows that half the populace worked happily and profitably at the weaving trade: "there were few or no beggars at all; poor people, whom God lightly blesseth with most children, did by means of this occupation, so order them, that by the time that they were come to six or seven years of age, they were able to get their own bread." Though intemperate living sometimes threatens Deloney's businessmen, they profit from their mistakes and from Thomas's gifts sufficiently to return to lucrative operations. Deloney creates no dishonest businessmen, at least not English businessmen; success transforms capitalists into philanthropists: they bequeath money to establish schools, support monasteries, and help young couples begin middle-class existence.

What insures Deloney's effectiveness is not this naively inspirational material, but a lively style that embodies economic growth and social decency in terms familiar to his audience. His homely euphuism domesticates exotic material: "Nay, quoth another, I'll lay my life that as the salamander cannot live without the fire, so Jack cannot live without the smell of his dame's smock"; yet his serious use of Lyly in romantic episodes predictably fails. Strengthening his colloquial tone is the anecdote invented to explain the genesis of familiar figures of speech, such as "St. Hugh's bones" for shoemaker's tools. And he has a talent for dialect, rustic and foreign, often involving malapropisms and often indecent. This humor condescendingly mocks those whose birth bars them from the English middle class. These elements and the illusion of ordinary life ("then shalt thou scoure thy pitchy fingers in a bason of hot water, with an ordinary washing Ball ...") support Deloney's translation of romance and mythic motifs to the ethical and aesthetic equivalents that suit the taste of his audience. Instead of winning princesses and kingdoms in heroic contests against princely rivals, Deloney's heroes aspire prosaically to the hands of mature widows, less for their beauty than for the businesses they control. Romantic love governs only foreigners, fools, and effete aristocrats (when Deloney does attempt a straightforward love theme, it reads like a poor imitation of an episode from a Greene romance). In *The Gentle Craft*, part 2, an apprentice wins his wealthy mistress by performing a variety of dirty kitchen tasks, a domestic version of Hercules' cleaning the Augean stables. Jack of Newbery's rivals vie with gifts of food in a ritual suggesting a childlike belief in the efficacy of material goods to establish the status of the giver and the extent of his devotion. One rival is understandably upset when the widow rejects him: "I never spent a pig and a goose to so bad a purpose before." But the suitors politely refuse the widow's offer to return their gifts: "although we have lost our labors, we have not lost our manners," a response affirming that fusion of public and private decency that characterizes Deloney.

The episodic nature of Deloney's works argues his inability to control plots, perhaps an inheritance from the jest-book tradition, but his good-humored, pragmatic tone unifies otherwise disparate anecdotes. Without Nashe's brilliant style that obviates any criticism of structure, or Greene's anguished personae whose authenticity makes plotting irrelevant, Deloney nevertheless creates a comforting world with a cohesive mood and system of values. Yet, though his fiction has considerable charm and wit, this world is so domestic and practical that the hierarchy of these values occasionally raises inadvertent questions. After an innkeeper and his wife murder Thomas of Reading in a gory episode that foreshadows Macbeth's murder of Duncan, and after Deloney's Providence administers the grimly appropriate punishment, he causes incipient laughter by implying that financial insolvency may be more serious a sin than homicide: "And yet notwithstanding all the money which they had gotten thereby, they prospered not, but at their deaths were found in debt."

—Burton Kendle

DENHAM, Sir John.   English.   Born in Dublin, Ireland, in 1615.   Educated at Trinity College, Oxford, 1631–34; Lincoln's Inn, London, 1634; called to the Bar, 1639.   Married 1) Anne Cotton in 1634 (died, 1647), two sons, two daughters; 2) Margaret Brooke in 1665 (died, 1667).   Succeeded to the family estate at Egham, Surrey, 1638; Sheriff for Surrey, 1642; a royalist: during Civil War defended Farnham Castle unsuccessfully, and imprisoned briefly in London; in Oxford, 1643, and France, 1646, possibly serving the Queen; exiled after 1648, in Charles II's entourage, though returned to England for various periods during the 1650's; after Restoration: Surveyor-General of Works, 1660–69, and Member of Parliament for Old Sarum, 1661–69.   Founding Member, Royal Society.   Knight, Order of the Bath, 1661. Became ill in 1666; confined to a mental asylum, 1666–67.   *Died 19 March 1669.*

PUBLICATIONS

Collections

    Poetical Works, edited by Theodore Howard Banks, Jr.   1928.

Verse

    Cooper's Hill.   1642; revised edition, 1655; edited by Brendan O Hehir, in *Expans'd Hieroglyphicks,* 1969.
    Mr. Hampden's Speech.   1643.
    The Destruction of Troy, from the *Aeneid* of Virgil.   1656.
    Panegyric on General Monck.   1659.
    A Relation of a Quaker That Attempted to Bugger a Mare near Colchester.   1659.
    The Second Advice to the Painter, in Imitation of Waller.   1667.
    Poems and Translations.   1668.
    A Version of the Psalms of David.   1714.

Plays

    The Sophy (produced 1641).   1642.
    Horace, by Katherine Phillips, completed by Denham, from a play by Corneille (produced 1668).   1678.

Other

    The Anatomy of Play.   1651.

    Translator, *Cato Major, Of Old Age,* by Cicero.   1669.

Bibliography: in *Poetical Works,* 1928.

Reading List: *The Subtler Language* by Earl R. Wassermann, 1959; *Harmony from Discords: A Life of Denham* by Brendan O Hehir, 1968.

*   *   *

In asserting that John Denham was the originator of "*local poetry*, of which the fundamental subject is some particular landscape," Dr. Johnson might seem to have overlooked or discounted some earlier seventeenth- or even sixteenth-century examples, but if Johnson had in mind the contemplation and celebration of a distant view or prospect of a place, then *Cooper's Hill* indeed initiated a "new species of composition," and one which was to be emulated, imitated, or burlesqued for more than a hundred years.

From the crown of the Hill, Denham surveys the Thames in its valley below, and exclaims:

> O could I flow like thee, and make thy stream
> My great example, as it is my theme!
> Though deep, yet clear, though gentle, yet not dull,
> Strong without rage, without o'erflowing full.

His verse should flow like the river which is the subject of his verse. This is the aspiration, and in these lines it could be said that the prescription is nearly met: the verse, if not profound, has, like the Thames contained within its banks, perspicuity, ease, strength. In general, here is the prescribed formula or model of the closed rhymed couplet which was to rule for several generations. Again Johnson, quoting Matthew Prior, recognizes this: "Denham and Waller improved our versification, and Dryden perfected it." Apart from the versification, *Cooper's Hill* set the pattern that a poetic contemplation of a landscape should provide, besides the description, a series of moralizing reflections on the events associated with the place.

The celebrity of *Cooper's Hill* has overshadowed the remainder of Denham's output which, though not large, is in several kinds. His blank-verse play, *The Sophy*, performed at Court in 1641 and "admired by all ingenious men," was daring inasmuch as the high-handed actions of Charles I, shortly to precipitate the civil war, appear to be clearly indicated by the behaviour of the Persian despot in the drama. When the war did break out, however, Denham – though, like Waller, "zealous against Ship-money" – was on the side of the Royalists.

A precursor of and an example in his poetic style for Dryden, Denham was eminently the poetic commentator on the current political events and personalities of his time. Unlike Dryden's verse though, Denham's rarely has the ring and magnificence to fire the modern reader who, unless he is an historian, may have slight interest in mid-seventeenth-century figures and controversies. Still, his lines "On the Earl of Strafford's Tryal and Death," representative of this main category of his writing, can be admired for their wit and incisiveness.

Of his verse translations from French, Latin, and Greek, "composing more than half the body of his work" as his editor T. H. Banks observes, the most interesting is his rendering of part of *The Aeneid*, Bk II, "The Passion of Dido for Aeneas." Conveying little or nothing of Virgil's emotive richness, the couplets have an elegance and neat rapidity of movement. The relation between these and Waller's and Dryden's renderings of Virgil is of interest. The latter certainly admired Denham's version.

From our present perspective, *Cooper's Hill* remains as Denham's one triumphant success as a poet.

—Francis Berry

DONNE, John.   English.   Born in London, January/June 1572; grandson of the writer John Heywood, great-grandson of the writer John Rastell. Educated at Hart Hall, Oxford, 1584–87; Cambridge University; Thavies Inn, London, 1591; Lincoln's Inn, 1592 (Master of the Revels, 1593–95). Married (secretly) Ann More in 1601 (died, 1617); six daughters, four sons. Took part in the Earl of Essex's expeditions to Cadiz, 1596, and to the Azores, 1597. Entered the service of the Lord Keeper, Sir Thomas Egerton, as Private Secretary, London, 1598; also, Member of Parliament for Brackley, 1601; discovery of his secret marriage to the Lord Keeper's niece caused him to be dismissed from his post and briefly imprisoned, and destroyed his hopes of political advancement. Lived in Pyrford, Surrey, 1602–06, and Mitcham, Surrey, 1606–11; travelled to the Continent, with Sir Walter Chute, 1605–06, with Sir Robert Drury, 1611–12. Born a Roman Catholic: at the instigation of King James, ordained in the Anglican Church, 1615; as royal chaplain attended James at Cambridge; Rector, Keyston, Hampshire, 1616–21, and Sevenoaks, Kent, 1616; Divine Reader (Preacher), Lincoln's Inn, 1616–21; Chaplain, Viscount Doncaster's embassy to Germany, 1619; Dean of St. Paul's, London, 1621; Rector, Blunham, Bedfordshire, 1622; Prebendary of Chiswick, 1622; Vicar, St. Dunstan's-in-the-West, London, 1624; Prolocutor of Convocation, 1626. Honorary Member of the Council, Virginia Company, 1622; Governor of the Charterhouse, London, 1626; Justice of the Peace, Kent and Bedfordshire, 1622, and Bedfordshire, 1626; served on the Court of Delegates, 1622–31. M.A.: Oxford University, 1610; D.D.: Cambridge University, 1615. *Died 31 March 1631.*

PUBLICATIONS

Collections

Poems, edited by H. J. C. Grierson.   2 vols., 1912.
Complete Poems and Selected Prose, edited by John Hayward.   1929; revised edition, 1936.
Complete Poetry, edited by John T. Shawcross.   1967.
Complete English Poems, edited by A. J. Smith.   1971.

Verse

The Anatomy of the World.   1611; *The Second Anniversary: Of the Progress of the Soul,* 1612; edited by Frank Manley, as *The Anniversaries,* 1963.
Poems.   1633.
Divine Poems, edited by Helen Gardner.   1952; revised edition, 1978.
Elegies, and Songs and Sonnets, edited by Helen Gardner.   1965.
Satires, Epigrams, and Verse Letters, edited by W. Milgate.   1967.
The Anniversaries, Epithalamions, and Epicedes, edited by W. Milgate.   1978.

Other

Pseudo-Martyr.   1610.
Conclave Ignati.   1611; as *Ignatius His Conclave,* 1611; edited by T. S. Healy, 1969.
Three Sermons.   1623.
Devotions upon Emergent Occasions.   1624; edited by Elizabeth Savage, 2 vols., 1975.
Four Sermons.   1625.
Five Sermons.   1626.

Juvenilia; or, Certain Paradoxes and Problems.   1633; edited by R. E. Bennett, 1936.
Six Sermons.   1634.
Two Sermons.   1634.
LXXX Sermons.   1640.
Biathanatos.   1646.
Catalogus Librorum Aulicorum, in *Poems.*   1650; edited by Evelyn M. Simpson, as *The Courtier's Library,* 1930.
Essays in Divinity, Interwoven with Meditations and Prayers.   1651; edited by Evelyn M. Simpson, 1952.
Letters to Several Persons of Honour.   1651; edited by E. E. Merrill, Jr., 1910.
Paradoxes, Problems, Characters, with Ignatius His Conclave.   1652.
Prayers, edited by Herbert H. Umbach.   1951.
The Sermons, edited by G. R. Potter and Evelyn M. Simpson.   10 vols., 1953–62.
Prebend Sermons, edited by Janel Mueller.   1971.

Bibliography: *A Bibliography of Donne* by Geoffrey Keynes, 1914, revised edition 1973; *Donne: An Annotated Bibliography of Modern Criticism 1912–1967* by John R. Roberts, 1973.

Reading List: *Life and Letters of Donne* by Edmund Gosse, 2 vols., 1899; *A Study of the Prose Works* by Evelyn M. Simpson, 1924, revised edition, 1948; *The Monarch of Wit* by J. B. Leishman, 1951; *Donne: A Collection of Critical Essays* edited by Helen Gardner, 1962; *Discussions of Donne* edited by Frank Kermode, 1963; *Five Metaphysical Poets* by Joan Bennett, 1963; *A Preface to Donne* by James Winny, 1970; *Donne: A Life* by R. C. Bald, 1970; *The Soul of Wit: A Study of Donne* by Murray Rosten, 1974; *Donne: The Critical Heritage* edited by A. J. Smith, 1975; *Essential Articles for the Study of Donne's Poetry* edited by John R. Roberts, 1976.

*   *   *

Perhaps at no period has a poet more strikingly embodied the characteristics of his age than John Donne, leader of the Metaphysical school. A time of transition like our own – which largely accounts for the modern revival of interest in the poets who reflected it – the seventeenth century was energized by a spirit of wide-ranging enquiry, both scientific and geographical. In *The Anniversaries* (*An Anatomie of the World* and *Of the Progresse of the Soule*) Donne powerfully indicates the currents of bewilderment and doubt in his contemporaries' response to the speculations of the "new" scientists and philosophers, so swiftly displacing the accustomed shape of the medieval world-picture. The late Elizabethan voyages of discovery had further expanded the frontiers of human consciousness; and here too Donne explores the events and ideas which were quickening public interest and imagination. "The Good-Morrow" charts the adventure of love through images of sea-discoverers, maps, new worlds, latitude and longitude; while its metaphor of the lovers' eyes as hemispheres, each reflecting the face of the other, recurs in "A Valediction: of Weeping." The souls of parted lovers in "A Valediction: Forbidding Mourning" are likened to the action of a pair of compasses. "The Sunne Rising" draws an analogy between the earth's riches – the spices of the East Indies and the gold mines of the West – and those the lover enjoys in his mistress. Even death, in "Hymne to God My God, in My Sicknesse," is envisaged as an exploration: the poet's physicians as cosmographers, his body as their map, and the evocative names of distant territories employed to interpret the spirit's final voyage of discovery. The art of alchemy, a strong attraction for the seventeenth-century mind, also furnishes Donne with metaphors as telling as others drawn from various aspects of belief inherited from medieval scholasticism (see especially "Aire and Angels" and the conclusion of "The Good-Morrow"). "The Canonization" ends with an image of the distillation of essences; while the refining of metals yields the magnificent simile, in "A Valediction: Forbidding Mourning," of two souls not divided by absence but expanded, "Like gold to ayery thinnesse beate." The alchemist's refining fire burns through the lovers' experience in "The Exstasie," as, in "A Nocturnall upon S. Lucies Day," it consumes and transmutes the bereaved spirit into an absolute of annihilation.

As a love poet Donne displays a range of mood more varied and a concept of passion more complex and profound than any of his predecessors. In reaction against the Petrarchan tradition favoured by Elizabethan sonneteers – the faithful lover for ever pining, prostrate and spurned, at the feet of a disdainful mistress – Donne's love poems often strike a defiantly disenchanted note. Conventional sentiment and diction are displaced by a testy aggressiveness in openings like "So, so, breake off this last lamenting kisse," or the still more irascible "For Godsake hold your tongue, and let me love." Prosaic adjectives and verbs – "spongy" for a weeping woman's eyes in "The Indifferent," "snorted" of the lovers in "The Good-Morrow" – are paralleled by the audacious conceit of the flea which, in uniting the blood of lover and mistress, becomes their "mariage bed, and mariage temple." "The Sunne Rising" disrespectfully apostrophizes its august subject as a "Busie old foole, unruly" and a "Sawcy pedantique wretch."

Such impudent colloquialism distressed the conservative Dryden, who lamented Donne's lack of "dignity of expression," as well as his tendency to "perplex the minds of the fair sex with nice speculations of philosophy, when he should engage their hearts, and entertain them with the softnesses of love." Certainly the subtle, close-knit, and often paradoxical argument, complicated syntax, and erudite allusions of the *Songs and Sonnets* make considerable demands upon Donne's readers; while their metrical flexibility drove Ben Jonson to declare that "for not keeping of accent" their author "deserved hanging." Yet in his greatest love poems, intellectual content and verbal ingenuity are charged with deep feeling. Describing himself, in "The Blossome," as the owner of a "naked thinking heart ... which lov'st to be/ Subtile to plague thy selfe," Donne crystallizes his unique blend of reason with passionate imagination. As T. S. Eliot said, "A thought, to Donne, was an experience; it modified his sensibility."

The metaphysical vision, which consistently seeks to establish the underlying unity of existence, is admirably summed up by Joan Bennett's observation (in *Five Metaphysical Poets*) that "The same flame that lights the intellect warms the heart; mathematics and love obey one principle ... one law is at work in all experience." Dr. Johnson attacked the Metaphysicals' habit of "ransacking" nature and art "for illustrations, comparisons, and allusions," their "heterogeneous ideas ... yoked by violence together." Yet Donne's most daring analogies and juxtapositions are invariably felicitous. Human love is enlarged, intensified, and dignified by its cosmic context, as it echoes and is echoed by the activity of sun and moon, seas and floods, tempest and earthquake, the very air itself.

The supremacy of a full relationship between man and woman is one of Donne's most constant themes. Love bestows safety upon the couple in "The Anniversarie"; encompasses and concentrates human experience, in "The Sunne Rising," "The Good-Morrow," and "The Canonization," to make "one little roome, an every where." Its ultimate aim is that fusion of two separate identities into a perfect whole explored with such metaphysical subtlety in "The Exstasie." Here, too, Donne expresses his most urgent and explicit recognition of the interdependence of body and soul in love. Passion, however rarefied, cannot exist indefinitely in abstraction; as he says in "Aire and Angels," "Love must ... take a body too."

But love, in Donne, is seldom unshadowed by mortality. He was, as Eliot said of Webster, "much possessed by death,/And saw the skull beneath the skin." In poems like "The Apparition," "The Legacie," or "The Dampe," the treatment is lighter and more ironic; but many others probe the mysteries of love and death at a profounder level. Both "The Canonization" and "The Relique" (with its unforgettable image of "A bracelet of bright haire about the bone") contemplate from beyond the grave the perfection of a past relationship. "The Anniversarie" triumphantly proclaims love's sole invincibility over corruption and dissolution; but the sombre finality of the St. Lucy's Day "Nocturnall" evokes a winter darkness of the soul from which there can be no rebirth. That poem provides the unassailable answer to Johnson's contention that the Metaphysicals' "courtship was void of fondness and their lamentation of sorrow."

In many of these poems Donne suggests affinities between earthly and divine love. The sardonic opening stanzas of "The Relique" develop into a searching investigation of the nature of miracles which makes human and heavenly implicitly synonymous. The concept of dead lovers worshipped as saints recurs in "The Canonization," with an insistence on love's other-worldliness which is echoed in the reference to the rest of mankind as "the layetie" in "A Valediction: Forbidding Mourning." This idea of love as divine revelation is perhaps strongest in "The Exstasie," whose lovers are liberated from their bodies into a mystical state of clarified perception unhampered by senses or reason.

The death of Donne's wife, two years after his ordination in 1615, strengthened the wholeness of his own surrender to religion. Yet in the Holy Sonnet "Batter my heart, three person'd God," he entreats the Almighty to storm his defences and penetrate the citadel of his spirit with an ardour as personal and passionate as for any of his human loves. In the audacity of the culminating erotic metaphor ("Nor ever chast, except you ravish mee") the experience is envisaged as an essentially similar invasion and possession of the self.

Donne does not hesitate to communicate this conviction through every poetic device at his command, even, in "A Hymne to God the Father," a boldly sustained punning on his own name. The metaphysical conceit is for him no mere frivolous decoration, but intrinsic to a poem's intensity and meaning. The geometrical "binding of a circle and the union of lovers," as Joan Bennett observes, "are equivalent symbols of eternity and perfection"; erudite abstract dialectic expresses the total desolation of loss experienced by the lover in the "Nocturnall"; and wit is equally compatible with the solemnity of sin, salvation, and the love of God.

From the tensions imposed by his vocation upon a turbulent and sensual nature flowed the power and passion of Donne's *Divine Poems*. Confessing in "A Hymne to God the Father" his fear of the finality of physical death, Donne invokes the light of God's Son to shine upon him at the last. The entreaty is answered in "Hymne to God My God, in My Sicknesse," where all doubts are submerged in certain hope of resurrection. Donne's supreme affirmation of faith triumphant over what, in a sermon, he called "the last and in that respect the worst enemy," is the conclusion of his Holy Sonnet "Death be not proud":

> One short sleepe past, wee wake eternally,
> And death shall be no more, Death thou shalt die.

—Margaret Willy

DRAYTON, Michael. English. Born in Hartshill, Atherstone, Warwickshire, in 1563. Educated (possibly) at a school in Coventry. Probably in the service of Henry, later Sir Henry, Goodere of Polesworth, and his brother Thomas, from age 10, and of Lucy Harrington, Lady Bedford, after 1595; possibly employed by Queen Elizabeth in a diplomatic mission to Scotland; writer for the Admiral's Players, London, 1597–1602; a friend of Jonson and Shakespeare; an esquire of Sir Walter Aston, 1603; associated with the Children of the King's Revels, at the Whitefriars Theatre, London, c. 1607. *Died in 1631.*

PUBLICATIONS

Collections

> Complete Works, edited by J. W. Hebel, Kathleen Tillotson, and Bernard H. Newdigate.   5 vols., 1931–41.
> Poems, edited by John Buxton.   2 vols., 1953.
> Poems (selection), edited by Vivien Thomas.   1977.

Verse

> The Harmony of the Church: Spiritual Songs and Holy Hymns.   1591; as A Heavenly Harmony, 1610.
> Idea: The Shepherds' Garland in Nine Eclogues.   1593.
> Piers Gaveston.   1593; revised edition, as The Legend of Piers Gaveston, with Robert, Duke of Normandy and Matilda, 1596.
> Idea's Mirror: Amours in Quaterzains.   1594; revised edition, as Idea, with England's Heroical Epistles, 1600.
> Matilda, The Daughter of Lord Fitzwater.   1594; revised edition, as The Legend of Matilda, with Robert, Duke of Normandy, and Piers Gaveston, 1596.
> Endymion and Phoebe: Idea's Latmus.   1594; edited by Elizabeth Story Donno, in Elizabethan Minor Epics, 1963.
> Mortimeriados: The Civil Wars of Edward the Second and the Barons.   1596; revised edition, as The Barons' Wars, 1603.
> The Tragical Legend of Robert, Duke of Normandy; The Legend of Matilda; The Legend of Piers Gaveston.   1596.
> England's Heroical Epistles.   1597; revised edition, 1598, 1600.
> Moses in a Map of His Miracles.   1604; revised edition, as Moses His Birth and Miracles, in The Muses' Elysium, 1630.
> The Owl.   1604.
> Poems.   1605.
> Poems Lyric and Pastoral.   1606(?); The Ballad of Agincourt edited by B. Juel-Jensen, 1951.
> The Legend of Great Cromwell.   1607.
> Polyolbion.   2 vols., 1612–22.
> The Battle of Agincourt, The Miseries of Queen Margarite, Nimphidia, The Quest of Cinthia, The Shepherd's Sirena, The Moon-Calf, Elegies upon Sundry Occasions.   1627; Nimphidia reprinted as The History of Queen Mab, 1751.
> The Muses' Elysium: Ten Nymphals, Noah's Flood, Moses His Birth and Miracles, David and Golia.   1630.

Plays

> Sir John Oldcastle, part 1, with others (produced 1599).   1600; edited by Peter Simpson, 1908.
> A Paean Triumphal for the Society of Goldsmiths Congratulating His Highness Entering the City.   1604.

Bibliography: Drayton: A Concise Bibliography by S. A. Tannenbaum, 1941; supplement by G. R. Guffey, 1967.

Reading List: *Drayton's Secondary Modes* by G. P. Haskell, 1936; *Drayton and His Circle* by Bernard H. Newdigate, 1941; *Drayton* by Paul G. Buchloh, 1964; *Drayton* by Joseph A. Berthelot, 1967; *The Spenserian Poets* by Joan Grundy, 1969; *Drayton and the Passing of Elizabethan England* by Richard F. Hardin, 1973; *The Evolution of Drayton's Idea* by Louise H. Westling, 1974.

*   *   *

When he was "scarse ten years of age," Michael Drayton asked his tutor to make him a poet, and his long literary life was spent achieving that end. While the doctrine of inspiration had a certain cachet in the Renaissance, the art of poetry was acknowledged as an acquired skill, the means spelled out in numerous treatises, most generally, if succinctly, by Sir Philip Sidney: art (rules), imitation (of the best models), and exercise (practice). In adhering to these precepts and in following poetic fashion, Drayton might well be called the representative Elizabethan poet except that he was also an innovator, introducing the ode into English and inventing, with a nudge from Ovid, the historical epistle. Stylistically ranging from the initial (unsatisfactory) imitation of Spenser (*Idea: The Shepherds' Garland*) to a special amalgam of the finer tones heard in many different poets – Sidney, Marlowe, Shakespeare, Donne – he seems quintessentially Elizabethan, but there are also notes anticipating the Cavaliers or even the Augustans.

Drayton opted for the pastoral mode early and late: the most effective passages, for example, in his epyllion *Endymion and Phoebe* (later, surprisingly, revised as a satire) have to do with pastoral description, while late examples – "The Shepherd's Sirena" and "The Muses' Elizium" – blend together the fanciful with realistic touches of country life. The early Spenserian imitations were also revised for 17th-century publication.

He responded too to the vogue for historical poetry, first by that popular derivative of the *Mirror for Magistrates*, the tragical complaint – *Piers Gaveston, Matilda*, and *Robert of Normandy* – and then by the *Mortimeriados*. In the latter, history is allied with epic and the hero projected in a romantic context. Again indicative of concern for his craft is the revision of that long poem, nearly 3,000 lines in rime royal, into the even longer *Barons' Wars* in ottava rima. In stressing its political and historical aspects, Drayton reduced the epical and romantic elements with a consequent sobering of tone and treatment. The most novel as well as popular example of his writing in this vein, however, was *England's Heroical Epistles*; here pairs of historical (rather than legendary) lovers exchange letters at a critical juncture in their relationship, creating a dramatic interaction that allows the poet to set forth shifting emotional states. The couplet is used with enormous skill, retaining in Drayton's hands a degree of openness and flexibility while anticipating something of the formality of the Augustans.

He was personally most concerned with his "Herculean toil," the composition of *Polyolbion*, a mammoth chorographical tribute to Great Britain, but his most assured achievement is the often revised collection of sonnets entitled *Idea*. Attacks on sonneteering by satirists induced him to inject an astringent cynical tone in describing his "oft-varying fate" as a lover or in counter-attacking his critics (hailing one as "crooked mimic," another as "leaden brain"). The lively colloquial tone of these sonnets is offset by an enchanting lyricism or by the immediacy of dramatic exchange. Furthermore, unlike most other examples, the sequence is structured: despite the astonishing variety of moods and motifs, according with the literary libertinism he openly adopts, the final sonnet brings it full circle. Having alternately extolled and abused his beloved, he challenges her:

I send defiance, since if overthrown,
Thou vanquishing, the conquest is mine own.

—Elizabeth Story Donno

DRUMMOND, William; Laird of Hawthornden.   Scottish.   Born in Hawthornden, near Edinburgh, 13 December 1585. Educated at Edinburgh High School; University of Edinburgh, M.A. 1605; also studied law at Bourges, and in Paris, 1607–08. Married Elizabeth Logan in 1632; five sons, four daughters. Succeeded to the estate of Hawthornden, 1610; a friend of Ben Jonson and Michael Drayton; also an inventor: patented various military and scientific instruments, 1627; a political moderate: worked for peace during the Scottish political turmoil, 1638, protested against the national league and convenant, 1643, and wrote in favor of negotiating with Charles I, 1646. *Died 4 December 1649.*

PUBLICATIONS

Collections

> *Works,* edited by John Sage and Thomas Ruddiman.   1711.
> *Poetical Works, with A Cypresse Grove,* edited by L. E. Kastner.   2 vols., 1913.
> *Poems and Prose,* edited by Robert H. MacDonald.   1976.

Verse

> *Tears on the Death of Moeliades.*   1613.
> *Poems.*   1614(?); revised edition, 1616.
> *In Memory of Euphemia Kyninghame.*   1616.
> *Forth Feasting: A Panegyric to the King's Most Excellent Majesty.*   1617.
> *Flowers of Sion.*   1623.
> *To the Exequies of the Honourable Sr. Antonye Alexander, Knight: A Pastoral Elegy.*   1638.
> *Polemo-Medinia inter Vitarvam et Nebernam.*   1645(?); as *Accedit Jacobi ...,* 1691.
> *Poems.*   1656.
> *Muckomachy; or, The Midden-Fecht.*   1846.

Play

> *The Entertainment of the High and Mighty Monarch Charles King of Great Britain* (produced 1633).   1633.

Other

> *Auctarium Bibliothecae Edinburgenae.*   1627.
> *A Midnight's Trance.*   1619; as *A Cypress Grove, with Flowers of Sion,* 1630; edited by Robert Ellrodt, 1951.
> *The Drunkard's Character.*   1646.
> *The History of Scotland 1423–1542.*   1655.
> *The Drunkard Forewarned.*   1680.
> *Conversations of Jonson with Drummond,* edited by D. Laing.   1842; edited by C. H. Herford and P. Simpson, in *Collected Works of Jonson 1,* 1925.
> *The Diary.*   1942.

Reading List: *Drummond* by A. Joly, 1935; *A Critical Study of Drummond* by French R. Fogle, 1952.

*   *   *

William Drummond of Hawthornden is generally thought of, and indeed thought of himself as the successor of Sidney, Daniel, and Drayton, carrying on the fashion for Petrarchan sonneteering into the age of Donne. But we should recognise his special position as the first important representative of Renaissance poetry in Scotland. Scottish poets, such as Drummond's friend Sir William Alexander (later Viscount Stirling), had only just begun to write in Southern English and to use the Italianate forms which had been established in England since the days of Wyatt and Surrey. Drummond not only modelled himself on his English predecessors, but also made a close study of the Italians, especially Petrarch, Tasso, Guarini, Sannazaro, and Marino, as well as Ronsard and other French poets of the sixteenth century. The influence of these foreign models, and the fact that Southern English would not have been Drummond's natural spoken tongue, make him imbue the language with special qualities. He gives it much of the smoothness and melody of Italian, while at the same time somewhat distancing it from actual speech. In this Drummond may be considered to anticipate Milton, with whom his characteristic Christian-Platonist humanism also gives him an affinity.

Drummond's earliest published poem was *Tears on the Death of Moeliades*, an elegy for Prince Henry, eldest son of James I. Its tone is heroic rather than pastoral and in his use of the couplet, Drummond almost anticipates the Augustans. Indeed the whole poem strongly suggests the vein of heroic panegyric later exploited by Waller and Dryden.

It is, however, for his sonnets that Drummond is chiefly remembered. The early death of his father enabled Drummond to retire to his family estate at Hawthornden, and to conform to the Renaissance ideal of rustic retreat and study adumbrated by Petrarch at Vaucluse. Drummond's betrothal, to Miss Cunningham of Barns, and her untimely death on the eve of their wedding, were the occasion for what is perhaps the most truly Petrarchan sonnet sequence in the English language. Petrarch's *Rime* are divided into two sections, the first telling of his wooing of Laura, the second mourning her death and treating of the poet's turning away from earthly joys to the contemplation of things heavenly. Drummond follows an exactly similar scheme. Furthermore, Petrarch interspersed his sonnets with lyrical forms – the ballata, the canzone, and the sestina. Drummond's equivalents for these are the madrigal, the song, and the sestain. The first two of these are written, not in the set Italian forms but in a very effective rhymed free verse; his sestains are also rhymed, but the rhyme words are repeated in each stanza and shift places according to the same formula as do the end-words in the Italian sestina. In his sonnets Drummond usually follows the general Elizabethan practice of concluding each poem with a couplet, rather than a strict Petrarchan form.

Drummond's later work, such as "Urania" and *Flowers of Sion*, is mainly religious in character. *Flowers of Sion* form an interesting parallel to the earlier sonnet sequence. It is likewise a sequence in which the sonnets are interspersed with lyrical forms, and narrate, instead of the courtship, death, and apotheosis of the beloved, the events of the Incarnation and earthly ministry of Christ culminating in His Passion, Resurrection, and Ascension. The sonnet on John the Baptist is the best known of these poems, and has power and simplicity. But equally fine in its own way is the extended lyric on the Ascension, in which Christ's ascent through the celestial spheres is imagined. The traditional scheme of the nine spheres and their harmony seems always to have fired Drummond's imagination. The final poem of this sequence, "The First Fair," written in couplets, is, together with his prose meditation *A Cypress Grove*, the fullest exposition of Drummond's Christian Platonism.

Other poems include *Forth Feasting*, written for King James's visit to Edinburgh in 1618, and *The Entertainment*, written for Charles I's visit to the same city in 1633. A macaronic satire on the Presbyterians *Polemo-Medinia*, was first printed as Drummond's work in 1691, but according to Daniel Defoe its author was Samuel Colvil. Various translations of mediaeval Latin hymns have also been attributed to Drummond but are doubtfully his. W. C. Ward also doubts the authenticity of "The Five Senses" among Drummond's posthumous poems, for no very cogent reasons. It is an outspoken but not distasteful satire alluding to King James's homosexuality.

—John Heath-Stubbs

FLETCHER, Giles, The Elder. English.   Born in Watford, Hertfordshire, in 1546. Educated at Eton College; King's College, Cambridge, 1565–68, B.A. 1569, M.A. 1573, LL.D. 1581. Married Joan Sheafe in 1580; one daughter, three sons, including Phineas Fletcher, *q.v.*, and Giles Fletcher the Younger, *q.v.* Fellow, King's College, Cambridge, 1568; Deputy Orator of Cambridge University, 1577; Commissary to the Chancellor of Ely, 1580; Member of Parliament for Winchelsea, 1585; undertook various diplomatic missions for the court to Scotland, Germany, Holland, and Russia, 1586–89; Remembrancer of the City of London, 1586–1605; Treasurer of St. Paul's Cathedral, London, 1597; granted lease of rectory at Ringwood, Hampshire, 1600. *Died in 1611.*

PUBLICATIONS

Collections

English Works, edited by Lloyd E. Berry.   1964.

Verse

Licia; or, Poems of Love, The Rising to the Crown of Richard the Third.   1593(?).
De Literis Antiquae Britanniae (in Latin), edited by Phineas FLetcher.   1633.

Other

Of the Russe Commonwealth.   1591; edited by Lloyd E. Berry and R. O. Crummey, in
    Rude and Barbarous Kingdom, 1969.
Israel Redux, with S. Lee.   1677.

Bibliography: "Fletcher: A Bibliography" by Lloyd E. Berry, in *Transactions of the Cambridge Bibliographical Society,* 1961.

Reading List: Introduction by R. Pipes to *Of the Russe Commonwealth,* 1966.

*   *   *

Giles Fletcher's poetic voice is quiet, but often unmistakably personal. At first sight the sonnets in *Licia* seem to be constructed out of the common properties of the Petrarchan hoard – "Roses and Lillies strive" in the loved one's face (Sonnet XXXV), but her heart is "Tyger-like," and she cannot love (VIII). The setting is appropriately pastoral, where "sweetest flowers enameld have the ground" (XXVI), and "Chrystal streames" join their murmurs to the lover's woe (XXVII). Yet a sudden genuine (as opposed to literary) perception breaks in from time to time; as when Cupid beats a hasty retreat from the lady, "as the foote, that treads the stinging snake, Hastes to be gone, for feare what may ensewe" (II). Occasionally, Fletcher seems to anticipate Donne, as in Sonnet XXIX where, with a conversational opening – "Why dy'd I not when as I last did sleepe" – he recounts a dream in which his mistress came to him. Commenting on her breasts and thighs, he passes with an Ovidian delicacy over "those sportes, in secret that are best" and longs for full consummation, either in dream or "indeede."

Fletcher, like so many of his contemporaries, plunders the writings of his continental counterparts: but he rarely attempts to pass off direct translation as his own work, and his borrowings are well assimilated into his English poems. His technique, more often than not, is to begin with a couple of lines translated from his source, and then develop the idea to a personal conclusion.

Included in *Licia* is a long poem somewhat in the manner of *The Mirror for Magistrates*, in which the speaker is Richard III. He recounts his triumphs with some pleasure, explaining that his entire family shared one dominant trait: "Sparkes of ambition did possesse us all" (line 62); given such a driving force, and the longing for a kingdom, Richard moved through blood ("For crownes with blood the brighter will they shine," line 70) until he achieved the throne. At the end of the poem he shows, unlike the *exempla* in *The Mirror for Magistrates*, no remorse for his deeds:

> Nor speake I now, as if I did repent,
> Unlesse for this a crowne I bought so cheap.
> For meaner things men wittes and lives have spent,
> Which blood have sowne, and crowns could never reap.
> Live *Richard* long, the honour of thy name,
> And scorne all such, as doe thy fortune blame.

In 1591 Fletcher published a prose work, *The Russe Commonwealth*, which proved to be the most important book on Russia by any sixteenth-century Englishman. He describes the geography of the country, and its hierarchy of government, deploring the servile condition of the common people who were so oppressed by their overlords that they "have no more courage in following their trades: for that the more they have, the more daunger they are in, not onely of their goods, but of their lives also." The Russian Orthodox Church – or rather, its ministers – shocked him: "As for preaching the worde of God, or any teaching, or exhorting such as are under them, they neyther use it, nor have any skill of it: the whole Cleargie beyng utterlie unlearned bothe for other knowledge, and in the word of God." Although parts of *The Russe Commonwealth* are derivative, there are occasional observations from personal experience; Fletcher spent at least a year in Russia, as ambassador specially commissioned to treat of trade matters. His letters tell how the Russians behaved "as if they had divised meanes of very purpose to shew their utter disliking both of the trade of the Marchant, and of the whole English nation."

—Roma Gill

FLETCHER, Giles, The Younger.   English.   Born in London c. 1585; son of Giles Fletcher the Elder, *q.v.*; younger brother of Phineas Fletcher, *q.v.* Educated at Westminster School, London; Trinity College, Cambridge, B.A. 1606. Married Anne, c. 1619. Fellow of Trinity College, Cambridge, 1608; Reader in Greek Grammar, 1615–18, and Reader in Greek Language, 1618–19, Cambridge University; Rector, Helmingham, Suffolk, 1617–18, and Alderton, Suffolk, 1619–23. *Died in 1623.*

PUBLICATIONS

Collections

Collections

> *Poetical Works of Giles and Phineas Fletcher,* edited by F. S. Boas.   2 vols., 1908–09.
> *Complete Poems,* edited by D. C. Sheldon.   1938.

Verse

> *Christ's Victory and Triumph in Heaven and Earth, over and after Death.*   1610; edited by N. Alexander, in *Elizabethan Narrative Verse,* 1967.

Other

> *The Reward of the Faithful.*   1623.
>
> Editor, *The Young Divine's Apology for His Continuance in the University, with Certain Meditations,* by Nathaniel Pownoll.   1612.

Reading List: *Spenser, The School of the Fletchers, and Milton* by Herbert E. Cory, 1912; "Fletcher and the Puritans," in *Journal of English and Germanic Philology,* 1955, and "Fletcher and the Catholics," in *Studies in Honor of T. W. Baldwin,* edited by D. C. Allen, 1958, both by A. Holaday; *The Spenserian Poets* by Joan Grundy, 1969.

*   *   *

Giles Fletcher the Younger is virtually the poet of a single poem. That poem, however, *Christ's Victory and Triumph,* itself consists of four poems that are at once separated and united, namely "Christ's Victory in Heaven," "Christ's Victory on Earth," "Christ's Triumph over Death," "Christ's Triumph after Death." Each has more independence than a book or canto, yet together they form a sequence sufficiently unified to give them the character of a "brief epic."

Beginning with a debate between Justice and Mercy in Heaven, they depict, dramatize, and celebrate (rather than simply narrate) the main events in the life of Christ, including the Temptation, Passion, Resurrection, and Ascension. Their treatment of these topics is at times allegorical and imitative of Spenser. This applies especially to the second poem, dealing with the Temptation. The stanza Fletcher adopts is itself a modified Spenserian stanza, having eight lines instead of nine but ending with an alexandrine. In style and temper, however, the poem's closest affinities are with the religious poetry of the counter-Reformation. Although Fletcher's Protestantism is never in doubt, his artistic sympathies with Catholic Italy are considerable. His writing is sensuous, often florid, passionate, fervent, and ecstatic. He employs the figures of rhetoric constantly, both in order to keep up the emotional temperature and to impress upon the reader, through paradox and antithesis especially, the wonder and mystery of his subject. The work as a whole is structured (through the juxtaposing of the four poems) in such a way as to illustrate or "enact" the central mystery of the Incarnation:

> And how the Infinite far greater grew
> By growing less, and how the rising Morn,
> That shot from heaven, did back to heaven return.

Fletcher's lyricism and genuine religious devotion make him at his best a fine and moving poet. His finest passages come in the celebration of the joys of heaven in the last poem, which achieves a sustained and exhilarating eloquence. But there is pathos too in his account of the Crucifixion, and tenderness in some of his lines on the Nativity. Milton knew Fletcher's poem and echoed it occasionally. His evident admiration of it was fully deserved.

Fletcher also wrote two short elegies, on the deaths of Queen Elizabeth and of Prince Henry, but the interest of these is slight. His prose work, *The Reward of the Faithful*, is a piece of devotional writing in which he again creates an ecstatic vision of the joys of heaven. Both here and in his major poem he appears essentially as a rapt, unworldly, rather Shelleyan spirit, pouring his full heart in strains of a highly conscious yet incantatory art.

—Joan Grundy

FLETCHER, Phineas.   English.   Born in Cranbrook, Kent, baptized 8 April 1582; son of Giles Fletcher the Elder, *q.v.*; elder brother of Giles Fletcher the Younger, *q.v.* Educated at Eton College; King's College, Cambridge, 1600–04, B.A. 1604, M.A. 1608, B.D. Married Elizabeth Vincent in 1615; four daughters, four sons. Fellow, King's College, Cambridge, 1611–16; ordained, 1611; Chaplain to Sir Henry Willoughby, Risley, Derbyshire, 1615–21; Rector, Hilgay, Norfolk, 1621–50. *Died in December 1650.*

PUBLICATIONS

Collections

> *Poetical Works*, with Giles Fletcher the Younger, edited by F. S. Boas.   2 vols., 1908–09.
> *Venus and Anchises − Britain's Ida − and Other Poems*, edited by Ethel Seaton.   1926.

Verse

> *Locustae: Vel Pietas Jesuitica* (Latin and English versions).   2 vols., 1627; English version edited by William B. Hunter, as *The Locusts, or Apollyonists*, in *The English Spenserians*, 1977.
> *Britain's Ida.*   1628.

Joy in Tribulation; or, Consolations for Afflicted Spirits.   1632.
The Purple Island; or, The Isle of Man, Together with Piscatory Eclogues and Other
     Poetical Miscellanies.   2 vols., 1633.
Sylva Poetica, in *De Literis Antiquae Britanniae*, by Giles Fletcher the Elder.   1633.

Play

Sicelides.   1631.

Other

The Way to Blessedness; or, A Treatise on the First Psalm.   1632.
A Father's Testament.   1670.

Editor, *De Literis Antiquae Britanniae*, by Giles Fletcher the Elder.   1633.

Reading List: *Spenser, The School of the Fletchers, and Milton* by Herbert E. Cory, 1912;
Fletcher, Man of Letters, Science, and Divinity by Abram B. Langdale, 1937; "Fletcher: His
Modern Readers and His Renaissance Ideals" by R. G. Baldwin, in *Philological Quarterly*,
1961; *The Spenserian Poets* by Joan Grundy, 1969.

                              *   *   *

Phineas Fletcher is remembered principally as the author of *The Purple Island; or, The Isle
of Man*, an allegorical poem in twelve cantos enlarging – to the point of absurdity, most
readers will feel – upon the idea that man is a microcosm or little world. The Island (man's
body – it is dew from its rivers – i.e., the blood-stream – that gives it its colour) is described in
elaborate geographical detail, the anatomical meaning of which is explained in lengthy and
learned marginal glosses. The poem's action concerns the battle fought between the Virtues
and Vices for possession of the King and Queen of the Island, Intellect and Will, who are
besieged in their castle by the Vices, and culminates in the triumphant overthrow of the
Dragon of the Apocalypse by a knight who is Christ himself. Much of the poem consists of
character-sketches of the various personifications, some florid, some satirical. The poem's
most attractive feature is its pastoral framework, in which the shepherd Thirsil is presented,
entertaining his friends with this story. As a whole, however, the poem is unappealing: its
allegory is at once over-ingenious and over-explicit, and lacks imaginative life.
     The *Piscatory Eclogues* use the image of the fisherman's life (instead of the more usual
shepherd's) to represent in pastoral form the various concerns of the poet – his poetry, his
love-affairs real or invented, his pursuit of preferment. The poems, whose setting is the river
(Cam, Medway, or Trent), not the sea, have a certain charm, if only for their novelty: it is
amusing to watch Fletcher devising "fishy" equivalents for the usual pastoral symbols. His
play *Sicelides*, also a "piscatory," is a very dull affair.
     Fletcher's narrative poem *Venus and Anchises* was published as Spenser's in 1628, under
the title of *Britain's Ida*. It is an ornate, heavily sensuous poem, centred on a love-encounter
of the type popularized by Marlowe's *Hero and Leander* and Shakespeare's *Venus and
Adonis*. Its sensuousness is surpassed in Fletcher's poetry only by the rapturous
Epithalamium of the Sion College manuscript.
     The Apollyonists, an English paraphrase of his Latin poem *Locustae*, is a "brief epic" on the
subject of the Gunpowder Plot, depicted as the work of the Jesuits who are portrayed as the
locusts of *Revelation*. The poem is effective, though harsh and repellent in tone. Fletcher's
representation of Satan may have been remembered by Milton in the Satan of *Paradise Lost*.

Fletcher's most attractive poems are the elegy "Elisa," the lyrics in *Poetical Miscellanies*, and the verses in his prose work *A Father's Testament*, itself an eloquent and quietly convincing devotional meditation. The personal themes of home, family, and friendship seem to have been near his heart, and he writes of them with a genuine tenderness and urgency. The religious "Verses and Translations" touch greatness in their intense spirituality and glowing moral fervour. The true poet in Fletcher, often obscured elsewhere by common-place subject-matter, platitudinous treatment, and an imitative manner, here asserts himself unmistakably.

—Joan Grundy

GASCOIGNE, George. English. Born in Cardington, Bedfordshire, in 1539. Educated at Trinity College, Cambridge, left without a degree; Middle Temple, London; Gray's Inn, London. Married Elizabeth Breton c. 1566; stepson, the poet Nicholas Breton, *q.v.* Soldier and courtier: Member of Parliament for Bedford, 1557–59; travelled in England and France, 1563–64; imprisoned for debt, 1571; elected Member of Parliament for Midhurst, 1572, but protests of his creditors caused him to flee to the Continent: served as Captain under William, Prince of Orange, in the Low Countries, 1572–75; returned to London and settled at Walthamstow; visited Kenilworth with Queen Elizabeth and Leicester, 1575. *Died 7 October 1577.*

PUBLICATIONS

Collections

Complete Works, edited by J. W. Cunliffe. 2 vols., 1907–10.

Verse

A Hundred Sundry Flowers, Bound Up in One Small Posie. 1573; as *The Posies,* 1575; edited by Charles T. Prouty, 1942.
A Delicate Diet for Daintymouthed Drunkards. 1576.
The Drum of Doomsday. 1576.
The Steel Glass: A Satire. 1576; edited by William L. Wallace, 1975.

Plays

Supposes, from a play by Ariosto (produced 1566). In *A Hundred Sundry Flowers,* 1573; edited by F. S. Boas, in *Five Pre-Shakespearean Comedies,* 1934.

Jocasta, with Francis Kinwelmershe (produced 1566).   In *A Hundred Sundry Flowers*, 1573; edited by J. W. Cunliffe, 1906.
A Device of a Masque for Viscount Montacute (produced 1572).   In *A Hundred Sundry Flowers*, 1573.
The Glass of Government (produced 1575?).   1575; edited by J. S. Farmer, 1914.
The Princely Pleasures at the Court at Kenilworth (produced 1575).   1821.
The Pleasant Tale of Hemetes the Hermit (produced 1575).   In *A Paradox Proving Baldness Better Than Bushy Hair*, by Synecius, 1579.

Fiction

A Pleasant Discourse of the Adventures of Master F. J., in *A Hundred Sundry Flowers*, 1573; edited by E. M. Moseley, in *Elizabethan Prose Fiction*, 1968.

Other

The Spoil of Antwerp.   1576(?).
The Whole Art of Venery or Hunting.   1611.

Editor, *A Discourse for a Discovery of a New Passage to Cataia*, by Humphrey Gilbert.   1576.

Reading List: *Gascoigne, Elizabethan Courtier, Soldier, and Poet* by Charles T. Prouty, 1942; *Gascoigne* by Ronald C. Johnson, 1972.

*   *   *

The main problem facing the modern reader of George Gascoigne is how to reconcile the lighthearted, erotic, courtly verse of "the Green Knight" (as he called himself in youth) with the grimly moralistic sermonising of the older man. The differences in themes, style, and attitude between his early productions and the works that he published in 1576 are so marked that at first it is hard to believe that they all emanate from the same pen.

The *Posies* contains most of Gascoigne's lyrical poetry. The first set (subtitled "Flowers") is composed largely of occasional amatory verse ("The Passions of a lover," "The lamentations of a lover," etc.), written in conventional mid-century manner after the style of Surrey and Vaux: "Amid my Bale I bath in blisse,/I swim in heaven, I sinke in hell." Sometimes a more satirical note is heard: in "*Sat cito, si sat bene*" he casts a critical eye on the beguiling lures of the "glistring Courte" and openly admits the fascination it has exercised upon his youthful mind, concluding, however, that in the long run "the gaines doth seldome quitte the charge." Also noteworthy is the plain, down-to-earth, proverbial style of "*Magnum vectigal parcimonia*." But on the whole it is difficult to justify Gascoigne's defence of his "Flowers" as exhibiting "rare invention and Methode before not commonly used" (Introductory Epistle to the Yong Gentlemen). The "Hearbes" follow much the same lines, though a trifle more moralistic in tone, while the "Weedes" consist of a series of complaints against fortune who smiled on him in his youth but now seems totally to have deserted him, leaving him "in prison pent,/ My gaines possessed by my foes, my friends against me bent." (Gascoigne was imprisoned for debt in 1571). Notable is "The Greene Knights farewell to Fansie" wherein he surveys his days amid the "glosse of gorgeous courtes," recollecting how he "liked sometimes well" to "lie along in Ladies lappes, to lispe and make it nice," but determining now, since it has proved to be all vanity, to bid a firm farewell to the fancies of the soldier and the courtier and seek instead the "comfort of Philosophie." It's an appealing poem – direct, frank, and unaffected. Indeed the most attractive quality of many of these early poems is their fresh, spontaneous tone: in "The Arraignment of a Lover," for example, Gascoigne manages successfully to combine a law-court allegory with a nicely balanced strain of self-directed irony.

It is a far cry from this to the morbid predictions of *The Droome of Doomes day* (with its woodcuts depicting the tortures of the damned in hell) or the thundering denunciations of *A delicate Diet, for daintiemouthde Droonkardes*. If we can safely ignore such obsessive ranting, there remains one later work well worthy our attention. This is Gascoigne's blank-verse satire *The Steele Glas*. The glass in question is not a crystal one that will reflect only the more pleasing side of life, but a mirror of steel to illuminate faults and vices — a satirical instrument to reaffirm the moral value of poetry in the face of its prevalent degeneration to mere courtly amusement. After a rueful glance in the mirror at his *own* failings, Gascoigne turns to survey the corruptions of the world. Desire for "glittring gold" lies at the root of the problem; and we are presented with a cogent and realistic picture of the decay of the countryside as all who can flock to town and court in pursuit of riches, the means to enjoy "A loytring life, and like an Epicure." All sectors of society are affected: soldiers, the defenders of the realm, have become drunken, lecherous boasters, despoilers, idlers, who set a dangerously bad example to honest craftsmen and ploughmen. Merchants and lawyers are no better.

The conclusion of the work is a tour de force: Gascoigne summons up a vision of the truly virtuous priests of the Church Militant whom he sets praying for all institutions and ranks of the realm, culminating with a celebration of the common people in the person of their representative, Peerce Plowman, the epitome of honest labour: "Behold him (priests) & though he stink of sweat/Disdaine him not: for shal I tel you what?/Such clime to heaven, before the shaven crownes." The poem ends with a Utopian vision of all trades engaged in virtuous toil and all things "ordred as they ought." Only then can the priest make holiday and the satirist lay down his pen.

Why do we find in Gascoigne this dramatic change from lyricist to moralist? It is tempting to say, as Gascoigne himself does, that age brings wisdom and with it the desire to "make amendes for the lost time which I misbetowed in wryting so wantonlie." But this is not enough to account for the obsessive quality of much of Gascoigne's later writing with its stress on the filthiness of the body, the futility of worldly ambitions, and the horrendous torments that await the sinner. These discourses are clearly allied to the Puritan tracts of men like Gosson and Stubbes, and it would not be amiss to see in the creative career of George Gascoigne a microcosm of the poetic problems of his age: there is a genuine erotic-lyrical impulse trying to find expression only to be stifled by the stern, anti-hedonistic weight of Puritan repression. Of the later works, only *The Steele Glas* successfully united the fervour of the moralist with the aesthetic claims of the poet; and of the earlier Gascoigne we are satisfied to discern in a few poems the seeds of the much greater lyrical achievement of later celebrated soldier-courtier-poets such as Sidney and Ralegh.

—A. W. Lyle

GODOLPHIN, Sidney. English. Born in Godolphin, Cornwall, baptized 15 January 1610. Educated at Exeter College, Oxford, 1624–27; entered one of the inns of court, London. Member of Parliament for Helston, Cornwall, 1628–43 (served in the Short Parliament and the Long Parliament, 1640); at outbreak of the Civil War joined Royalist forces commanded by Sir Ralph Hopton, and was killed in action in Devonshire. *Died (buried) 10 February 1643.*

PUBLICATIONS

Collections

Poems, edited by William Dighton.   1931.

Verse

The Passion of Dido for Aeneas, with Edmund Waller.   1658.

Play

Pompey the Great, with others, from a play by Corneille (produced 1664).   1664.

Reading List: "Godolphin and the Muses Fairest Light" by M. Teresa, in *Modern Language Notes,* 1946; *Private Men and Public Causes* by Irene Coltman, 1962.

*   *   *

Sidney Godolphin is an almost perfect example of a truly minor poet. He followed the poetic tastes of his time – the witty amorous lyric, the epitaph, the Psalm paraphrase, the occasional poem, the Horatian epistle, the pretty pastoral. Of the nearly 1000 lines of his original verse, not one is memorably bad; nor is there a single line that is memorably good. Though he wrote poems in tribute to both Donne and Jonson, Godolphin's verse is never fully committed to either of the two great exemplars of 17th-century English poetry. In Suckling's "A Session of the Poets" Apollo calls him "Little Cid" and advises him "not to write so strong." The term "strong" may refer to Godolphin's attempts to be witty in Donne's manner. His song, "Or love me less or love me more," ends with a witty turn reminiscent of Donne's "The Prohibition."

> Then give me more, or give me less:
>   Do not disdain a mutual sense;
> Or your unpitying beauties dress
>   In their own free indifference.
> But show not a severer eye
>   Sooner to give me liberty,
> For I shall love the very scorn
>   Which for my sake you do put on.

But Godolphin owes far more to Jonson. Ben's great legacy to his sons was the octosyllabic couplet and Godolphin is a true son of Ben. In his octosyllabics he catches the grace and poise of courtly lyric. His "Madam 'tis true, your beauties move" first appeared in Jonson's *Underwoods* (1640) as if it were Ben's own. He also has the Jonsonian preference for plain statement and courtly wit:

> Delighted by the diverse grace
> Of music and so fair a face,
> First all my soul is in mine eye;
> But then the sweet voice doth deny
> Your beauty's title and presence,
> And sows division twixt my sense.

Like many other minor poets, Godolphin never quite found his own voice. The preceding lyric sounds as much like Carew as Jonson. The short poem "Cloris, may I unhappy prove" could be by Robert Herrick. And his song "Shepherd, we do not see our looks" is in the vein of Andrew Marvell. All of Godolphin's poems illustrate the very high level of grace and sophistication which English lyric verse achieved in the 17th century.

—Thomas Wheeler

GOOGE, Barnabe.   English.   Born in Alvingham, Lincolnshire, 25 July 1540. Educated at Christ's College, Cambridge; New College, Oxford; Staple Inn, London. Married Mary Darrell c. 1563; eight children. Courtier, and member of the household of Sir William Cecil; travelled to Spain with Sir Thomas Challoner, 1561–62; appointed one of the queen's gentlemen-pensioners, 1565; sent to Ireland by Cecil to report on Essex's expedition to Ulster, 1574; performed numerous commissions in Ireland, and served as Provost Marshal of the Presidency Court of Connaught, 1582–85; returned to England and retired to his Lincolnshire estate, 1585. *Died in February 1594.*

PUBLICATIONS

Collections

Selected Poems, edited by Alan Stephens.   1961.

Verse

The Zodiac of Life, 3 books, from a work by Marcellus Palingenius.   1560; 6 books, 1561; 12 books, 1565.
Eclogues, Epitaphs, and Sonnets.   1563.
The Ship of Safeguard.   1569.

Other

A Prophecy Predicting the Rising and Falling of the United Provinces.   1572.

Translator, *The Popish Kingdom; or, Reign of Antichrist,* by Thomas Naogeorgus.   1570; edited in part by R. C. Hope, 1880.
Translator, *The Overthrow of the Gout,* by C. Balista.   1577.
Translator, *Four Books of Husbandry,* by C. Heresbach.   1577.
Translator, *The Proverbs of Sir James Lopez de Mendoza with the Paraphrase of Peter Diaz of Toledo.*   1579.
Translator, *The Virtues of a New Terra Sigillata Lately Found Out in Germany,* by Andrew Bertholdus.   1587.

Reading List: Introduction by Rosamond Tuve to *The Zodiac of Life*, 1947; *Googe: Poet and Translator* by Brooke Peirce, unpublished dissertation, Harvard University, 1954; "Googe: A Puritan in Arcadia" by Paul E. Parnell, in *Journal of English and Germanic Philology 60*, 1961; "A Timely Anachronism: Tradition and Theme in Googe's *Cupido Conquered*"by William E. Sheidley, in *Studies in Philology,* April 1972.

*   *   *

Barnabe Googe was a respected poet and translator of the first Elizabethan generation. Educated at Christ's College, Cambridge, and Staple Inn, Googe was an ethical humanist, a strong Reformer, and an exponent of Elizabethan literary nationalism. As a distant relative of Sir William Cecil, he found opportunities to serve the Crown and the Protestant cause – at home, as courtier and member of Cecil's household; abroad, with an embassade to Spain and as intelligencer and officeholder in Ireland. But Googe best served his country with his pen, translating a series of useful and improving works, including an anti-Catholic tract, a treatise on farming, a compendium of Spanish moral proverbs, and two medical works. His version of a popular philosophical compendium, *The Zodiake of Life* by Palingenius, occupied Googe through a good part of his career. With his contemporaries, he considered it his *chef d'oeuvre*; it provided a training ground for his skills as a writer and remains useful to the modern student of Renaissance ideas.

Googe is chiefly known today, however, for his original verse in *Eglogs, Epytaphes, and Sonettes*, the first collection of poetry by a single Elizabethan author to appear in print. The eight pastoral eclogues with which the volume opens are inspired by Mantuan and contain the first English borrowings from Montemayor's *Diana*. Structurally and thematically unified into an effective analysis of and attack upon conventional amatory passion, Googe's eclogues anticipate much of what Spenser would accomplish in *The Shepheardes Calender*. Googe also mastered the visionary allegory. In "Cupido Conquered," the dreaming poet overcomes the debilitating effect on his muse of unrequited love by witnessing a psychomachy in which the army of Diana defeats the forces of Cupid. Though it cleverly exploits the ancient convention, Googe admits that his "Dreame" is "to hastely fynyshed." He took more care with the short poems that make up the rest of the collection, several of which ring with a clear and emphatic voice of personal concern that cuts through the humdrum of metrical regularity and copious elaboration typical of early Elizabethan verse. As much may not be said for Googe's longest original poem, *The Shippe of Safegarde*, which describes emblematic islands, castles, and monsters reminiscent of *The Faerie Queene*.

Critics expounding the tradition of the native plain style have praised Googe's fusion of its resources with those of the learned and rhetorical style favored in his day. In poems like "To Doctor Bale," "To the Translation of Pallingen," and the epitaph on Nicholas Grimald, Googe further channels his feelings through deftly realized particular situations, heightening their sincerity and force. In "Of Money" and elsewhere, he raises self-awareness to the level of devastating ironic wit. His best work is marked by a degree of subtlety and control unusual among the early Elizabethan writers. We may regret that Googe abandoned poetry for the "more serious" activities of translation and civil service, but his varied and innovative literary achievement continues to invite admiration.

—William E. Sheidley

GREENE, Robert.   English.   Born in Norwich, Norfolk, baptized 11 July 1558. Educated at St. John's College, Cambridge, 1575–78, B.A. 1578; Clare Hall, Cambridge, M.A. 1583; incorporated at Oxford, 1588. Married in 1585, but later deserted his wife; one illegitimate son. Travelled in Italy and Spain, 1579–80; writer from 1580; settled in London, 1586, and quickly became known as a pamphleteer and romancer; associated with the University Wits; known for his profligate life. *Died 2 or 3 September 1592.*

PUBLICATIONS

Collections

Life and Complete Works in Prose and Verse, edited by A. B. Grosart.   15 vols., 1881–86.
Plays and Poems, edited by J. C. Collins.   2 vols., 1905.
Complete Plays, edited by T. H. Dickinson.   1909.

Fiction

Mamillia: A Mirror or Looking Glass for the Ladies of England.   1583; augmented edition, 1583(?).
Arbasto: The Anatomy of Fortune.   1584.
Gwydonius: The Card of Fancy.   1584; edited by George Saintsbury, in *Shorter Novels 1,* 1929.
Morando the Tritameron of Love.   1584; augmented edition, 1587.
The Mirror of Modesty.   1584.
Planetomachia.   1585.
Euphues His Censure to Philautus.   1587.
Penelope's Web.   1587.
Pandosto: The Triumph of Time.   1588; as *Dorastus and Fawnia,* 1636; edited by James Winny, in *The Descent of Euphues,* 1957.
Perimedes the Blacksmith.   1588.
Ciceronis Amor: Tullie's Love.   1589; edited by Charles Howard Larson, 1974.
The Spanish Masquerado.   1589.
Menaphon: Camilla's Alarum to Slumbering Euphues.   1589; as *Greene's Arcadia,* 1610; edited by G. B. Harrison, with *A Margarite of America* by Thomas Lodge, 1927.
Greene's Never Too Late.   1590.
Greene's Mourning Garment.   1590.
Greene's Farewell to Folly.   1591.
The Black Book's Messenger: The Life and Death of Ned Browne.   1592; edited by A. V. Judges, in *The Elizabethan Underworld,* 1930.
Philomela: The Lady Fitzwater's Nightingale.   1592.
Greene's Groatsworth of Wit, Bought with a Million of Repentance.   1592; edited by A. C. Ward, 1927.
Greene's Orpharion, Wherein Is Discovered a Musical Concord of Pleasant Histories.   1599 (first extant edition).
Alcida: Greene's Metamorphosis.   1617 (first extant edition).

Plays

Alphonsus, King of Aragon (produced 1587?).   1599; edited by W. W. Greg, 1926.
Friar Bacon and Friar Bungay (produced 1589?).   1594; edited by J. A. Lavin, 1969.
A Looking Glass for London and England, with Thomas Lodge (produced 1590?).   1594; edited by T. Hayashi, 1970.
Orlando Furioso, One of the Twelve Peers of France (produced 1591?).   1594; edited by W. W. Greg, in *Two Elizabethan Stage Abridgements,* 1923.
The Scottish History of James the Fourth (produced 1591?).   1598; edited by Norman Sanders, 1970.
A Knack to Know a Knave (produced 1592).   1594.
George à Greene, The Pinner of Wakefield (produced before 1593).   1599; edited by E. A. Horsman, 1956.

Verse

A Maiden's Dream: Upon the Death of Sir Christopher Hatton.   1591.

Other

A Notable Discovery of Cozenage.   1591; *The Second Part of Cony-Catching,* 1591; *Third and Last Part,* 1592; edited by A. V. Judges, in *The Elizabethan Underworld,* 1930.
A Disputation Between a He Cony-Catcher and a She Cony-Catcher.   1592; as *Thieves Falling Out, True Men Come by Their Goods,* 1615; edited by A. V. Judges, in *The Elizabethan Underworld,* 1930.
A Quip for an Upstart Courtier.   1592.
The Repentance of Robert Greene, Master of Arts.   1592; edited by G. B. Harrison, with *Greene's Groatsworth of Wit,* 1923.

Translator, *An Oration at the Burial of Gregory the 13th,* from the French.   1585.
Translator, *The Royal Exchange,* by Orazio Rinaldi.   1590.

Bibliography: *Greene Criticism: A Comprehensive Bibliography* by T. Hayashi, 1971; *Greene* by A. F. Allison, 1975.

Reading List: *Greene* by J. C. Jordan, 1915; *The Professional Writer in Elizabethan England* by E. H. Miller, 1959; *L'Opera Narrativa di Greene* by F. Ferrara, 1960; *The Aphorisms of Orazio Rinaldi, Greene, and Lucas Gracian Dantisco* by C. Speroni, 1968.

*   *   *

Robert Greene, in the few years between his graduation with an M.A. from Cambridge in 1583 and his early death in 1592, was a restless and indefatigable free-lance writer with a massive output. He turned his hand to several currently popular genres in succession. Beginning with prose romances (of which he wrote some dozen), he was then briefly involved in the Marprelate controversy, an angry exchange of theological pamphlets written for popular appeal deliberately in colloquial style. This led him to experiment with a series of prose pamphlets on "conny catching," for which he drew on his considerable knowledge of the seamy (and criminal) side of London life. These pamphlets, ostensibly designed to expose the "cosenages and villainies" of the Elizabethan underworld, met with great popular success as lively pieces of crime fiction.

Greene was associated with Lodge, Nashe, and other of the "university wits" and was inescapably drawn into working for the theatre. The full extent of his involvement (considering the collaborative writing common at the time) is not exactly determinable, but he is the certain author of five plays, four of them comedies produced by Queen Elizabeth's Men between 1589 and 1591.

Greene began by writing for a leisured and cultured audience – his romance, *Menaphon*, is, typically, dedicated to a noble lady and its preface is addressed "To the Gentlemen Readers." For these he wrote his prose romances (the best-known are *Menaphon* and *Pandosto*, the source of Shakespeare's *The Winter's Tale*), Arcadian love-tales marked by lively plotting, pastoral settings, interspersed lyrics, and a highly mannered prose style. His involvement with public controversy led to a great change in his attitude to writing. The later conny-catching and other pamphlets exploit the resources of a colloquial prose based on the speech of ordinary Londoners. With his friend Nashe, Greene expanded "downwards" the whole range of vocabulary and prose structures that could be admitted into literary English, and so paved the way for Defoe and the establishment of the English novel.

His skill in plotting, acquired in his prose fiction, is evident in all his work for the theatre. His best-known comedy, *Friar Bacon and Friar Bungay*, owes something to the magic scenes in Marlowe's *Faustus*, but Greene shows an independent mastery of the resources of the Elizabethan stage (the inset "glass perspective" scene, where he presents simultaneously scenes in two different places, both actions integrated into the forward movement of the plot). His portraits, in prose and drama, of lively and independent-minded young women (Margaret in *Friar Bacon*, Fawnia in *Pandosto*) foreshadow, and perhaps helped towards creating, the Rosalinds and Beatrices of Shakespeare; in one of his early works he announced himself as a "Homer of women."

Like many Elizabethan writers of any genre, in an age when poetry and music went hand-in-hand, he had an instinctive facility for lyric poetry. Twenty of his lyrics (from his plays and his prose romances) are included in the *Oxford Book of Sixteenth Century Verse*.

—Ian A. Gordon

GREVILLE, Sir Fulke; 1st Baron Brooke. English. Born at Beauchamp Court, Warwickshire, 3 October 1554. Educated at Shrewsbury School, Shropshire, where he met Sir Philip Sidney, 1564–68; Jesus College, Cambridge (Fellow-Commoner), from 1568. Served in the courts of both Queen Elizabeth I and James I: travelled with Sidney to Heidelberg, 1577; with Walsingham on diplomatic mission to Flanders, 1578; accompanied Sidney's friend Languet to Germany, 1579; with Sidney, Sir Edward Dyer, and Gabriel Harvey, formed the Areopagus literary society, an important center of literary influence at court; served under Henry of Navarre in Normandy, 1591; Member of Parliament for Warwickshire, 1592–93, 1597, 1601, 1620; Secretary for the Principality of Wales, 1583 until the end of his life; Treasurer of the Navy, 1598–1604; Chancellor and Under-Treasurer of the Exchequer, 1614–21, and Commissioner of the Treasury, 1618; Member, Council of War, 1624, and Committee on Foreign Affairs, 1625. Granted Wedgnock Park by Elizabeth, 1597; and Warwick Castle, 1605, and extension of his family estates, Knowle Park, 1606, by

James. Knight of the Bath, 1603; created Baron Brooke, 1621. Murdered by a discontented servant. *Died 30 September 1628.*

PUBLICATIONS

Collections

> *The Works in Verse and Prose,* edited by Alexander B. Grosart.   4 vols., 1870.
> *Poems and Dramas,* edited by Geoffrey Bullough.   2 vols., 1939.
> *Selected Poems,* edited by Thom Gunn.   1968.
> *Selected Writings,* edited by Joan Rees.   1973.

Verse

> *Two Elegies,* with William Browne.   1613.
> *Caelica,* in *Certain Learned and Elegant Works.*   1633; edited by Una Ellis-Fermor, 1936.
> *The Remains: Poems of Monarchy and Religion.*   1670; edited by G. A. Wilkes, 1965.

Plays

> *Alaham* (produced 1600?).   In *Certain Learned and Elegant Works,* 1633.
> *Mustapha* (produced 1603–08?).   1609.

Other

> *Certain Learned and Elegant Works.*   1633.
> *The Life of the Renowned Sir Philip Sidney.*   1652; edited by Nowell Smith, 1907.

Reading List: *Greville tra il Mondo e Dio* by Napoleone Orsini, 1941; *Greville's Caelica: An Evaluation* by William Frost, 1942; *Die Anschauungen über Wissenschaft und Religion im Werke Grevilles* by H. W. Utz, 1948; *The Life of Greville* by Ronald A. Rebholz, 1971; *Greville: A Critical Biography* by Joan Rees, 1971; *The Fatal Mirror: Themes and Techniques in the Poetry of Greville* by Richard Waswo, 1972.

*   *   *

Sir Fulke Greville brought to the pursuit of poetry a powerful and individual mind. Stimulated by Sidney in his young manhood, he composed lyrics on the theme of love, using sometimes the devices of Petrarchan rhetoric and sometimes plainer styles. These form part of the sequence *Caelica,* a collection of 109 short poems of which 41 are sonnets. The sonnets are composed in the English form, not, like Sidney's, in the Italian, but this is only one of many differences between Greville's "love" poetry and that of his friend. It seems likely that the first 76 of the *Caelica* poems were written before Sidney's death and, at points where *Caelica* and *Astrophil and Stella* are close, Greville can be seen to be making an ironic commentary on Sidney's idealisation of sexual love. Even in these early poems, the mark of Greville's writing is a cool and sceptical intelligence and the lyrics display a shrewd and sardonic wit. A few of them adopt the neo-Platonic attitude of reverence towards the beloved but an increasingly ironic tone makes itself heard and Greville's use of religious reference and vocabulary comes to be, not a compliment to a mistress, but a means of exposing the relative worthlessness of earthly pursuits and earthly desires. The dates of the later poems of *Caelica* are unknown but Greville may have gone on composing and revising throughout his long life. Whatever the chronology, the poems in effect constitute a record of his maturing mind and temperament. In LXXXIV he says farewell to secular love, and the religious feeling, present by ironic implication earlier, reaches full expression in some subtle and splendid later poems. Greville's picture of the inner hell of man cut off from God and his sense of the saving grace offered through Christ lead to some of his most powerful and successful writing.

The later *Caelica* poems include some on political themes. In a sequence which mirrors as fully as this one does the mind of the poet, such material has a proper place. To the older Greville, a man much experienced in court and state affairs, political situations offered themselves as the perfect ground on which to observe the interplay of dominant forces in human nature: desire for power, and fear. After the early years, he treated love itself in a political context, for his temperament led him easily to a perception of sexual relations as a species of power struggle. Political choices, moreover, could be used to focus the tension between temporal advantage and eternal values, man's bondage to sin leading him always to seek the things of this world at the expense of the claims of another. Greville wrote a number of verse treatises in which the contending claims of the world and of God confront each other. Practising politician as he was, his analysis of the ways of the world is detailed and incisive but sooner or later he matches them against another conception of life in which renunciation and obedience to a higher law replace cupidity and aggression. There is much of interest in these treatises but the expression is often so sinewy and elliptical that for long passages they make tough reading.

Greville's two dramas, *Alaham* and *Mustapha*, deserve, on the other hand, to be much more read than they are. *Alaham* takes an extreme political situation and through it exposes the full capacity of human evil. *Mustapha* also treats of the worst corruptions of lust for power and makes out of its material a profound and wide-ranging drama of ultimate choices. Most men and women, as the play shows them, are selfish, or at best only partly committed to what they themselves recognise as virtue. The one truly good and innocent man is murdered and accepts death without resistance for he is really free of worldly entanglements. Such souls, Greville knows, are rare. In his so-called *Life of Sidney*, a prose work originally intended as a dedication of his poems, he is inclined to present the friend of his youth, long dead, as being among them. But for most men the conflict of God's will with the way of the world produces no sainthood but a sad awareness of the "wearisome condition of humanity / Born under one law, to another bound," as the chorus of priests in *Mustapha* puts it.

Mustapha is a parable with religious and political meanings and it offers, besides, a keen analysis of human nature. It does on an extended scale what some of the *Caelica* poems also do; that is, it evolves a distinctive language of multiple reference which enables Greville to make his commentary on human experience at several levels simultaneously. Because of the packed meaning, and because also in non-lyrical work he rarely makes concessions to the beauty and music of language and phrasing, he is often a difficult poet to read, but there should be no doubt that he is a considerable one. His use of images bespeaks a poetic imagination, and his world view, by its coherence and force and penetration, becomes itself an imaginative creation. The two completest works that Greville wrote, *Caelica* and *Mustapha*, stand out among the rest as the most remarkable achievements of a most remarkable writer.

—Joan Rees

HABINGTON, William.   English.   Born in Hindlip, Worcestershire, 4 November 1605. Educated at St. Omer's, and in Paris. Married Lucy Herbert c. 1630; one son. *Died 30 November 1654.*

PUBLICATIONS

Collections

Poems, edited by Kenneth Allott.   1948.

Verse

Castara.   2 vols., 1634; revised edition, 1635, 1640.

Play

The Queen of Aragon; or, Cleodora (produced 1640).   1640; edited by W. C. Hazlitt in *Dodsley's Old Plays 13,* 1875.

Other

The History of Edward the Fourth.   1640.
Observations upon History.   1641.

*   *   *

"To write this," William Habington tells readers of his *Castara,* "love stole some hours from business, and my more serious study." But in fact he was serious and high-minded in his love-poetry as in all else. Distressed that English verse had been corrupted by licentious French models, he traces under the names Araphil (altar-lover) and Castara (chaste altar) his own exemplary courtship and marriage to the fair and virtuous Lucy Herbert – a courtship in which, he assures us, he "never felt a wanton heat."

It is evidence of Habington's independent spirit that, in an age when the love-sonnet had passed out of fashion, more than half the poems in *Castara* are "sonnets" – or at least fourteen-line poems in decasyllabic verse. But except for one sonnet, which follows the English form, all these fourteen-line poems are rhymed in couplets. It is hard to imagine what advantages Habington could have seen in such "sonnets." Perhaps, without wanting to write in a deliberately outmoded manner, he thought of the fourteen-line limitation as at least a gesture toward an older discipline. Meanwhile much of his imagery and subject-matter ("To Roses in the Bosom of Castara," "To Castara, Upon a Sigh") is the common stock of poets of his time, or at least a fastidious selection from that stock.

A Catholic and Royalist, he derived from his religion and politics strong reinforcement for his moral creed; one of his lyrics, "To Castara, Upon the Mutual Love of Their Majesties," points to Charles I and Henrietta Maria as models of married love.

His single play, a tragi-comedy called *The Queen of Aragon,* received a highly successful performance before the King and Queen at Whitehall. The lofty sentiments of the play, expressed in eloquent blank verse, could hardly have failed to appeal to the royal couple, who in their own way were as serious-minded as Habington. By all criteria it is one of the best-written of the highly artificial dramas of the period; when it was revived after the Restoration, Samuel Pepys found it "so good that I am astonished at it." Along with its nobler elements it offers mild amusement and satire in the characters of a witty lady and a foolish lord.

Besides some short *Observations upon History*, Habington wrote a *History of Edward the Fourth*, which he dedicated to King Charles. This is no less a moral work than his poems and play – so moral, indeed, that it avoids any mention of King Edward's famous mistress, Jane Shore. More importantly, it is a tract for the times, since Edward IV had succeeded in imposing a "happy calm" on his kingdom after a long period of strife. "May your Majesty long continue in peace," Habington tells King Charles in the dedicatory epistle. "But if you shall be forced to draw your sword, may your enemies submit and taste part of your mercy: if not, perish in your victories." In 1640, when this was published, neither Habington nor his King could reasonably have suspected that they were united in a losing cause.

—Rhodes Dunlap

HALL, Joseph. English. Born in Ashby-de-la-Zouch, Leicestershire, 1 July 1574. Educated at a grammar school in Ashby; Emmanuel College, Cambridge, B.A. 1592, M.A. 1596, B.D. 1603, D.D. 1612. Married Elizabeth Winiffe in 1603; two daughters. Fellow, Emmanuel College, Cambridge, 1595; took holy orders c. 1600; given the living of Halstead, Suffolk, 1601, and Waltham, Essex, 1608; appointed a chaplain to James I, 1608; sent by the king as chaplain to Lord Doncaster in his embassy to France, 1616; appointed Dean of Worcester, 1616; accompanied James to Scotland in an attempt to establish the Episcopacy, 1617; Delegate to the Synod of Dort, 1618; Bishop of Exeter, 1627–41; appointed Bishop of Norwich, 1641: protested against exclusion of the bishops from Parliament, and was imprisoned in the Tower of London, 1642; released, but deprived of the bishopric, 1647; retired to a farm in Higham, Norfolk. *Died 8 September 1656.*

PUBLICATIONS

Collections

Works, edited by P. Wynter.   20 vols., 1863.
Devotions, Sacred Aphorisms, and Religious Table-Talk, edited by J. W. Morris.   1867.
Collected Poems, edited by Arnold Davenport.   1949.

Verse

Virgidemiarum: First Three Books of Toothless Satires.   1597; *Three Last Books of Biting Satires*, 1598.
The King's Prophecy; or, Weeping Joy.   1603.
Some Few of David's Psalms Metaphrased, for a Taste of the Rest, in Holy Observations.   1607.

Other

The Anatomy of Sin.   1603; as *Two Guides to a Good Life,* 1608.
Meditations and Vows Divine and Moral.   1605; revised edition, 1607.
Mundus Alter et Idem.   1605(?); edited by Huntington Brown, 1937.
Heaven upon Earth.   1606.
The Art of Divine Meditation.   1606; edited by Rudolf Kirk, with *Characters of Virtues and Vices,* 1948.
Holy Observations.   1607.
Characters of Virtues and Vices.   1608; edited by Rudolf Kirk, 1948.
Epistles.   4 vols., 1608–11.
Salomon's Divine Arts.   1609.
The Peace of Rome.   1609.
A Common Apology of the Church of England.   1610.
Contemplations upon the Principal Passages of the Holy Story.   8 vols., 1612–26; edited by C. Wordsworth, 1871.
Polemices Sacrae Par Prior: Roma Irreconciliabilis.   1611.
A Recollection of Such Treatises as Have Been Heretofore Severally Published and Are Now Revised.   1614; revised edition, 1621.
Quo Vadis? A Just Censure of Travel as It Is Commonly Undertaken by the Gentlemen of Our Nation.   1617.
The Honour of the Married Clergy Maintained.   1620.
Works.   1625; revised edition, 2 vols., 1628; 3 vols., 1662.
The Old Religion.   1627.
An Answer to Pope Urban, His Inurbanity.   1629.
The Reconciler.   1629.
Occasional Meditations.   1630.
A Plain and Familiar Explication of the Old and New Testament.   1632.
An Explication by Way of Paraphrase of All the Hard Texts in the Old and New Testament.   1633.
Propositiones Catholicae.   1633; translated as *Certain Catholic Propositions,* 1633.
The Residue of the Contemplation upon the New Testament, with Sermons.   1634.
Antochediasmata; vel, Meditatiunculae Subitaneae.   1635.
The Remedy of Prophaneness.   1637.
Certain Irrefragable Propositions.   1639.
An Humble Remonstrance to the High Court of Parliament.   1640.
Christian Moderation.   1640.
Episcopacy by Divine Right.   1640.
A Defense of the Humble Remonstrance.   1641.
Osculum Pacis.   1641.
A Modest Confutation.   1642.
A Modest Offer to Some Meet Considerations.   1644.
The Devout Soul.   1644.
The Peace-Maker.   1645.
The Remedy of Discontentment.   1645.
The Balm of Gilead.   1645.
Three Tractates.   1646.
Christ Mystical.   1647.
Hard Measures.   1647.
Satan's Fiery Darts Quenched; or, Temptation Repelled.   1647.
The Breathings of the Devout Soul.   1648.
Pax Terris.   1648.
Select Thoughts: One Century.   1648.
Resolutions and Decisions of Diverse Practical Cases of Conscience.   1649.

The Revelation Unrevealed.   1650.
Susurrium cum Deo.   1651.
Holy Raptures.   1652.
The Great Mystery of Godliness.   1652.
The Holy Order.   1654.
The Invisible World.   1659.
The Apostolic Institution.   1659.
The Shaking of the Olive-Tree: Remaining Works.   1659.
Diverse Treatises, vol. 3.   1662.
Psicittacorum Regis.   1669.
Contemplations upon the Remarkable Passages in the Life of Holy Jesus.   1679.
Episcopal Admonition.   1681.

Reading List: "Bishop Hall, 'Our English Seneca' " by Philip A. Smith, in *Publications of the Modern Language Association 63,* 1948; "Hall's Imitation of Juvenal" by Arnold Stein, in *Modern Language Review 43,* 1948; *The Life and Works of Hall* by Tom F. Kinloch, 1951; "Hall's *Characters of Vertues and Vices:* Notes Toward a Revaluation" by Gerard Muller-Schwefe, in *Texas Studies in Language and Literature 14,* 1972; *Hall: A Biographical and Critical Study* by Frank Livingstone Huntley, 1978.

*   *   *

To the modern reader, the most familiar passage in the works of Joseph Hall is almost certainly the long description of the Golden Age that opens the third book of his *Virgidemiarum.* But it should be noted that this celebration of the days of Saturn owes as much to Juvenal as it does to Ovid, and that Hall's main claim for his collection is that it comprises the first full-scale set of Juvenalian satires in English. The pastoral primitivism lauded in Book III, Satire I, in fact serves almost entirely as a positive prelapsarian backdrop against which Hall can vilipend with savage vehemence the follies, villainies, and abuses of degenerate modern days. This he does with a relish that combines the moral indignation of the Puritan preacher with the obsessive harshness of the original Juvenal.

All satire to some extent subscribes to a belief in progressive deterioration, and Hall is never tired of comparing the virtue of the past to the viciousness and decay of the present, when "Ech Muck-worme will be rich with lawlesse gaine" (IV, vi), when sons squander their patrimony in harlots' beds (IV, iii), when fools abandon the "home-spun *Russet*" of former days for the garish "far-fetched liuery" of France, Italy, Germany and Spain (III, i), when fops forsake the martial valour of their ancestors for effeminate rose-pulling (IV, iv). In short, all the customary targets of satire are to be found in the *Virgidemiarum.* Like Juvenal, Hall sees greed for money as the root cause of so much contemporary corruption: lawyers look only at the client's hand "lined with a larger fee" (II, iii), doctors abandon "the leane reward of Art" (II, iv), in favour of more liberal emolument from gouty peers, chaplains are treated with ignominy and paid no more than a mere serving-man (II, vi).

Of particular interest, perhaps, in terms of content is the first book. Here Hall turns his attention specifically to the failings of contemporary poetry, and, in surveying what he considers to be its decayed status, comes to the not unexpected conclusion that satire alone should be allowed to survive. Erotic poetry is now obscene ("*Cythéron* hill's become a Brothel-bed," I, ii), the high decorum of tragedy is lost "when vile *Russetings,*/Are match't with monarchs" (I, iii), even religious poetry is polluted with secular taints (I, viii). Hall's editor, Arnold Davenport, is quite right in regarding his author as a one-sided but highly perceptive literary critic.

The style of the *Virgidemiarum* is probably something of a stumbling-block to present-day readers. At its best, it is harsh, vigorous, and crude – not at all "toothlesse" as the description on the title-page would have us believe. The usual metaphors of whipping and scourging occur regularly, and Hall himself compares satire to a porcupine "That shoots sharpe quils out in each angry line" (V, iii). His imagery is, predictably, drawn from disease and dirt – adjectives such as *rotten, festering, scabby* proliferate throughout. Sexual aberration especially seems to arouse Hall to heights of Juvenalian frenzy, as he contemplates, for example, the "close adultresse" coming "crauling from her husbands lukewarme bed,/Her carrion skin bedaub'd with odours sweete.... Besmeared all with loathsome smoke of lust" (IV, i). Unfortunately Hall is not always so direct as that, and, despite his disclaimer of "ridle-like" darkness (III, Prol.), there is much obscurity in his *Virgidemiarum* – the result both of the prevailing Renaissance tradition which prescribed a crabbed obliquity for the satiric muse and of Hall's own determination to conceal the identities of the persons he is attacking (they include Nashe, Harvey, and Greene) under the cloak of pseudonyms.

Hall lived until 1656, but none of his later work (gratulatory verse, religious verse, sermons, pamphlets, etc.) is of any literary interest. It is to the *Virgidemiarum* that we return for a fascinating array of corrupt characters, a richly-detailed survey of various moral and social abuses, and a comprehensive critique of the failing of the poets of the 1590's – all delivered with a rhetorical zest and vigour that show Hall (like all the best satirists) as much intrigued by the vices he assails as repulsed by them. Like Ben Jonson a few years later, Hall finds in the corruptions of his time a vivid source of poetic energy, and, in giving dramatic embodiment to these, becomes the first writer to naturalise in England the Juvenalian satire.

—A. W. Lyle

HARINGTON, Sir John. English. Born in Kelston, near Bath, Somerset, 4 August 1560; godson of Queen Elizabeth I. Educated at Eton College, from 1570; King's College, Cambridge, 1576–81, B.A. 1578, M.A. 1580; Lincoln's Inn, London, 1581. Married Mary Rogers in 1583; nine children. Gave up legal career when he succeeded to the family estates at Kelston, 1582; thereafter a courtier of Queen Elizabeth; High Sheriff of Somerset, 1592; banished from the court for suspected slur against Leicester, 1596, but forgiven by the queen, 1598; accompanied Essex on expedition to Ireland, 1599; knighted by Essex, 1599; because of queen's displeasure at his attempt to justify Essex's actions, he retired to Kelston; returned to the court of James I as tutor to Prince Henry. *Died 26 November 1612.*

PUBLICATIONS

Collections

   The Letters and Epigrams, with The Praise of Private Life, edited by Norman E. McClure. 1930.

Verse

   Epigrams Both Pleasant and Serious. 1615; revised edition, as *The Most Elegant and Witty Epigrams,* 1618.

Other

A New Discourse of a Stale Subject, Called the Metamorphosis of Ajax.   1596; edited by
    Elizabeth S. Donno, 1962.
An Anatomy of the Metamorphosed Ajax.   1596.
Ulysses upon Ajax.   1596.
A Brief View of the State of the Church of England, edited by John Chetwind.   1653.
Nugae Antiquae: A Miscellaneous Collection of Original Papers, with others, edited by
    Henry Harington.   2 vols., 1769–75; edited by Thomas Park, 2 vols., 1804.
A Short View of the State of Ireland Written in 1605, edited by W. D. MacCray.   1879.
A Tract on the Succession to the Crown, edited by Clements R. Markham.   1880.

Editor, with John Harington of Kelston, *The Arundel Harington Manuscript of Tudor
    Poetry,* edited by Ruth Hughey.   2 vols., 1960.

Translator, *Orlando Furioso in English Heroical Verse,* by Ariosto.   1591; edited by
    Robert McNulty, 1972.
Translator, *The Englishman's Doctor; or, The School of Salerne,* by J. de
    Mediolano.   1607; edited by F. R. Packard and F. H. Garrison, 1920.

Reading List: *Harington and Ariosto* by Townsend Rich, 1940; *The Harington Family* by Ian
Grimble, 1957; *Harington of Stepney, Tudor Gentleman: His Life and Works* by Ruth
Hughey, 1971.

*   *   *

When Harington translated the *Orlando*, he demonstrated fluency in the use of the Italian
language. Ariosto's sense of high seriousness, and, paradoxically, of mockery, was congenial
to Harington, who had a fine sense of the comic, which could move quickly to the pathetic.
Both poets enjoyed introducing themselves, their families, and friends into the notes, though
Harington has been criticized for compressing and expanding his original, and for adding
details in his attacks on women. Although use of the *ottava rima* stanza is praiseworthy, his
translation lacks the well-structured design of the Italian. Ariosto is the better poet, but
Harington has, nevertheless, created a worthy achievement of his own. In the prefixed
Apologie, Harington's purpose is not to refute the Puritans but to defend the *Orlando*, its
author, and its translator. He begins by using common refutations against the critics, often
referring to Sidney.

The *Metamorphosis of Ajax* is in the form of a mock encomium, but it also emphasizes the
utility of the cloacal invention (a jakes, or privy). The thrust is satiric but not cynical; it is
paradoxical: if man is god-like, he is also an animal.

For Harington, "of all poems the epigram is the wittiest, and of all that write epigrams,
Martial is counted the pleasantest." Some of Sir John's epigrams are drawn from Martial, but
his most effective verses are inspired by homely incidents of his own experience, to form
oblique compliments to friends or family, especially his wife, "Sweet Mall." A satiric line
could reverse the point of the epigram. Harington also introduced merry tales which pleased
the privileged few who had access to the circulating manuscripts.

Harington was a delightful letter-writer. He tells of the exploits of his ancestors, or of the
antics of his little dog Bungay, or of the Irish campaign in 1599, or of his painful interview
with the Queen on his return. No other contemporary account reveals so penetrating an
understanding of the old Queen, still the awe-inspiring monarch, but at the same time, the
woman, deeply hurt, disillusioned, and alone.

—Ruth Hughey

HERBERT OF CHERBURY, Lord; Edward Herbert, 1st Baron Herbert of Cherbury. Welsh. Born at Eyton-on-Severn, Shropshire, 3 March 1582; elder brother of George Herbert, *q.v.* Educated by tutors, 1589–96, and at University College, Oxford, 1596–99. Married his kinswoman Mary Herbert in 1598 (died, 1634); several children. Courtier and Diplomat: presented himself at court, 1600; Sheriff of Montgomeryshire. 1605; toured the Continent, 1608–09; served with the English expedition to recapture Juliers, 1610; joined the Army of the Prince of Orange, 1614, and subsequently toured Germany and Italy, and was persuaded to give help to the Savoyards but was briefly imprisoned in Lyons, 1615; returned to London: became acquainted with Ben Jonson, Donne, and Carew; Privy Councillor, and Ambassador to the French court, 1619–24; Member, Council of War, 1632–39; attended Charles I on Scottish expedition, 1639–40; briefly imprisoned for Royalist speech in the House of Lords, 1642, but otherwise neutral during the Civil War: admitted parliamentary force into Montgomery Castle to save his library, 1644; submitted to Parliament and was granted a pension, 1645; appointed Steward of the Duchy of Cornwall and Warden of the Stanneries, 1646. Knight of the Order of Bath, 1603; Irish peer, of Castle Island, County Kerry, 1624; created Baron Herbert of Cherbury, 1629. *Died 20 August 1648.*

PUBLICATIONS

Collections

> *Poems,* edited by G. C. Moore Smith. 1923.
> *Minor Poets of the Seventeenth Century,* edited by R. G. Howarth. 1931; revised edition, 1953.
> *Correspondence,* edited by W. J. Smith. 1963.

Verse

> *Occasional Verses.* 1665.

Other

> *De Veritate.* 1624; translated by M. H. Carre, 1937.
> *De Causis Errorum.* 1645.
> *De Religione Laici.* 1645; edited and translated by H. R. Hutcheson, 1944.
> *The Life and Reign of King Henry the Eighth.* 1649; edited by W. Kennett, in *Complete History of England,* 1706.
> *Expeditio in Ream Insulam, Anno 1630,* edited by T. Baldwin. 1656; as *The Expedition to the Isle of Rhé,* 1860.
> *De Religione Gentilium.* 1663; translated by W. Lewis, 1705.
> *The Life of Lord Herbert Written by Himself,* edited by Horace Walpole. 1765; edited by J. M. Shuttleworth, 1976.
> *A Dialogue Between a Tutor and His Pupil.* 1768.
> *Religio Laici,* edited by H. G. Wright, in *Modern Language Review.* 1933.

Reading List: *La Vita, le Opere, i Tempi di Herbert* by M. M. Rossi, 3 vols., 1947; "The Platonic Love Poetry of Herbert" by C. A. Hébert, in *Ball State University Forum 11,* 1970.

*   *   *

Edward Herbert was a courtier, soldier, and diplomatist, handsome, dashing, and proud of his ancestry. The self-portrait he left in his autobiography concentrates on these aspects of his life and personality. It is an extraordinarily lively picture, but it quite fails to do justice to the range of his gifts and intellectual interests. He was a considerable scholar, whose Latin philosophical treatises on Truth and Natural Religion later earned him the title Father of the English Deists. Little is said about his speculative studies in the autobiography, and nothing at all about his poetry. No doubt he took it for granted. He was the eldest son of Magdalen Herbert, and thus on familiar terms with John Donne. George Herbert was a younger brother. He knew and admired Ben Jonson, and among his more courtly literary friends were Thomas Carew and Aurelian Townshend. Naturally he wrote poetry, just as he sang, rode, danced, and duelled. But his occasional verses, collected long after his death by a nephew and dedicated to his eldest grandson, are much more interesting than we should expect if we took Lord Herbert at his own estimation. They bear the imprint of a powerfully argumentative mind. They are stylistically varied, and at their best achieve a distinctive beauty.

"Metaphysical" is an epithet truly applicable to the poetry of Edward Herbert. The relation of appearance to reality, of time to eternity, of body to spirit, were matters of major consequence to him. Even his complimentary poems move from the concrete to the abstract. His conceits have a philosophical basis, more often than not, and the framework of most of the poems is logical. Sometimes, when the topic is a trivial one, the result is a rather chilly artefact. But Herbert has lyrical as well as intellectual power. His "Elegy over a Tomb" is justly famous, and the finest of his poems, "An Ode upon a Question Moved, Whether Love Should Continue for Ever," is as beautifully cadenced as it is subtly argued. Like Donne's "The Ecstasy," it is a dramatised meditation on the nature of love, but it also has affinities with Sidney's love-dialogue "In a Grove most rich of shade." Both poems may well have provided Herbert with inspiration. To associate him solely with Donne, however, is to ignore the grace and lucidity of many of his poems. The heritage from Sidney and the links with Jonson are no less significant.

Edward Herbert was versatile in poetic invention; satires, sonnets, verse epistles, epigrams, epitaphs, songs to be sung to specific melodies, madrigals, elegies (including one on Donne), and meditative lyrics – he could produce with panache whatever the occasion called for. Yet perhaps it is understandable that, when, an elderly and disillusioned man, Lord Herbert recalled and recorded his earlier years, he made no mention of his poems. They seldom give the impression of having much emotional impetus behind them. To him, they may have been no more than pastimes; pleasurable in the execution but, because not heartfelt, of no lasting personal interest. To posterity, however, their value is beyond doubt.

—Margaret Bottrall

HERBERT, George.   Welsh.   Born at Montgomery Castle, Wales, 3 April 1593; younger brother of Lord Herbert of Cherbury, *q.v.* Educated at Westminster School, London, 1605–09; Trinity College, Cambridge, B.A. 1613, M.A. 1616. Married Jane Danvers in 1629. Minor Fellow, 1614, and Major Fellow, 1616, Trinity College, Cambridge; also, Reader in the Rhetoric School, 1618, Deputy Orator, 1618, and Public Orator, 1619–27, Cambridge University; frequently attended the court of James I, 1620–25; Member of Parliament for Montgomery, 1624–25; presented to the prebend of Layton Ecclesia, with an estate at Leighton Bromswold, Huntingdon, and ordained deacon, 1626; restored the ruined church at Leighton, with the help of Nicholas Ferrar, 1627; ordained priest, 1630; Rector, Bemerton, Salisbury, Wiltshire, 1630–33. *Died 1 March 1633.*

PUBLICATIONS

Collections

> Works, edited by F. E. Hutchinson.   1941; revised edition, 1945.
> Poems, edited by Helen Gardner.   1961.
> The Latin Poetry: A Bilingual Edition, edited and translated by Mark McCloskey and
>   Paul R. Murphy.   1965.
> Selected Poems, edited by James Reeves.   1971.
> English Poems, edited by C. A. Patrides.   1974.

Verse

> The Temple: Sacred Poems and Private Ejaculations.   1633.

Other

> Remains (includes A Priest to the Temple, or, The Country Parson His Character, and A
>   Rule of Holy Life and Jacula Prudentum), edited by Barnabas Oley.   1652; selections
>   from A Priest to the Temple edited by G. M. Forbes, as Herbert's Country Parson,
>   1949.

> Translator, A Treatise of Temperance and Sobriety, by L. Lessius.   1634; as The
>   Temperate Man, 1678; as How to Live for 100 Years, 1933.

Bibliography: Herbert: A Concise Bibliography by S. A. and D. R. Tannenbaum, 1946.

Reading List: A Reading of Herbert by Rosemond Tuve, 1952; Herbert: His Religion and Art
by Joseph H. Summers, 1954; Herbert by Margaret Bottrall, 1954; Herbert by T. S. Eliot,
1962; Utmost Art: Complexity in the Verse of Herbert by Mary E. Rickey, 1966; Herbert's
Lyrics by Arnold Stein, 1968; Herbert: Idea and Image: A Study of The Temple by Sister
Thelka, 1974; The Poetry of Herbert by Helen Vendler, 1975; A Life of Herbert by Amy
Charles, 1977.

*   *   *

The poetry of George Herbert is usually associated today with the poetry of the
seventeenth-century "metaphysical poets," particularly with that of John Donne, the close
friend of Herbert's mother and elder brother. As poets, however, Herbert and Sir Philip
Sidney, the uncle of his patrons and distant cousins (the earls of Pembroke and Montgomery),
had more in common with each other than with most of their contemporaries. Both
experimented extraordinarily with varying patterns of rhymes and line-lengths, as well as
with patterns of persuasion, argument, repetition, and variation. In their major collections
both arranged shorter poems within a larger whole which gave a context and increased
significance to the separate poems. Both conceived their major poetic works as embodying an
account of a single love, and both wrote most of the poems within those works within a
range of the tones of intimate address, as if they were speaking, privately or semi-privately, in
their own persons. Both were convinced that an effect of sincerity was essential for such
poems, and, in their practices and their attacks on the clichés of others, they showed unusual
consciousness of the difficulties in achieving such an effect. Both explored the languages

proper to courtesy and humility as well as to love. Although they used different kinds of diction for differing purposes, both usually employed the most direct language truly adequate to the occasion, and both showed a frequent preference for the monosyllabic line. Both poets usually created a limpid surface which invited the reader into a poem with the promise of immediate and full understanding; once within it, the reader might discover complexities of which he initially had no notion. Finally, neither Sidney nor Herbert seems to have allowed the poems in his major work to circulate in manuscript among friends – the usual manner of "publication" in an age when most gentlemen still eschewed the vulgarity of print: each seems to have felt his "love poems" in some ways too private to be generally read within his lifetime, although each carefully arranged his poems for potential readers. On his deathbed in 1633 Herbert sent the manuscript of *The Temple* to his friend Nicholas Ferrar with the instructions that Ferrar should have the poems printed if he thought they might do good to "any dejected poor soul"; otherwise, he should burn them.

In two sonnets sent from Cambridge to his mother for New Year's Day of 1610, the young poet wittily expressed his determination to devote his poetry to religious rather than secular love. Except for a few doubtful (and brief) translations, epitaphs, and dedications, Herbert seems to have abided by that determination in his English poems and in a good many of his Latin poems (particularly the epigrams of *Passio Discerpta* and the collection *Lucus*). But it may somewhat stretch the concept of religious love to consider it the primary subject of *Musae Responsoriae*, the witty collection of epigrams he may have begun at Westminster School in response to Andrew Melville's Puritanical attack on the universities and the Church of England; and it is the love of Magdalene Herbert which is primary in the fourteen Latin and five Greek poems of *Memoriae Matris Sacrum* published within a month of his mother's death in 1627. Herbert's duties as Latin Orator at Cambridge required him to provide poems as well as orations for royal and official occasions, but his poems in praise of Bacon went far beyond his official duties. Bacon acknowledged his indebtedness to Herbert (supposedly for help in translating *The Advancement of Learning* into Latin), and Bacon's influence may still be evident in the remarkably clear and effective prose of the work which Herbert almost certainly called *The Country Parson*.

The Temple, however, is Herbert's masterpiece. In his description of the source of his inspiration for its poems, Herbert begins "Jordan (II)" with his initial effort for richness ("Nothing could seem too rich to clothe the sun,/Much less those joys which trample on his head") and neatly makes the connections between over-ornamentation, vulgar display, egoism and commercialism; his conclusion may shock modern readers:

> As flames do work and winde, when they ascend,
> So did I weave my self into the sense.
> But while I bustled, I might heare a friend
> Whisper, *How wide is all this long pretence!*
> *There is in love a sweetnesse readie penn'd:*
> *Copie out onely that, and save expense.*

To "Copie out onely" the sweetness that is "readie penn'd" in love involved a wider activity than Sidney's contemplation of the beautiful image of Stella within his heart, since the work of Herbert's Love is God's work in creating and redeeming and sustaining heaven and earth, nature as well as man, that work of which man's love for God is only a reflection, made possible by God's gracious love for man. It encompasses everything that truly exists or has existed. The work of the one Love, for which all the hyperbolic praises of the Petrarchan lovers and the arguments about the mysteriously indestructible union of lovers might become simply statements of fact, is the largest subject possible.

But *The Temple* does not strike us as at all grandiose. Except in "The Sacrifice" (where Christ is the speaker) and perhaps in "The Church Militant," Herbert rarely approached the heroic mode in his English poems. He is neither epic nor thoroughly systematic in his treatment of his largest subject. Instead, he is selective, episodic, personal. It is as if he attempted to sketch only individually observed aspects or details of the vast activity of Love in the belief that any one might be suggestive of a larger whole. The altar for "The Church" is not an elaborate liturgical one, but "A broken A L T A R, .../Made of a heart, and cemented with teares," a speaking altar embodying as well as providing a place for the human sacrifice of praise and thanksgiving.

Herbert was fascinated with common speech. He made a collection of "Outlandish Proverbs," and he used proverbs in his poems – "Let losers talk" or "Most take all," for example. The Bible and proverbial speech proved as stimulating to Herbert's poetic imagination as scholastic and neoplatonic definitions and doctrines did to Donne's. (The poets shared an interest in what could be done in poetry with conversational phrases and rhythms.) At the same time, Herbert loved the intricate and the artful. Some poems ("The Fore-runners," for one) suggest that Herbert loved the English language and poetry so much that he had to put them to God's service if they were not to prove rival loves. In "A Wreath" Herbert developed one of his most elaborate forms as part of his demonstration that in spiritual matters the straight is to be preferred before the circuitous, simplicity before deception.

Herbert included at least one example of almost every known poetic species within his microcosmic ark. There are so many ingenious formal experiments and so many fine poems (sometimes the same poems, but not always) that it may seem arbitrary to discuss specific ones. *The Temple* includes an anagram, an echo poem ("Heaven"), a hidden acrostic (*"Our life is hid with Christ in God"*), poems based on the punning interpretation of initials, syllables, and a word ("Love-joy," "Jesu," and "The Sonne"), a "pruning" poem ("Paradise"), different kinds of circular poems ("Sinnes round" and "A Wreath"), different kinds of broken forms ("Denial" and "Grief"), the inner transformation of external form in "Aaron," the dissolution of form in "Church-monuments," in addition to the more startling "pattern poems," "The Altar" and "Easter-wings." Apart from his unusual sonnets (at least two of them, "Redemption" and "Prayer (I)," among his finest poems), Herbert rarely repeated a form. Concentration on the experimentation, variety, and wit, however, may prove more dazzling than illuminating. One may more readily come to understand and respond to Herbert's achievement by reading a sequence of the poems in their final order in *The Temple*.

An early manuscript collection (now in Dr. Williams's Library, London) contains slightly less than half the poems, none of which refers to Herbert's being a priest. In *The Temple*, six of those poems are omitted, and many others revised or recast or retitled. (Herbert seems to have been the first English poet who provided a significant title for every poem.) The two collections begin and end with the same groups of poems, but the remaining poems are reordered, along with many new poems, in a manner to reflect the fluctuations of mood and achievement in the spiritual life. After the introductory "The Church-porch" and "Superliminare," the opening sequence moves from "The Altar," "The Sacrifice," "Thanksgiving" and "The Reprisal" to "Josephs coat" and "The Pulley," includes two of Herbert's most moving poems concerning suffering and renewal, "The Crosse" and "The Flower," and may be thought to conclude with "The Sonne," a sonnet expressing Herbert's delight in the pun on "Sonne" and "A true Hymne," which insists that for the religious poet neither wit, ingenuity, nor craft is as important as the state of the heart: in the final line God supplies the rhyme for a poem about the poet's inability to construct a poem.

Often imagery and details within a poem anticipate its "turn" or conclusion (the fruit, the thorn, and the wine and corn in "The Collar," for example, anticipate the surprising final discovery that the hard taskmaster against whom the speaker revolts is really Love), but the syntax moves so firmly from point to point, usually temporally as well as logically, that the dramatic final "discovery" is not blunted. As we come to further understanding within the course of the poem, we are invited, not to collapse or deny the reality or importance of the initial experience or response, but to see it within a larger context – as if we viewed an event simultaneously in the lights of both time and eternity. The comforting "subtexts" no more undercut or destroy the "texts" than the Resurrection denies or casts doubt upon the reality of the Crucifixion.

Although all the poems are devoted to God, our chief impression of *The Temple* is not of monotony but of richness and variety. The volume imitates both the formal perfection and the surprising inventiveness of that provident love which hates nothing that it has made. Its workings are particularly imaged where they are usually most difficult to see: in the changes and the sufferings of an imperfect human life. Herbert's language establishes (or discovers) relationships between the most disparate human experiences and voices.

—Joseph H. Summers

HERRICK, Robert. English. Born in London, baptized 24 August 1591. Possibly educated at Westminster School, London: apprenticed to his uncle, Sir William Herrick, goldsmith and jeweller to the king, London, 1607–13; at St. John's College, Cambridge, 1613–16, and Trinity Hall, Cambridge, 1616–17, B.A. 1617, M.A. 1620. Associated with the "Sons of Ben," London, 1617–29; ordained in the Anglican Church, 1623; Chaplain to the Duke of Buckingham on the Isle of Rhé expedition, 1627; Vicar of Dean Prior, Devon, 1629 until ejected by the Puritans, 1647; lived in London, 1647–62; returned to Dean Prior, 1662–74. *Died 15 October 1674.*

PUBLICATIONS

Collections

> *Poetical Works*, edited by L. C. Martin.   1956.
> *Selected Poems*, edited by John Hayward.   1961.
> *Complete Poetry*, edited by J. Max Patrick.   1963.
> *Cavalier Poets*, edited by Thomas Clayton.   1978.

Verse

> *Hesperides; or, The Works Both Humane and Divine.*   1648.

Bibliography: *Herrick: A Concise Bibliography* by S. A. and D. R. Tannenbaum, 1949.

Reading List: *Herrick, The Last Elizabethan* by Leon Mandel, 1927; *Herrick* by John Press, 1961; *Herrick* by Roger B. Rollin, 1966; *A Study of Herrick* by S. Ishii, 1968; *Herrick* (biography) by George Walton Scott, 1974; *Ceremony and Art: Herrick's Poetry* by Robert H. Deming, 1974; *Trust to Good Verses: Herrick Tercentenary Essays* edited by Roger B. Rollin and J. Max Patrick, 1978.

*   *   *

In his youth Robert Herrick achieved some literary renown as a follower of Ben Jonson although his poems circulated only in manuscript. Between his graduation from Trinity Hall, Cambridge, in 1617 and his appointment to the living of Dean Prior in Devonshire in 1629 we know little of his life: he took Holy Orders in 1623, went as the Duke of Buckingham's Chaplain on the expedition to the Isle of Rhé in 1627, and became acquainted with the court musicians William Lawes and Henry Lawes. He probably spent much of his time in London, where he made friends with poets and wits who frequented taverns. He resided in what he called "dull" and "loathed" Devonshire from 1629 until his death in 1674, except for the years 1647 to 1660, having been expelled for his refusal to subscribe to the Solemn League and Covenant, and returning only at the Restoration of Charles II.

Hesperides, a volume containing his profane and sacred poems, was published in 1648. In 1869 there appeared the first collection of *Hesperides* to contain poems other than those printed in the 1648 edition: we do not know whether he wrote them after 1648 (apart from the elegy on Lord Hastings written in 1649).

Herrick was endowed with an unusually powerful and discriminating sensuality. His love of jewels and of glittering surfaces may, like his fondness for ritual, have been nurtured in the years when he was apprenticed to his uncle, Sir William Herrick, a rich London goldsmith who played a prominent role in the pomp and ceremony indulged in by the great City of London Guilds. Herrick's five senses apprehend the things of this world with a quivering eagerness. He loves to contemplate, to touch, to inhale, to hear, and to savour whiteness, softness, sweetness, smoothness. He is attracted by variety and contrast, a theme often discussed in seventeenth-century aesthetics. "The Lilly in a Christal" argues that lilies, roses, grapes, cherries, cream, and strawberries are more alluring if partially shaded. Women also can arouse men's desires more fiercely if they half conceal their soft, white nakedness:

> Yet, when your Lawns & Silks shal flow;
> And that white cloud divide
> Into a doubtful Twi-light; then,
> Then will your hidden Pride
> Raise greater fires in men.

Although many of Herrick's poems are erotic, he is capable of writing gravely and delicately about the love of man and woman. One of his best-known poems, "To Anthea, who may command him anything," is a declaration of tenderness and fidelity:

> Bid me to live, and I will live
> Thy Protestant to be;
> Or bid me love, and I will give
> A loving heart to thee.

He admires the aristocratic ideal of early seventeenth-century England, following his mentor Ben Jonson in his praise of the great country-house whose owner cares for the well-being of his tenants. He loves the English countryside, where blossom gives way to fruition, and he celebrates the pleasures of feasting after an abundant harvest. His years of living among his Devon parishioners made him acutely aware of the relics of paganism present in every aspect of country life. "The Hag" is a poem about the darkness and terror of the rural world, the other side of the medal that depicts the elves and fairies of popular superstition.

Many of Herrick's finest poems are rooted in his sense of mortality. Even his most joyous celebrations of human gaiety and of nature's fruitfulness are overshadowed by his awareness of death: the sense of life's brevity pervades poems such as "To Daffodils," "To Blossoms," and the magnificent "Corinna's Going A-Maying," Nor does his faith as a Christian priest banish his grief and fear, although he expresses a devotion to his Saviour and prays the Holy Spirit to comfort him. His "Noble Numbers" (comprising the divine poems) are greatly inferior to the remainder of *Hesperides*.

Herrick's responsiveness to language is as acute and subtle as his responsiveness to the sensuous properties of the world. He shows a remarkable skill in handling the Anglo-Saxon and the Romance elements of the English language, and often lends variety to the verse by introducing unexpectedly a Latinism as a contrast to the monosyllabic, everyday words that make up the body of the poem: "Shew me thy feet; shew me thy legs, thy thighes;/Shew me Those *Fleshie Principalities.*" He achieves weight and conciseness by incorporating into his poems reminiscences of and phrases from other writers of verse and prose. Since it is possible to date only about fifty of his poems, we cannot trace the way in which his art developed; but it seems as if his early verse draws on Catullus, Horace, and Ovid, while his later poetry owes more to Martial. The probabilities are that he picked up quotations from those writers in Florio's translation of Montaigne and in Burton's *Anatomy of Melancholy.*

When we speak of Herrick's lyrical perfection we may recall that, in the eighteenth century, when he was largely neglected, some of his poems were known in their musical settings. Indeed, certain of his sacred and profane poems had originally been designed to be sung, for Herrick writes in the tradition of the English lutanists. As for his perfection, we can tell how carefully he revised his work by comparing earlier versions of his poems with their final versions in *Hesperides.* Despite changes in taste, Herrick's place as a minor poet of consummate artistry seems secure.

—John Press

HOBBES, Thomas. English. Born in Westport, Wiltshire, 5 April 1588. Educated at a church school in Westport from age 4; Robert Latimer's school, 1599–1603; Magdalen Hall, Oxford, 1603–08, B.A. 1608. Had one illegitimate daughter. Tutor and Travelling Secretary to William Cavendish, later 2nd Earl of Devonshire, 1608–28; travelled with Sir Gervase Clinton's son, 1629–31; Tutor and Travelling Companion to William Cavendish, 3rd Earl of Devonshire, 1631–40; lived in Paris, 1640–51: tutored Charles II in mathematics, 1646–48; received a pension from the Earl of Devonshire, 1651; returned to England, 1652, and settled in London; granted a pension from the king, 1660. *Died 4 December 1679.*

PUBLICATIONS

Collections

   English and Latin Works, edited by William Molesworth.   16 vols., 1839–45.
   Selections, edited by J. E. Woodbridge.   1930.

Prose

   A Brief of the Art of Rhetoric (on Aristotle).   1635(?).

Elementorum Philosophiae:
1. *De Corpore.*   1655; edited by C. von Brockdorff, 1934; translated as *Philosophical Rudiments Concerning Government and Society*, 1651.
2. *De Homine.*   1658.
3. *De Cive.*   1642; edited by Sterling P. Lamprecht, 1949.

Human Nature; or, The Fundamental Elements of Policy.   1650.

De Corpore Politico; or, The Elements of Law, Moral and Politic.   1650; edited by Ferdinand Tönnies, 1889.

Epistolica Dissertatio de Principiis Justis et Decori.   1651.

Leviathan; or, The Matter, Form, and Power of a Commonwealth.   1651; edited by C. B. MacPherson, 1968.

Of Liberty and Necessity.   1654; edited by C. von Brockdorff, 1938.

The Questions Concerning Liberty, Necessity, and Chance.   1656.

Aretelogia; or, Marks of the Absurd Geometry of John Wallis.   1657.

Examinatio et Emendatio Mathematicae Hodiernae Qualis Explicatur in Libris Johannis Wallisii.   1660.

Dialogus Physicus: Sive de Nature Aeris.   1661.

Problemata Physica.   1662.

Mr. Hobbes Considered in His Loyalty, Religion, Reputation, and Manners.   1662.

De Principiis et Ratiocinatione Geometrarum.   1666.

Quadratura Circuli.   1669.

Rosetum Geometricum cum Censura Brevi Doctrinae Wallisianae de Motu.   1671.

Three Papers Presented to the Royal Society Against Dr. Wallis.   1671.

Lux Mathematica Excussa Collisionibus Johannis Wallisii et Thomae Hobbesii.   1672.

Principia et Problemata Aliquot Geometrica.   1674.

A Letter about Liberty and Necessity.   1676.

Decameron Physiologicum; or, Ten Dialogues of Natural Philosophy.   1678.

Behemoth; or, An Epitome of the Civil Wars of England.   1679; edited by Ferdinand Tönnies, 1889.

An Historical Narration Concerning Heresy and the Punishment Thereof.   1680.

A Dialogue Between a Philosopher and a Student of the Common Laws of England.   1681; edited by Joseph Cropsey, 1971.

Historia Ecclesiastica Carmine Elegiaco Concinnata.   1688.

Verse

De Mirabilibus Pecci Carmen (in Latin).   1666(?).

Other

Translator, *Eight Books of the Peloponnesian War*, by Thucydides.   1629; edited by Richard Schlatter, 1975.

Translator, *The Iliads and Odyssey of Homer.*   1673.

Bibliography: *Hobbes: A Bibliography* by Hugh Macdonald and M. Hargeaves, 1952.

Reading List: *Sir William Davenant's "Gondibert," Its Preface, and Hobbes's Answer: A Study in English Neo-Classicism* by Cornell March Dowlin, 1934; *The Hunting of Leviathan* by Samuel I. Mintz, 1962; *The Divine Politics of Hobbes: An Interpretation of Leviathan* by F. C. Hood, 1964; *The Anatomy of Leviathan* by F. S. McNeilly, 1968; *The Logic of Leviathan* by D. P. Gautheir, 1969; *Hobbes and the Epic Tradition of Political Theory* by Sheldon S.

Wolin, 1970; *Hobbes in His Time* edited by Ralph Ross, Herbert W. Schneider, and Theodore Waldman, 1975; *The Golden Lands of Hobbes* by Miriam M. Reik, 1977.

*   *   *

"Mr. Hobbes is and will in future ages be accounted the best writer at this day in the world." If James Harrington's contemporary assessment of the merits of Hobbes's prose style appears a little fulsome, it is as well to remember that it was not untypical. Harrington disliked the political philosophy propounded by Hobbes, but he recognised the lucidity and forcefulness of the language in which his "noxious and combustible" doctrines were made public. Perhaps Hobbes is known today first and foremost for his pessimistic view of human nature – an opinion which profoundly influenced several generations of English writers – the consequence of which was the belief that, without strong government, "the life of man" would degenerate to a state in which it was "solitary, poore, nasty, brutish, and short." But, in addition to his philosophy, his psychology, and his mathematics, he was a literary critic of some weight, and a translator of not merely Thucydides, but of Homer's epics, the *Iliad* and the *Odyssey*. His literary significance was such that Sir William Davenant worked on Hobbes's aesthetic theories in the heroic poem *Gondibert*. Not only did Hobbes scrutinise Davenant's composition daily, as it was being written, but the publication of the first two books of *Gondibert* were accompanied, in 1650, by a preface by the poet addressed to Hobbes, and by an answer from the pen of Hobbes himself. Together, these critical essays formulated "a manifesto from the classical school" of some critical importance (Edmund Gosse, *From Shakespeare to Pope*, 1885). In his tersely argued essay, Hobbes asserted that it was the role of the poet, "by imitating humane life in delightful and measur'd lines, to avert men from vice and incline them to vertuous and honorable actions," and he put forward the critical axioms on which the "New Aesthetics" should be based.

But Hobbes's criticism and translations should be put into perspective alongside his thought. Pierre Bayle, in his *Dictionary*, referred to Hobbes as "one of the greatest minds of the seventeenth century," while Hobbes himself claimed that his translation of the *Odyssey* was published merely to "take off my Adversaries from shewing their folly upon my more serious Writings, and set them upon my Verses to shew their wisdom." It is these "more serious Writings," and *Leviathan* in particular, that still interest us today. His philosophy was consistent, but the definitive version was given in 1651 in *Leviathan*. When Hobbes was writing, England had been plunged into the turmoil of civil war, and he was in exile in France. The firmness of the bonds which held society together within its hierarchical framework was being tested to the utmost. Anarchy threatened, and, once law and order was submerged, property would be unprotected. Basing his system on a shrewd list of psychological truisms, Hobbes postulated the consequences of anarchy in a vision of total and incessant war of every man against every man. He sought to analyse society and social behaviour in scientific terms, to demonstrate what would happen should society fall apart, or cease to function properly.

At the root of all of Hobbes's theories is the truism that man is a rational egoist. From this starting-point, he works on three quasiaxiomatic observations: that men perpetually seek power; that, to all intents and purposes, men are equal "in the faculties of body, and mind"; and that there is a scarcity of resources. From these propositions, he deduces his system. Without the restraints imposed upon society by a sovereign power which maintains law and order, a state of war would exist, because "Competition of Riches, Honour, Command, or other power, enclineth to Contention, Enmity, and War." But because man is a *rational* egoist, he can see that it is in his interests to escape from the prevalent conditions of a "state of nature." Reason "suggesteth convenient Articles of Peace" – the so-called laws of nature. By surrendering to a sovereign, along with all other men, his natural right to do anything that is in any way conducive to self-preservation, man can get round this impasse. The social contract – "the mutuall transferring of Right" – is the crux of Hobbes's system. Once the sovereign has been set up, he has the power and authority to ensure that no-one breaks the contract, punishing transgressors impartially. In Hobbes's view this was, in effect, the situation in England in 1651. He was a royalist, but the sovereign did not necessarily have to be a king, simply an absolute power able to maintain law and order. The sovereign was the Leviathan, or artificial man, "a common Power to keep them all in awe," without which society would quickly decline into a state of nature.

It was Hobbes's horrific view of human nature, rather than his totalitarianism, which troubled his contemporaries. As proof of his psychological analysis, he asked men to observe the lack of real altruism in society. He denied that man was a social or sociable animal, and in so doing he had contrived to render God irrelevant to his system. In 1676 one clergyman suggested that his doctrines had been "the debauching of this generation." Although, as Quentin Skinner points out (in *The Historical Journal*, September 1966), Hobbes's opinions were not unique, he was the figure at which all darts were levelled. We can sense a reaction to Hobbes in the literature of the Augustan age, in the thought of Shaftesbury, and in the cult of sentimentality, which was not only anti-Puritan and anti-Stoic, but implicitly anti-Hobbesian (see R. S. Crane in *Journal of English Literary History*, December 1934). It is possible that in *Gulliver's Travels* the Yahoos are the epitome of the popular view of Hobbesian man, while in *Tom Jones* Blifil is a perfect specimen of the rational egoist, in contrast to the good-nature, benevolence, and altruism of Tom himself. It is a measure of the influence of Hobbes's opinions on human nature that they are reflected and refuted in many works of the Augustan imagination, and that they were recognisable as Hobbesian without explicit statement.

—J. A. Downie

HUME, Alexander.   Scottish.   Born, probably at Polwarth, Berwickshire, c. 1560; son of Baron Polwarth. Studied at the University of St. Andrews, and probably graduated B.A. in 1574; studied law for four years in Paris. Married Marione Duncanson; one son, two daughters. Unsuccessfully sought an appointment in law and subsequently at court; took holy orders, 1597; Minister of Logie, near Stirling, 1598–1609. *Died 4 December 1609.*

PUBLICATIONS

Collections

The Poems, edited by Alexander Lawson.   1902.

Verse

Hymns or Sacred Songs, Wherein the Right Use of Poesie May Be Espied.   1599.

Other

A Treatise of Conscience.   1594.
A Treatise of the Felicity of the Life to Come.   1594.
The Practice of Sanctification, edited by R. M. Fergusson.   1901.

Reading List: *Hume, An Early Poet-Pastor of Logie, and His Intimates* by R. M. Fergusson, 1899.

*   *   *

Alexander Hume's poetry is significant in two respects. In its treatment of nature, it is a link in the chain which connects the Scottish poetic tradition of Gavin Douglas with that of Thomson and ultimately Burns; and, as Alexander Lawson observes (in the introductory essay to his edition of Hume's works), it is proof, occasionally, that poetry was possible even in as rigorous and repressive a time as the late sixteenth century in Scotland. His best (and best-known) poem, "A Day Estival," has been called the best poem written in the late sixteenth century by a Scot. It is a lyric celebration of a May morning, in places evocative of Thomson's descriptive passages in *The Seasons.*

The rest of Hume's work — poetry and prose — is narrowly religious and in many ways typical of post-reformation Scottish writing. His themes are sin, damnation, gratitude to God, and earthly resignation.

—John J. Perry

JONSON, Ben(jamin).   English.   Born in Westminster, London, probably 11 June 1572. Educated at Westminster School, London, under William Camden. Fought for the Dutch against the Spanish in the Low Countries. Married Anne Lewis c. 1593; had several children. Actor, then playwright, from 1595; acted for Philip Henslowe, 1597; killed a fellow actor in a duel, 1598, but escaped the gallows by pleading benefit of clergy; enjoyed the patronage of Lord Albany and Aurelian Townshend; appointed Poet Laureate, and given royal pension, 1616, and wrote and presented masques at court, 1616–25; gained a reputation as the "literary dictator" of London and in later life attracted a circle of young writers who styled themselves the "Sons of Ben"; visited Scotland, and William Drummond of Hawthornden, 1618–19: elected a Burgess of Edinburgh, 1619; appointed City Chronologer of London, 1628. M.A.: Oxford University, 1619. *Died 6 August 1637.*

Collections

> *Works*, edited by C. H. Herford and P. and E. M. Simpson.   11 vols., 1925–52.
> *Complete Masques*, edited by S.Orgel.   1969.
> *Complete Poems*, edited by Ian Donaldson.   1975.

Plays

> *The Case Is Altered* (produced 1597–98?).   1609.
> *Every Man in His Humour* (produced 1598).   1601; edited by G. B. Jackson, 1969.
> *Every Man Out of His Humour* (produced 1599).   1600.
> *The Fountain of Self-Love; or, Cynthia's Revels* (produced 1600).   1601.
> *Poetaster; or, The Arraignment* (produced 1601).   1602.
> *Sejanus His Fall* (produced 1603).   1605; edited by W. Bolton, 1966.
> *Entertainment of the Queen and Prince at Althorp* (produced 1603).   1604.
> *King James His Royal and Magnificent Entertainment*, with Dekker (produced 1604).   With *Entertainment of the Queen and Prince at Althorp*, 1604.
> *A Private Entertainment of the King and Queen at Highgate* (produced 1604).   In *Works*, 1616.
> *Eastward Ho*, with Chapman and Marston (produced 1605).   1605; edited by C. G. Petter, 1973.
> *Volpone; or, The Fox* (produced 1605).   1607; edited by J. Creaser, 1978.
> *The Masque of Blackness* (produced 1605).   In *The Characters of Two Royal Masques*, 1608.
> *Hymenaei* (produced 1606).   1606.
> *The Entertainment of the Two Kings of Great Britain and Denmark at Theobalds* (produced 1606).   In *Works*, 1616.
> *An Entertainment of King James and Queen Anne at Theobalds* (produced 1607).   In *Works*, 1616.
> *The Masque of Beauty* (produced 1608).   In *The Characters of Two Royal Masques*, 1608.
> *The Hue and Cry after Cupid* (produced 1608).   In *Works*, 1616.
> *The Description of the Masque Celebrating the Marriage of John, Lord Ramsey Viscount Haddington* (produced 1608).   In *Works*, 1616.
> *The Masque of Queens* (produced 1609).   1609.
> *Epicoene; or, The Silent Woman* (produced 1609).   In *Works*, 1616; edited by L. A. Beaurline, 1966.
> *The Speeches at Prince Henry's Barriers* (produced 1610).   In *Works*, 1616.
> *The Alchemist* (produced 1610).   1612; edited by Alvin B. Kernan, 1974.
> *Oberon, The Faery Prince* (produced 1611).   In *Works*, 1616.
> *Love Freed from Ignorance and Folly* (produced 1611).   In *Works*, 1616.
> *Catiline His Conspiracy* (produced 1611).   1611; edited by W. Bolton and J. F. Gardner, 1972.
> *Love Restored* (produced 1612).   In *Works*, 1616.
> *The Irish Masque* (produced 1613).   In *Works*, 1616.
> *A Challenge at Tilt* (produced 1614).   In *Works*, 1616
> *Bartholomew Fair* (produced 1614).   1631; edited by Edward B. Partridge, 1964.
> *The Golden Age Restored* (produced 1616).   In *Works*, 1616.
> *Mercury Vindicated from the Alchemists* (produced 1616).   In *Works*, 1616.
> *The Devil Is an Ass* (produced 1616).   1631; edited by M. Hussey, 1967.

Christmas His Masque (produced 1616).   In *Works*, 1640.

The Vision of Delight (produced 1617).   In *Works*, 1640.

Lovers Made Men (produced 1617).   1617.

Pleasure Reconciled to Virtue (produced 1618).   In *Works*, 1640; revised version, as *For the Honour of Wales* (produced 1618), in *Works*, 1640.

News from the New World Discovered in the Moon (produced 1620).   In *Works*, 1640.

An Entertainment at the Blackfriars (produced 1620).   In *The Monthly Magazine; or, British Register*, 1816.

Pan's Anniversary; or, The Shepherd's Holiday (produced 1620).   In *Works*, 1640.

The Gypsies Metamorphosed (produced 1621).   In *Works*, 1640; edited by W. W. Greg, 1952.

The Masque of Augurs (produced 1622).   1622.

Time Vindicated to Himself and to His Honours (produced 1623).   1623.

Neptune's Triumph for the Return of Albion.   1624; revised version, as *The Fortunate Isles and Their Union* (produced 1625), 1625.

The Masque of Owls (produced 1624).   In *Works*, 1640.

The Staple of News (produced 1625).   1631; edited by Devra Rowland Kifer, 1976.

The New Inn; or, The Light Heart (produced 1629).   1631.

Love's Triumph Through Callipolis (produced 1631).   1631.

Chloridia (produced 1631).   1631.

The Magnetic Lady; or, Humours Reconciled (produced 1632).   In *Works*, 1640.

A Tale of a Tub (produced 1633).   In *Works*, 1640.

The King's Entertainment at Welbeck (produced 1633).   In *Works*, 1640.

Love's Welcome at Bolsover (produced 1634).   In *Works*, 1640.

The Sad Shepherd; or, A Tale of Robin Hood (incomplete), in *Works*.   1640; edited and completed by Alan Porter, 1944.

Other

Works (plays and verse).   1616; revised edition, 2 vols., 1640.

Timber; or, Discoveries Made upon Men and Matter, in *Works*.   1640; edited by R. S. Walker, 1953.

The English Grammar, in *Works*.   1640; edited by S. Gibson, 1928.

Leges Convivales.   1692.

Literary Criticism, edited by J. D. Redwine.   1970.

Translator, *Horace His Art of Poetry*, in *Works*.   1640; edited by E. H. Blakeney, 1928.

Bibliography: *Jonson: A Concise Bibliography* by S. A. Tannenbaum, 1938; supplement 1947; supplement in *Elizabethan Bibliographies Supplements 3* by G. R. Guffey, 1968.

Reading List: *Jonson, Poet* by George B. Johnston, 1945; *Jonson of Westminster* (biography) by Marchette Chute, 1953; *The Accidence of Jonson's Plays, Masques, and Entertainments* by Astley C. Partridge, 1953; *Jonson and the Comic Truth* by John J. Enck, 1957; *The Broken Compass: A Study of the Major Comedies of Jonson* by Edward B. Partridge, 1958; *Jonson and the Language of Prose Comedy* by Jonas A. Barish, 1960; *Jonson's Plays: An Introduction* by Robert E. Knoll, 1965; *Jonson's Dotages: A Reconsideration of the Late Plays* by L. S. Champion, 1967; *Vision and Judgment in Jonson's Drama* by Gabriele B. Jackson, 1968; *The Aristophanic Comedies of Jonson* by Coburn Gum, 1969; *Jonson* by John B. Bamborough, 1970; *Jonson's Moral Comedy* by A. C. Dessen, 1971; *Jonson, Public Poet and Private Man* by George Parfitt, 1976.

*   *   *

The opening lines of T. S. Eliot's famous essay on Ben Jonson are now nearly sixty years old, yet they are almost as applicable today as when they were first written: "The reputation of Jonson," Eliot wrote, "has been of the most deadly kind that can be compelled upon the memory of a great poet. To be universally accepted; to be damned by the praise that quenches all desire to read the book; to be afflicted by the imputation of the virtues which excite the least pleasure; and to be read only by historians and antiquaries – this is the most perfect conspiracy of approval." Substitute "academics and students" for "antiquaries" and you have a fair summary of Jonson's current reputation. That this state of affairs is partly of Jonson's own making is certainly true but hardly sufficient justification. In his own day Jonson saw himself as the self-appointed arbiter of true critical taste, the upholder of classical standards of decorum, construction, and moral didacticism against the undiscriminating popular appetite for sensation and extravagant spectacle, and the champion of high erudition against barbarous ignorance. So successful was he in imposing this version of himself on his own age and those that followed that it was not long before the contrast was drawn by which Jonson's reputation is still largely defined – the contrast between the warm spontaneous, generous-hearted inclusiveness of the "romantic" Shakespeare and the chilly learning and cold perfection of the "classical" Jonson. Like all such sweeping contrasts, this one has enough plausibility to survive as the received truth, though it is as misleading about Shakespeare as it is about Jonson.

By way of building up a fairer picture of the nature of Jonson's achievement we may begin by recalling one of Drummond's remarks about him: "He hath consumed a whole night in lying looking to his great toe, about which he hath seen Tartars and Turks, Romans and Cartheginians, fight in his imagination." Such a detail serves to draw attention to an element in Jonson's work which meets us at every turn and which is at least as important as his undoubted learning and his emphasis on classical precept and precedent. It is a facet of his imagination at once childlike, romantic, and grotesque, and one which clearly contributed to some of his finest comic creations as well as to his tenderest lyrics and his most savage satirical epigrams.

The exuberance of Jonson's imagination is already apparent in his first great stage success, *Every Man in His Humour* first performed in 1598 by the Lord Chamberlain's Men, the most famous theatrical company of the time. (The tradition that Shakespeare himself arranged for his company to present the play is attractive, though it cannot be traced beyond the eighteenth century.) In terms of plot and setting there is nothing to distinguish Jonson's play from many others deriving from classical Roman Comedy, with its conflict of generations and the convoluted manoeuvrings of wily servants. Jonson's distinctive contribution appears in his conception of the "humorous man," a dramatic character whose personality is shaped by some leading trait (or "humour") in his temperament which was itself, according to prevailing medical notions, based on the predomination of one of the four bodily fluids, blood, choler, melancholy, and phlegm. Jonson's contemporary George Chapman had been the first to put "humorous" characters on the stage (in *A Humorous Day's Mirth* performed a year before Jonson's comedy), but the vigour and extravagance of Jonson's presentation set it apart. The sharp distinction he draws between true "humour" as an element of character and mere affectation is typical of the energy and inventiveness of Jonson's imagination:

> As when some one peculiar quality
> Doth so possess a man, that it doth draw
> All his affects, his spirits, and his powers,
> In their confluctions, all to run one way,
> This may truly said to be a Humour.
> But that a rook, in wearing a pied feather,
> The cable hat-band, or the three-piled ruff,
> A yard of shoe-tie, or the Switzer's knot
> On his French garters, should affect a Humour!
> Oh, 'tis more than most ridiculous.

Like most sequels, Jonson's attempt to capitalize on the success of his play with *Every Man Out of His Humour* was a comprehensive failure and appears to have led to the Chamberlain's Men dispensing with his services. The Children of the Queen's Chapel, one of the companies of boy actors which sprouted up towards the end of the century, were his new theatrical patrons and for them he wrote the satiric comedies which involved him in the "war of the theatres" with his contemporaries John Marston and Thomas Dekker. In spite of occasional passages of great satirical energy and some beautiful lyrics such as "Queen and huntress, chaste and fair," Jonson's contributions to this "war" are not by any means among his best plays. *Cynthia's Revels* deserves to be remembered for its portrait of Jonson himself as Crites, the impartial and well-informed judge of society and the arts; and in *The Poetaster* Jonson as Horace feeds Marston (Crispianus) an emetic that makes the latter spew great quantities of words in his typically turgid style. But Jonson's greatest achievements in drama were yet to come.

This achievement is certainly not to be found in Jonson's two classical tragedies *Sejanus His Fall* and *Catiline His Conspiracy*; though the latter especially has some magnificent speeches as well as dramatic moments of great intensity, both suffer by comparison with Shakespeare's excursions into Roman history, especially *Julius Caesar*. Jonson's enduring reputation as a dramatist rests squarely on three great comedies, *Volpone; or The Fox*, *The Alchemist*, and *Bartholomew Fair*. Each of them exemplifies Jonson's enormous capacity to dramatize the grotesque aberrations of human appetite, his zest for the variety of life, and his unfailing delight in the villain as artist. *Volpone* is scrupulously classical in its didactic import, yet what delights us is chiefly the artistry of Volpone and his henchman Mosca. *The Alchemist* is a model of the observance of the Aristotelian unities, but its dramatic appeal lies in the breakneck momentum of its plot and the almost unbearable comic tension created by it. And in *Bartholomew Fair* Jonson abandoned even the pretence of being the classical moralist in favour of the unbuttoned enjoyment of Jacobean London in all its colour and richness.

The opening years of the seventeenth century witnessed Jonson's finest dramatic productions, not only for the public stage, but in the sphere of royal entertainment, when Jonson's collaboration with the scene designer and architect Inigo Jones led to a splendid flowering of that most ephemeral of theatrical forms, the court masque. Rooted as it was in time, place, and occasion, the masque can give us little sense of its splendour through the text alone, though Jonson's scripts for such works as *Pleasure Reconciled to Virtue* and *The Gypsies Metamorphosed* are eloquent enough in the reading. It was precisely the disagreement between Jonson and Jones as to the relative importance of words versus spectacle in masque which led to the dissolution of this brilliant partnership in 1631.

Jonson's last years present a sad picture of commercial failure, declining creative powers, and increasing bodily decrepitude. Apart from the comedies already mentioned, *The Silent Woman*, *The Devil Is an Ass*, and *The Staple of News* deserve to be remembered for their occasional inventiveness and keen-eyed observation of London life and manners. But if Jonson's principal claim to fame lies in his three great comedies, his achievements as lyric and epigrammatic poet are not inconsiderable. Contemporary practitioners of verse esteemed him so highly that a group of them, which included Herrick, Suckling, and Carew styled themselves the Sons of Ben and produced a commemorative volume *Jonsonus Virbius* after his death in 1637. As a critic, too, Jonson was of the first rank, forthright, well-informed, and catholic in taste by the standards of the time. All these qualities are well illustrated in the splendid commendatory verses which he contributed to the Folio edition of Shakespeare's works published in 1623.

That Jonson was a classicist and an erudite one need not be disputed, though he was by no means the most learned classical scholar of his day (his mentor Camden and his contemporary John Selden were far better versed in the classics). But the emphasis should finally fall on the originality of his imagination, his roots in the popular idiom he affected to despise, and his enormous sense of theatre which is illustrated by the continued success on the stage of his great comedies.

—Gāmini Salgādo

KING, Henry.   English.   Born in London, 16 January 1592. Educated at Westminster School, London; Christ Church, Oxford, M.A. 1614, D.D. 1625. Married Anne Berkeley in 1617 (died, 1624); six children. Prebendary of St. Paul's, London, 1616; subsequently Archdeacon of Colchester, Chaplain to the Court, and Canon of Christ Church, Oxford; Dean of Rochester, 1638; Bishop of Chichester, 1642 until deprived of his title by the Puritans; returned after the Restoration. *Died 30 September 1669.*

PUBLICATIONS

Collections

Poems, edited by Margaret Crum.   1965.

Verse

An Elegy upon Charles I.   1648.
A Groan Fetched at the Funeral of Charles the First.   1649.
The Psalms of David Turned into Meter.   1651.
Poems, Elegies, Paradoxes, and Sonnets.   1657; revised edition, 1664.

Other

Two Sermons Preached at White-Hall in Lent.   1627.
An Exposition upon the Lord's Prayer Delivered in Certain Sermons in the Cathedral Church of St. Paul.   1628.

Bibliography: *A Bibliography of King* by Geoffrey Keynes, 1977.

Reading List: *King and the Seventeenth Century* by Ronald Berman, 1964.

*   *   *

A member of a distinguished ecclesiastical family, Henry King had a professional career that is suggested by the sermons he published, his *Exposition on The Lord's Prayer*, and his metrical paraphrases of the Psalms ("To Be Sung after the Old Tunes Used in the Churches"). But, as the last item suggests, like George Herbert and many other of his contemporaries at Westminster School, he wrote verse throughout much of his life. Many of his poems were responses to public occasions common among university men: from the death of Prince Henry in 1612 until that of the Countess of Leinster in 1657, he marked public, as well as a number of private, losses with elegies. In some of his later, and most distinguished, ones, such as those on the third Earl of Essex and on Sir Charles Lucas and Sir George Lisle, King's hostility to the victorious forces of the Commonwealth led him to anticipate the pointed satire of a later age. In his elegy for Charles I he ironically congratulated the new rulers for their "preposterous Wisdoms" in both actions and propaganda:

> For as to work His Peace you rais'd this Strife,
> And often Shot at Him to Save His Life;
> As you took from Him to Encrease His wealth,

And kept Him Pris'ner to secure His Health;
So in revenge of your dissembled Spight,
In this last Wrong you did Him greatest Right,
And (cross to all You meant) by Plucking down
Lifted Him up to His Eternal Crown.

Some of King's brief stanzaic poems (such as "The Vow-Breaker" or "The Double Rock") are more or less in the manner of Donne, and others nearer that of Jonson: "Tell mee no more how faire shee is" is one of the most graceful lyrics of the age, and King also imitated Jonson's epigrams and epistles. His characteristic vein is valedictory, whether mortuary or amatory. He is frequently "Content/... to Lament," whether particular individuals or imaginary loves or the condition of man. His characteristic couplets are frequently marked by a sort of dying fall when the major cadence occurs after the third, fourth, or fifth syllable rather than at the end of the line.

As his contemporary James Howell remarked, one finds in King's verse "not only heat and strength, but also an exact concinnity and evenness of fancy." "*Sic Vita*," for example, is a miniature masterpiece constructed of materials which served a number of other versifiers only for undistinguished exercises in commonplaces. Perhaps King's most remarkable achievement was the creation of a verse and tone proper for the most intimate personal and familial uses. "To my Sister Anne King who chid mee in verse for being angry" is a charming end to a domestic quarrel, and King's masterpiece, "An Exequy to his Matchlesse never to be forgotten Freind," written for the death of his young wife, is one of the wittiest as well as most moving personal elegies in English. King's formal and ingenious funeral rite ends with a direct and tender address to the dead loved one:

But hark! My Pulse, like a soft Drum
Beats my Approach, Tells Thee I come;
And, slowe howe're my Marches bee,
I shall at last sitt downe by Thee.
    The thought of this bids mee goe on,
And wait my dissolution
With Hope and Comfort. Deare! (forgive
The Crime) I am content to live
Divided, with but half a Heart,
Till wee shall Meet and Never part.

—Joseph H. Summers

LODGE, Thomas.   English.   Born in West Ham, London, c. 1558. Educated at the Merchant Taylors' School, London, 1571–73; Trinity College, Oxford, matriculated 1573, B.A. 1577, M.A. 1581; entered Lincoln's Inn, London, 1578; later studied medicine at Avignon: M.D. 1600; awarded M.D. at Oxford, 1602; admitted to the College of Physicians, London, 1610. Married 1) Joan Lodge in 1583, one daughter; 2) Mrs. Jane Aldred. Settled in London, 1578; gave up study of law for a literary career, c. 1580; a friend of Robert Greene, and probably of Rich, Daniel, Drayton, and Lyly; served with Captain Clarke on an expedition to the Terceras and Canary Islands, 1588, and with Thomas Cavendish on an expedition to Brazil and the Straits of Magellan, 1591–93; returned to London, and resumed literary career, 1593–96; converted to Roman catholicism; abandoned literature, and practised medicine, in London, from 1600. *Died in September 1625.*

PUBLICATIONS

Collections

Complete Works, edited by Edmund Gosse.   4 vols., 1883.

Fiction

An Alarum Against Usurers, The Delectable History of Forbonius and Prisceria, The Lamentable Complaint of Truth over England.   1584.
Rosalynde: Euphues' Golden Legacy.   1590; as *Euphues' Golden Legacy,* 1612; edited by Geoffrey Bullough, in *Narrative and Dramatic Sources of Shakespeare 2,* 1958.
The Famous, True, and Historical Life of Robert Second Duke of Normandy.   1591.
Euphues' Shadow, The Battle of the Senses, The Deaf Man's Dialogue.   1592.
The Life and Death of William Long Beard, with Many Other Histories.   1593.
A Margarite of America.   1596; edited by G. B. Harrison, 1927.

Plays

The Wounds of Civil War, Lively Set Forth in the True Tragedies of Marius and Sylla (produced 1588?).   1594; edited by Joseph W. Houppert, 1969.
A Looking Glass for London and England, with Robert Greene (produced 1590?).   1594; edited by T. Hayashi, 1970.

Verse

Scilla's Metamorphosis, Interlaced with the Unfortunate Love of Glaucus, with Sundry Other Poems and Sonnets.   1589; as *A Most Pleasant History of Glaucus and Scilla,* 1610; edited by N. Alexander, 1967.
Phillis: Honoured with Pastoral Sonnets, Elegies, and Amorous Delights; The Tragical Complaint of Elstred.   1593; edited by M. F. Crow, 1896.
A Fig for Momus, Containing Satires, Eclogues, and Epistles.   1595.

Other

A Defence of Poetry, Music, and Stage Plays.   1579(?).
Catharos: Diogenes in His Singularity.   1591.
The Devil Conjured.   1596.
Wit's Misery and the World's Madness.   1596.
Prosopopoeia: Containing the Tears of the Mother of God.   1596.
The Poor Man's Talent, in *Complete Works.*   1883.

Translator, *The Flowers of Lodowicke of Granado,* by Michael ab Isselt.   1601.
Translator, *The Famous Works of Josephus.*   1602.
Translator, *A Treatise of the Plague,* by F. Valleriole.   1603.
Translator, *The Works of Seneca.*   1614; selections edited by W. Clode, 1888, and by
    W. H. D. Rouse, 1899.
Translator, *A Learned Summary upon the Famous Poem of William of Saluste, Lord of
    Bartas, Translated Out of French.*   1621.

Bibliography: *Lodge: A Concise Bibliography* by S. A. Tannenbaum, 1940; *Lodge 1939–65*
by R. C. Johnson, 1968.

Reading List: *Lodge* by Edward A. Tenney, 1935; *Lodge, Gentleman* by Pat M. Ryan, 1958;
Lodge by W. D. Rae, 1967.

*   *   *

Thomas Lodge's main claim to literary recognition lies in his pastoral romance, *Rosalynde:
Euphues Golden Legacie.* For all the title's apparent indebtedness to Lyly, the work derives
less from *Euphues* itself than from classical sources common to both Lyly and Lodge. Two
fables intertwine in *Rosalynde.* Dominant much of the time is the narrative concerning the
fates of two girls, Rosalynde and Alinda, who escape into the Forest of Arden to avoid the
wrath of King Torismond, Alinda's father and Rosalynde's uncle. In the Forest they
encounter Rosader, one of the three sons of Sir John of Bordeaux. Rosalynde is secretly in
love with Rosader, and he with her; but because Rosalynde is disguised as a page, calling
herself Ganymede, she is naturally unrecognized by her lover. The second narrative concerns
Sir John's sons and the ways in which they succeed or fail in living up to their dead father's
precepts. With the meeting of Rosalynde and Rosader, the two narratives combine. The
lovers compete in impromptu versifying, after Rosalynde has challenged Rosader to
demonstrate, in "some amorous eclogue," the depth of his love for the mistress he cannot see
in her.
  Rosalynde is, of course, the source for Shakespeare's *As You Like It,* but it is important to
acknowledge the work for its own merits. Lodge's medium, a highly polished prose
interspersed with gentle songs, is appropriate for the stories he has to tell and for his neat, if
conventional, antithesis of court and country. His pastoral idyll knows few hardships, as the
philosophical Corydon tells Alinda: "Envy stirs not us, we covet not to climb, our desires
mount not above our degrees, nor our thoughts above our fortunes. Care cannot harbour in
our cottages, nor do homely couches know broken slumbers: as we exceed not in diet, so we
have enough to satisfy: and, mistress, I have so much Latin, *Satis est quod sufficit.*" As well
as the thought, the style of this passage speaks proudly of its origins; in the sentence "Care
cannot harbour in our cottages, nor do homely couches know broken slumbers," Lodge
achieves with the uninflected language a chiastic symmetry that Ovid would have approved.
  Lodge treats the lovers' verses with a delicate seriousness. The situation, with Alinda
playing on her pipe while Rosalynde and Rosader vie with each other in lyrics, is, in the
extreme, artificial. Yet Lodge's tact in avoiding excess, either in the verse or in the prose, is
such that the comedy is gentle, but never ludicrous; disbelief is always willingly suspended.

> Love in my bosom like a bee
>   Doth suck his sweet:
> Now with his wings he plays with me,
>   Now with his feet.
> Within mine eyes he makes his nest,
> His bed amidst my tender breast;
> My kisses are his daily feast,

And yet he robs me of my rest.
Ah, wanton, will ye?

Lyrics such as this deserve a place in the Elizabethan anthology. Lighter in touch than some of Wyatt's, they have also a whimsical humour which his poems often lack.

In *A Looking Glass for London*, which he wrote with Robert Greene, Lodge takes a stern look at the sorry state of the nation. A conqueror who rivals Tamburlaine ("*Rasni* is God on earth and none but he") indulges his lust for women; his extravagant wife scents herself with all the perfumes of Arabia; a usurer deprives a poor man of his cow and then bribes the judge to pervert the course of justice; the blacksmith's servant beats his master – all are comically exaggerated characters, and all, of course, are properly punished. Jonah's Nineveh is the meeting-place for these incongruous characters, and there is always at hand the doom-laden prophet Oseas, who can extend the moral to sixteenth-century London:

If such escapes ô London raigne in thee:
Repent, for why each sin shall punisht bee.
Repent, amend, repent, the houre is nie,
Defer not time, who knowes when he shall die?

Lodge also attempted writings in other popular Renaissance genres, and although there is nothing especially striking about, for instance, his satires in *A Fig for Momus* there is, equally, nothing to be ashamed of. He is always careful and competent, applying the best of his skill to the matter in hand, whether as a pastoral sonneteer in *Phillis*, or as a medical practitioner in a pamphlet giving advice to the poor and sick on the management of the plague. Like other writers of his time, he held literature in the highest esteem; in his *Reply* to Stephen Gosson's attack on the stage, he wrote: "Poetes were the first raysors of cities, prescribers of good lawes, mayntayners of religion, disturbors of the wicked, advancers of the wel disposed, inventors of laws, and lastly the very fot-paths to knowledge, and understanding."

—Roma Gill

LOVELACE, Richard. English. Born in Woolwich, London, in 1618. Educated at Charterhouse School, London; Gloucester Hall, Oxford, 1634–36, honorary M.A. 1636; incorporated at Cambridge, 1637. Ensign in Lord Goring's Regiment in the first Scottish expedition, 1639, and Captain in the second expedition, 1640. Inherited the family estates in Kent, 1639. Courtier and royalist: imprisoned for presenting the "Kentish Petition" to the Long Parliament, 1642, and subsequently released on bail; took up arms on behalf of the king, 1645; after defeat of the Royalists left England, served with the French Army against the Spanish, and was wounded at Dunkirk, 1646; returned to England, and was imprisoned by the Puritan government, 1648–49; depleted his estate in the king's cause and probably lived his last years in poverty in Gunpowder Alley, London. *Died in 1658.*

PUBLICATIONS

Collections

> Poems, edited by C. H. Wilkinson. 1930.
> Cavalier Poets, edited by Thomas Clayton. 1978.

Verse

> Lucasta: Epodes, Odes, Sonnets, Songs, etc., to Which Is Added Amarantha: A Pastoral. 1649.
> Lucasta: Posthume Poems, edited by Dudley Posthumus Lovelace. 1659–60.

Bibliography: A Bibliography of Lovelace by C. S. Ker, 1949.

Reading List: The Cavalier Spirit and Its Influence on the Life and Work of Lovelace by C. H. Hartmann, 1925; Lovelace by Manfred Weidhorn, 1970.

*   *   *

Richard Lovelace shares with the other so-called "Cavalier poets" like Thomas Carew and Sir John Suckling the traits of wit and ease, "ease" being a seventeenth-century critical term contrasted to "strength" and comprising such traits as metrical regularity, dilation of thought and image rather than compression, and care for the whole poem rather than strikingly original parts of it.

The quality that distinguishes Lovelace's verse from that of the other Cavalier poets is complexity of view, a quality that is exhibited both by his handling of his subjects and by his subtle tone. In "Gratiana dauncing and singing," for an example of the first, he sees in dancing proliferating meanings for the action of love and the operation of the universe. Similarly, in his many poems on animals and insects, Lovelace is intent on seeing the great in the small, the great usually taking the form of necessary conflict and death in a Nature seen objectively – and at a distance – as brutal (as noted by Manfred Weidhorn); one of the best of these is "The Grasse-hopper" (which alludes to the plight of the Cavaliers after the death of Charles I), in which the grass-hopper is not only praised as trusting and open but also condemned (and pitied) as heedless, and in which the Horatian conclusion advising retirement is not only serious but playful as well. "To Amarantha, That she would dishevell her hair" develops microcosmic conceits around her loosened hair so as to make it an emblem of a life as fully natural as the sunrise and as enjoyable as love; her untying the ribbon at her lover's insistence is imaged as deflowering, and with that act the lover's emotions pour forth in all their complexity – first eagerness, then acceptance of both joy and pain in the act ("I'le drink a teare out of thine eyes"), finally a realization of the limits, and even desperation, of the act of love in a fleeting world. This poem shows Lovelace's ability to keep such distance between himself and his emotions as to accept calmly disparate views of love and of reality in general, and disparate emotions toward them – enjoyment, cynicism, tenderness, brutality, grief (see Marius Bewley, "The Colloquial Mode of Byron," Scrutiny 16); so too does "La Bella Bona Roba," which presents the wholehearted gusto of the lover's preference for plump women against the dark background figure of a death's head, and encloses the whole within the playful yet brutal image of love as a hunt. Love and death combine with an amazing harmony in Lovelace's most famous lyric, "To Lucasta, Going to the Warres," where the serious adjustment of love with honor in facing death at the end of the lyric is achieved within a context of tender humor (treating the beloved's breast hyperbolically as a "Nunnerie," for instance) and reckless playfulness (treating war as if it were actually the sexual infidelity she thinks it is). Lovelace's is the poetry of poise – distant, judicious, open to conflict.

—Walter R. Davis

LYLY, John. English. Born in the Weald of Kent c. 1553. Educated at King's School, Canterbury, Kent; Magdalen College, Oxford, B.A. 1573, M.A. 1575; also studied at Cambridge University, M.A. 1579. Married Beatrice Browne in 1583; two sons and one daughter. In the service of Lord Delawarr, 1575–80, and the Earl of Oxford, from 1580; leased Blackfriars Theatre, London, 1584, but subsequently gaoled for debt in the same year; wrote for the children's acting companies of the Chapel Royal and St. Paul's, London, until 1591; Member of Parliament for Hindon, Aylesbury, and Appleby, 1589–1601. *Died* (buried) *30 November 1606.*

PUBLICATIONS

Collections

> *Dramatic Works,* edited by F. W. Fairholt.   2 vols., 1858–92.
> *Complete Works,* edited by R. W. Bond.   1902.

Fiction

> *Euphues: The Anatomy of Wit.*   1578; augmented edition, 1579; edited by J. Winny, 1957; *Euphues and His England,* 1580; *Euphues* (both parts), 1617; edited by M. W. Croll and H. Clemons, 1916.

Plays

> *Alexander, Campaspe, and Diogenes* (produced 1584).   1584; as *Campaspe,* 1584; edited by W. W. Greg, 1933.
> *Sappho and Phao* (produced 1584).   1584.
> *Galathea* (produced 1584–88?).   1592; edited by A. B. Lancashire, with *Midas,* 1969.
> *Mother Bombie* (produced 1587–90?).   1594; edited by A. Harriette Andreadis, 1975.
> *Endymion, The Man in the Moon* (produced 1588).   1591; edited by W. H. Neilson, 1911.
> *Love's Metamorphosis* (produced 1589–90?).   1601.
> *Midas* (produced 1590?).   1592; edited by A. B. Lancashire, with *Galathea,* 1969.
> *The Woman in the Moon* (produced 1590–95?).   1597.

Other

> *Pap with a Hatchet, Alias a Fig for My Godson; or, Crack Me This Nut; or, A Country Cuff, That Is, A Sound Box of the Ear, for the Idiot Martin.*   1589.

Bibliography: *Lyly: A Concise Bibliography* by S. A. Tannenbaum, 1940; *Lyly 1935–65* by R. C. Johnson, 1968.

Reading List: *Lyly and the Italian Renaissance* by V. M. Jeffery, 1928; *Lyly: The Humanist and Courtier*, 1962, and *Lyly and Peele*, 1968, both by George K. Hunter; *The Court Comedies of Lyly; A Study in Allegorical Dramaturgy* by Peter Saccio, 1969.

*   *   *

John Lyly graduated as Master of Arts from Oxford, where he had enjoyed the patronage of Lord Burleigh, Queen Elizabeth's Lord High Treasurer. He gained a position as secretary to the Earl of Oxford, Burleigh's son-in-law and a supporter of a company of boy actors. Lyly's humanistic education, and his entry as a young man to court circles, determined both his audience and his entire literary output. He first appeared in print with a pastoral prose romance *Euphues: The Anatomy of Wit* and followed it up with an even more successful sequel *Euphues and his England*, both parts continuing during his lifetime to be regularly reprinted.

He was appointed vice-master of Paul's Boys (the cathedral choristers who also acted as boy actors) and later to a position in the Revels Office, which was responsible for mounting the Queen's entertainments. He was (with Nashe) drawn in for a time on the side of the bishops in the theological Marprelate controversy to which he contributed one pamphlet *Pappe with an Hatchet* in colloquial prose. But unlike Nashe, who found in the pamphlet a new and effective prose style, Lyly preferred the prose style of which he was a master and the audience with which he was familiar. His later work, all theatrical, was written to be acted (and sung) by Paul's Boys for performance before Elizabeth and her court.

Euphues, a love-romance, was directed particularly towards an audience of leisured ladies. "*Euphues* had rather lie shut in a lady's casket than open in a scholar's study," claims its preface. Lyly drew on the stylistic devices of medieval and renaissance rhetoric to produce a skilled, highly mannered, prose (which has always since Lyly's time been termed Euphuism, the sentence quoted above being a relatively simple example). Euphuism was characterised by (a) a balance of similar parts of speech in successive clauses, the matching words generally reinforced by alliteration or by "like endings," (b) equal-length phrases or clauses used in a parallel series, (c) the repetition of words derived from the same stem, (d) the use of antithesis, and (e) frequent far-fetched similes many of them drawn from the natural world and derived from Pliny's *Natural History*. The style was much admired and was fashionable for a few years. It was brilliantly parodied by Shakespeare in a speech by Falstaff, and echoes of it can be found in mannered prose as late as that of Dr. Johnson.

When Lyly came to write for the theatre, he generally used some variation of his Euphuistic prose style, though he could vary it with a more colloquial (but never vulgar) idiom if the situation demanded. Apart from *Campaspe* (derived from Classical history) and *Mother Bombie* (a Terence-type comedy on an English folk-theme), his plays are fantasies based on themes and characters from Classical mythology. The format encouraged lavish spectacle, allegorical references to current affairs in court (in *Endymion*, Cynthia and Endymion could be readily interpreted as Elizabeth and Leicester), aristocratic comedy to evoke what the preface to *Sapho and Phao* called "soft smiling, not loud laughing"; and it could very easily (as in the close of *Endymion*) be diverted to open praise of the monarch who was present at the performance. All was presented with a high degree of wit and dazzling verbal displays.

With a cast of boy actors and choristers, and an audience who demanded glitter, Lyly made no attempt to present real human feelings. His comedy was pantomimic and non-realistic, and (given the terms in which it was written) extremely effective. He made full use of the resources at his disposal. *Endymion*, for instance, contains several lyrics for his choristers, a dumb-show representing a dream, a dance of fairies for his troop of boy actors, and indications in the stage directions for spectacular costumes, changing scenic effects, and a final transformation in full view ("Bagoa recovers human shape").

The drama of the Elizabethan and Jacobean period ranges over a spectrum. At one end is the "drumming decasyllabon" of Marlowe's *Doctor Faustus* and *Tamburlaine* and the poetry and human insights of Shakespeare. Lyly's plays are at the other end of the spectrum. They are scripts for a kind of extended *commedia dell' arte*, and their real affinities are with the later Court Masque of Inigo Jones and Ben Jonson.

—Ian A. Gordon

MARLOWE, Christopher. English. Born in Canterbury, Kent, 6 February 1564. Educated at King's School, Canterbury, 1579; Benet College, now Corpus Christi College, Cambridge, matriculated 1581, B.A. 1584, M.A. 1587. Settled in London c. 1587: wrote plays for the Lord Admiral's Company and Lord Strange's Company; charged with heresy, 1593: stabbed to death in a tavern brawl before the case was considered. *Died 30 May 1593.*

PUBLICATIONS

Collections

Works, edited by R. H. Case and others. 6 vols., 1930–33.
Poems, edited by Millar Maclure. 1968.
Plays, edited by Roma Gill. 1971.
Complete Works, edited by Fredson Bowers. 2 vols., 1973.
Complete Plays and Poems, edited by E.D. Pendry. 1976.

Plays

Tamburlaine the Great, Divided into Two Tragical Discourses (produced 1587). 1590; edited by Irving Ribner, 1974.
Doctor Faustus (produced 1588 or 1592?). 1604; alternative text, 1616; both texts edited by W. W. Greg, 1950; edited by Keith Walker, 1973.
The Rich Jew of Malta (produced 1589?). 1633; edited by N. W. Bawcutt, 1977.
Edward the Second (produced 1592?). 1594; edited by Irving Ribner, 1970.
Dido, Queen of Carthage (produced 1593?). 1594.
The Massacre at Paris (produced 1593?). 1594(?).

Verse

> Epigrams and Elegies of Ovid, with John Davies.   1595(?); as All Ovid's Elegies: 3
> Books, with Epigrams by John Davies, 1598(?).
> Hero and Leander, Begun by Marlowe, Completed by Chapman.   1598; edited by Louis
> L. Martz, 1972.
> Lucan's First Book Tanslated Line for Line.   1600.

Bibliography: Marlowe: A Concise Bibliography by S. A. Tannenbaum, 1937, supplement,
1947; supplement by R. C. Johnson, 1967.

Reading List: Marlowe by M. Poirier, 1951; The Overreacher: A Study of Marlowe by Harry
Levin, 1952; Marlowe and the Early Shakespeare by F. P. Wilson, 1953; Suffering and Evil
in the Plays of Marlowe by D. Cole, 1962; Marlowe: A Collection of Critical Essays edited by
Clifford Leech, 1964; Marlowe: A Critical Study by J. B. Steane, 1964; In Search of Marlowe:
A Pictorial Biography by A. D. Wraight and V. F. Stern, 1965; Marlowe by R. E. Knoll,
1968; Critics on Marlowe edited by J. O'Neill, 1969; Marlowe's Agonists by C. C. Fanta,
1970; Marlowe, Merlin's Prophet by Judith Weil, 1977.

*   *   *

A "Coblers eldest son" (as Robert Greene jealously scorned him), Christopher Marlowe
earned for himself the education of a gentleman at the University of Cambridge, and almost
immediately after graduating as Master of Arts startled London with Tamburlaine. The play's
"high astounding terms" (Prologue to Part 1) conquered the new world of the theatre with
the same éclat as its eponymous hero overcame the Turks and Persians; for many years after
its presumed first production, no dramatist could shake himself free of its cadences.

The echoes of Tamburlaine in other sixteenth-century plays whose dates are more certain
is almost the only objective means of establishing a date for the play; the same is true of all
Marlowe's works. Subjective evidence, from its style, suggests that Dido, Queen of Carthage
was his earliest dramatic production, and that it belongs with the translations of Lucan and
Ovid, perhaps accomplished while he was still at Cambridge. Translating the Latin taught
him to handle his native language, and a steady progression can be observed in the facility
with which he treats the classical authors. Book 1 of his version of Lucan's Pharsalia is a line-
for-line rendering of the original; the Elegies convert Ovid's verse form (hexameter followed
by pentameter) into racy, sometimes witty, English heroic couplets. Dido takes the whole of
the first part of Virgil's Aeneid as its provenance; the plot centres on Book 4, but details of
character and episode are snatched up with easy deliberation from Books 1 to 6.

The titlepage presents Dido as having been performed by the Children of the Chapel Royal,
and it ought to be judged by the criteria obtaining for children's plays written by such authors
as Lyly and Marston. Its distinction is unmistakable. Marlowe exploits the delight in costume
and effect, making his characters draw attention to what they are wearing or to the efforts of
the stage technicians. Children's plays aspired to verisimilitude only in the accidentals of a
performance; by no stretch of the imagination could boys with unbroken voices imitate to the
life the great heroes of classical mythology who were the protagonists of these plays. But if
they could not act, they could recite; they had been chosen for their voices, and they were
highly trained in all the Renaissance arts of elocution. In Aeneas's account of the fall of Troy
Marlowe writes a stirring "aria" which augurs well for his subsequent career as a dramatist
writing for the public theatres.

The Prologue to the first part of Tamburlaine, written perhaps in 1585, disdains the
"jigging veins of rhyming mother-wits," preferring language more appropriate to its tale of
the Scythian shepherd whose personal magnetism and force of arms raised him to imperial
status and won the love of his captive Egyptian princess, Zenocrate. The success of Part 1

"made our poet pen his second part" (Prologue to Part 2), and the two parts together show the complete revolution of Fortune's Wheel. Tamburlaine is not vanquished by any human power; mortality itself brings about his overthrow: he falls sick, and dies, lamenting that he must "die, and this unconquered." The play is a tragedy only in the Elizabethan sense; the hero suffers no Aristotelian flaw, and the dramatist does not presume to criticize any of his callous slaughters as errors. The pride with which Tamburlaine identifies himself as "the scourge of God" is no hubris but a factual description of the English drama's first superman, larger than life in every sense. In comparison with Tamburlaine, the rest of the *dramatis personae* are two-dimensional, of interest merely as they enhance their conqueror's achievement in Part 1, and show in their deaths the waning of his power in Part 2.

In *Tamburlaine* the famous "mighty line" praised by Ben Jonson (in a poem prefixed to the First Folio of Shakespeare's works) is appropriate to the "aspiring mind" of its great hero. In Marlowe's next play, *The Jew of Malta*, rhetoric is inflated for comic purposes. In this story of a Jew's battle against Christians, neither of the opposing factions is worthy of respect; admiration is compelled only for the skill of unscrupulous dealings, and sentiment is dismissed by cruel laughter. The Jew's daughter is murdered by her father, but calls upon two friars to witness that she dies a Christian; any pathos arising from this situation is dispelled by the friar's response: "Ay, and a virgin too; that grieves me most." The audience's sympathy is with the Jew, Barabas – not because he is virtuous but because he makes no secret of his double-dealings, confiding in elaborate asides his schemes to outwit the no-less villainous, but hypocritical, Christians. Barabas of course overreaches himself and meets an appropriate end in the boiling cauldron that he had prepared for his chief enemy – but not until he has engineered the deaths of his daughter and her two suitors, an entire convent of nuns, the two friars, the army of Turkish soldiers, a prostitute, her pimp, and one of her clients (who happens to be Barabas's blackmailing slave). Like Tamburlaine, Barabas is larger than life; the rest of the characters, in this play too, are insignificant in comparison with the protagonist, and chiefly remarkable as objects or agents of his malevolence.

Marlowe probably wrote *The Massacre at Paris*, which survives only in a mangled, reported text, at much the same time as he wrote *The Jew of Malta*. Both have the same black comedy, in which murder is committed with a jest – and the laugh is the murderer's. *The Massacre at Paris* is a political play, dealing with recent events in the struggle between Catholics and Protestants in France in the late 1580's. The central figure is the Duke of Guise, a professed villain like Barabas but more menacing than him because the crimes are not imagined but historical. In a reported text, which relies on the memory of actors, poetry suffers more damage than plot, but one can still detect in the Guise the note of true Marlovian aspiration:

> What glory is there in a common good,
> That hangs for every peasant to achieve?
> That like I best that flies beyond my reach.

In *The Jew of Malta* and *The Massacre at Paris* Marlowe makes great play with the popular concept of the machiavellian "politician" who parodied the Florentine statesman by putting self before state. In *Edward II* he treats Machiavelli's ideas more seriously, showing in the character of Young Mortimer a hot-headed patriot who, for the first half of the play, is genuinely distressed by the king's weakness and profligacy. But as the play progresses, covering twenty-three years of chronicled history, Mortimer loses principle as he gains power until, when Edward is imprisoned in the dungeon sewers of Kenilworth Castle and he himself is, as he believes, secure as Protector over the prince and lover of the queen, he manifests all the characteristics of the Italianate villain who so appealed to the Elizabethan imagination: "Fear'd am I more than lov'd; let me be fear'd,/And when I frown, make all the court look pale." Mortimer contrasts with Edward, passively homosexual and ambitious for nothing more than "some nook or corner" in which to "frolic with [his] dearest Gaveston."

Marlowe manipulates the sympathies of the audience, turning them away from Edward and his recklessness to support Mortimer and the barons in their care for the realm. But this care is not flawless: pride and ambition vitiate it from the start. Mortimer's regime is hateful, and the treatment meted out to Edward is brutal and obscene. There is no "mighty line" in this play, but the quick cut and thrust of conversations between conspirators and enemies. Isabella, Edward's queen, is allowed a languid romanticism as the despised wife, but when she comes under Mortimer's domination her speeches are at first hollow and hypocritical, and later subdued by fear. In some ways *Edward II* is Marlowe's best play: its structure is shapely, with Mortimer's fortunes rising as Edward's decline; its characterisation is diversified, and for the first time the protagonist has a worthy antagonist and a supporting cast who are characters and not merely names; its verse, though businesslike to the point of drabness, is nevertheless suited to the unheroic action. *Dr. Faustus*, the play that followed *Edward II* and which was Marlowe's last play (though some scholars think it was earlier), has none of these qualities. But while *Edward II* is a good play, *Dr Faustus* is a great one.

Two texts of *Dr Faustus* survive, but neither represents the play as Marlowe intended it. The earlier was published in 1604 and seems to be the work of actors who repeated their lines inaccurately, were sometimes vague about meaning, and often confused about which speech came next. The 1616 text is longer and more coherent, being based probably upon some theatrical document such as a prompt-book. But this too is unreliable. An "editor" has been at work, simplifying, censoring, and adding the extra material for which Henslowe, the actor-manager, paid Bird and Rowley four pounds in 1602. A twentieth-century text can only be eclectic in its attempts to approach the play that Marlowe wrote.

The plot of *Dr. Faustus* is simple: a brilliant scholar, frustrated by the limitations imposed on human learning, sells his soul to the devil for four and twenty years of knowledge, power, and voluptuousness. At the end of the play only one hour is left, after which "The devil will come, and Faustus must be damn'd." The play is remarkable for its first two and last acts. In the first, Faustus reviews the whole scope of learning available to Renaissance man in a speech where the names of Aristotle, Galen, and Justinian glitter for a while until they are extinguished by the logic which sees death as the inevitable climax of all human endeavour, and by the perverse will that presents necromancy as the only means of escaping human bondage. An interview with Mephostophilis, one of the "Unhappy spirits that fell with Lucifer," does nothing to shake Faustus's resolution even though the troubled spirit begs him to "leave these frivolous demands/Which strikes a terror to my fainting soul." The play disintegrates in the middle acts, where clownage distracts Faustus's mind from contemplation of his deed. The 1616 text's comic scenes are fully developed, but the rudiments are present in the 1604 text, forcing the conclusion that although Marlowe may not have written them himself, he nevertheless acquiesced to their presence in his play. Parts of 1616's Act V, however, are not to be found anywhere in 1604; among them is the interchange between Faustus and Mephostophilis where Faustus blames the devil for his damnation and Mephostophilis proudly claims responsibility. Eleven lines (V, ii, 80–91) are crucial to an interpretation of the play. If they are included as part of Marlowe's design, then Dr. Faustus is no more than a puppet, manipulated by external forces of good and evil, and in no way responsible for his fate; the play is in that case a Morality Play which lacks the traditional happy ending in which God's mercy prevails over His justice. But if the lines are discarded (as I think they should be), Faustus appears as an independent being who, of his own free will, although with imperfect knowledge, chooses damnation; and the play is a true tragedy.

Plague raged in London during the last year of Marlowe's life. The theatres were closed, to avoid the spread of infection; and there was consequently no demand for new plays. Like Shakespeare, Marlowe spent some of the time writing a long narrative poem. His subject, the love between Hero and Leander, is a tragic one, but the poem stops with the consummation of the love; it is not clear whether Marlowe intended to proceed to the catastrophe. The eight hundred lines that he wrote reveal a marvellously rich invention that combines tenderness with sardonic wit in a form that is, in the best sense, artificial. Describing his two protagonists, Marlowe counterpoises the elaborateness of Hero's garments with the sensuous simplicity of Leander's naked body. Of "Venus' nun" he tells us:

> Buskins of shells all silver'd used she
> And branch'd with blushing coral to the knee,
> Where sparrows perch'd, of hollow pearl and gold,
> Such as the world would wonder to behold.

Sight and sound predominate in the description of Hero, but Marlowe refers to touch and taste when he speaks of Leander:

> Even as delicious meat is to the taste,
> So was his neck in touching, and surpass'd
> The white of Pelops' shoulder. I could tell ye
> How smooth his breast was, and how white his belly.

The ease with which he moves through the polished couplets is assurance enough that Marlowe, when he died in the spring of 1593, had by no means exhausted his genius.

—Roma Gill

MARSTON, John.   English.   Born in Wardington, Oxfordshire, baptized 7 October 1576. Educated at Brasenose College, Oxford, 1592–94, B.A. 1594; Middle Temple, London, 1595–1606. Married Mary Wilkes c. 1605; one son. Wrote for Paul's boys company after 1599, and shareholder in the Queen's Revels company after 1604; imprisoned (for unknown reasons), 1608; ordained deacon, then priest, 1609, and ceased writing for the theatre after taking orders; Rector of Christchurch, Hampshire, 1616 until his resignation, 1631. *Died 25 June 1634.*

PUBLICATIONS

Collections

Works, edited by A. H. Bullen.   3 vols., 1887.
Plays, edited by H. H. Wood.   3 vols., 1934–39.
Poems, edited by Arnold Davenport.   1961.

Verse

The Metamorphosis of Pygmalion's Image; and Certain Satires.   1598; edited by Elizabeth Story Donno, in *Elizabethan Minor Epics,* 1968.
The Scourge of Villainy: Three Books of Satires.   1598; revised edition, 1599.

Plays

Antonio and Mellida, part 1 (produced 1599).   1602; edited by G. K. Hunter, 1965.
Antonio's Revenge (part 2 of *Antonio and Mellida*) (produced 1599).   1602; edited by Reavley Gair, 1977.
Histriomastix; or, The Player Whipped, from an anonymous play (produced 1599).   1610.
Jack Drum's Entertainment; or, The Comedy of Pasquill and Katherine (produced 1600).   1601.
What You Will (produced 1601?).   1607.
The Dutch Courtesan (produced 1603–04?).   1605; edited by Peter Davison, 1968.
The Malcontent (produced 1604).   1604; edited by Bernard Harris, 1967.
Parasitaster; or, The Fawn (produced 1604–05?).   1606; edited by David A. Blostein, 1978.
Eastward Ho, with Chapman and Jonson (produced 1605).   1605; edited by C. G. Petter, 1973.
The Wonder of Women; or, The Tragedy of Sophonisba (produced 1606).   1606.
The Argument of the Spectacle Presented to the Sacred Majesties of Great Britain and Denmark as They Passed Through London (produced 1606).   In *Poems,* edited by Arnold Davenport, 1961.
The Honorable Lord and Lady of Huntingdon's Entertainment at Ashby (produced 1607).   In *Works,* 1887; in *Poems,* 1961.
The Insatiate Countess, completed by William Barksted (produced 1610?).   1613.
Works (tragedies and comedies).   1633.

Bibliography: *Marston: A Concise Bibliography* by S. A. Tannenbaum, 1940; supplement in *Elizabethan Bibliographies Supplements 4* by C. A. Pennel and W. P. Williams, 1968.

Reading List: *Marston: Satirist* by A. Caputi, 1961; *The Satire of Marston* by M. S. Allen, 1965; *Jacobean City Comedy: A Study of Satiric Plays by Jonson, Marston, and Middleton* by B. Gibbons, 1968; *Marston of the Middle Temple: An Elizabethan Dramatist in His Social Setting* by P. J. Finkelpearl, 1969.

*   *   *

John Marston's crabbed and bitter satire quickly established his literary reputation. In the "Parnassus Plays" of 1598–1601 at Cambridge University, Marston's satiric style was parodied in the Character of "W. Kinsayder": "What, Monsieur Kinsayder, lifting up your leg and pissing against the world? Put up, man, put up for shame. Methinks he is a ruffian in his style." His literary quarrels with Ben Jonson and Joseph Hall created a furor at the time; Drummond of Hawthornden notes that Jonson "had many quarrels with Marston, beat him and took his pistol from him, wrote his Poetaster on him." Jonson also attacked him in *Every Man Out of His Humour* and *Cynthia's Revels,* since Marston had "represented him on the stage." This so-called *Poetomachia* was not enduring, though, and the two eventually became friends.

Marston's tendency to stumble in and out of quarrels, jails and royal favour has marked him for centuries of literary criticism as a railing and often incoherently self-defeating malcontent. This is not entirely justified, however, as in all his works, from the most violent to the most flippant, there is an underlying moral concern. Many details of Marston's life are anomalous, but it is not altogether surprising that at the age of thirty-two he set aside his writing and, like his fellow satirists John Donne and Joseph Hall, took Holy Orders.

Marston's literary career begins with two collections of verse satires: the semi-erotic *Metamorphosis of Pygmalion's Image* and the snarling and snapping *Scourge of Villainy,* in which Marston ridicules the poses and pretenses of the young gallants of the Inns of Court and London. In both volumes, the satire shifts uneasily from a range of effete social pastimes to vulgar depravities; both were considered immoral, and burned in 1599. The harsh and contentious style of the verse satires is carried over to Marston's first play, *Histriomastix*, a pageant-like allegory performed at the Inns of Court, which deals with the function of law in a crumbling society. *Jack Drum's Entertainment* and *What You Will* reflect the lighter side of the verse satires, again attacking the foppish young gallants, though love themes and Shakespearean echoes complement the satire in these romantic comedies.

Antonio and Mellida and *Antonio's Revenge* introduce the dark qualities of Marston's satiric vision. In spite of its tentative comic reconciliation, the first play is largely influenced by evil and unjust characters, and the moral climate of the Venetian court is oppressive and sordid. The second play, however, lurches into perhaps the most violent and painful revenge tragedy in Elizabethan drama. As the protagonist degenerates both psychologically and morally, his "barbarism and blood lust" confirm the play's assertion that men are "vermin bred of putrifacted slime."

The Malcontent is generally considered Marston's greatest play. His tragi-comic satire of the court and of a morally degenerating world is successfully accomplished, while at the same time the play is well-structured and temperate in plot, character, and language. Through the character of Malevole, Marston probes the moral complexities of the human condition by dramatically juxtaposing neo-stoicism with worldly epicurianism. The play's Induction reveals that the King's Men stole it from the Children of Blackfriars in response to their theft of *The First Part of Jeronimo*. While *The Malcontent* was clearly influenced by Shakespeare's *Measure for Measure*, and particularly by *Hamlet*, it was also performed at the Globe, and the title role of Malevole was played by Shakespeare's Hamlet, Richard Burbage.

After *The Malcontent*, *The Dutch Courtesan* is perhaps Marston's next best work. It is a very entertaining comedy dealing again with complex moral values, in particular the relationship of love and lust, set against a colourful city background of prostitutes, rakes, and mountebanks. The satire in *Parasitaster; or, The Fawn* is to a large degree directed against James I and his Court: flattering and deluded courtiers, corrupting and corrupted governors. The Fawn's speeches expose the moral vacuum in this society, but the play ends on a reconciliatory note with a masque that acknowledges both the "Ship of Fools" and the "Parliament of Cupid." These two comedies are more epicurian than Marston's earlier works.

Marston's part in the collaborative *Eastward Ho!* with Ben Jonson and George Chapman is generally accepted as the entirety of the first act, as well as various parts throughout the play, though it is difficult to determine his specific authorship beyond this point. The play is a delightful parody of the "citizen comedy" tradition that was so popular on the London stage in the first decade of the seventeenth century. Several references to the Scots proved objectionable enough to James to result in the imprisonment of Chapman and Jonson, though Marston apparently escaped.

In his preface to *The Fawn*, Marston observes that comedies are "writ to be spoken, not read" because they consist solely in action. He wrote *The Wonder of Women; or, The Tragedy of Sophonisba*, however, as a tragedy that "shall boldly abide the most curious perusal." While sensation and spectacle abound, the highminded rhetoric in such an austere Roman tragedy demands our close reading, or "curious perusal." The play is often quite moving, and the moral dichotomy in this classical world is presented in great earnest, though there is little memorable action. Contrasted with the Stoic integrity of Sophonisba is the pathological lust of the heroine in Marston's unfinished play, *The Insatiate Countess*. Marston presumably left the various plots and characters in the play unresolved when he was sent to prison in 1608, though his hand is traceable in the 1613 edition completed by William Barksted.

Recent criticism has begun to acknowledge the considerable range and variety of Marston's dramatic works. His bold experimentation and unique characterization, particularly in the *Antonio* plays and *The Malcontent*, were completely new to Elizabethan audiences. Studies of the individual plays reveal a dramatic craftsmanship and originality that liberate him from his contemporary reputation as Kinsayder, "pissing against the world." There are many aspects of Marston's life and writings that deserve further critical analysis. His greater defects are very apparent, but T. S. Eliot's observation is still true: "for both scholars and critics he remains a territory of unexplored riches and risks."

—Raymond C. Shady

MARVELL, Andrew. English. Born at Winestead in Holderness, Yorkshire, 31 March 1621. Educated at Hull, Yorkshire Grammar School; Trinity College, Cambridge, 1633–41 (scholar, 1638), B.A. 1638. Evidently never married, though Mary Marvell claimed to be his widow. Travelled in Holland, France, Italy, and Spain, 1642–46; Tutor to Mary, daughter of Lord Fairfax, Lord-General of the Parliamentary Forces, 1650–52; resided at Eton College, as tutor to Cromwell's ward, William Dutton, 1653–57; Assistant to the poet John Milton, *q.v.*, then Latin Secretary for the Commonwealth, 1657–58 (intervened on Milton's behalf after the Restoration); Member of Parliament for Hull, 1659–78; Secretary to Lord Carlisle's embassy to Russia, Sweden, and Denmark, 1663–65. *Died 16 August 1678.*

PUBLICATIONS

Collections

Complete Works in Verse and Prose, edited by Alexander B. Grosart. 4 vols., 1872–75.
Poems and Letters, edited by H. M. Margoliouth. 2 vols., 1927; revised by Pierre Legouis and E. E. Duncan-Jones, 1971.
Complete Poems, edited by Elizabeth Story Donno. 1972; as *Complete English Poems,* 1974.

Verse

The First Anniversary of the Government under His Highness the Lord Protector. 1655.
The Character of Holland. 1665.
Advice to a Painter. 1679(?).
Miscellaneous Poems, edited by Mary Marvell. 1681.

Other

The Rehearsal Transprosed. 2 vols., 1672–73; edited by D. I. B. Smith, 1971.
Mr. Smirke; or, The Divine in Mode. 1676.
An Account of the Growth of Popery. 1677.
Remarks upon a Late Disingenuous Discourse by T.D. 1678.
A Short Historical Essay. 1680.

Translator, *The History of the Twelve Caesars,* by Suetonius. 1672.

Bibliography: in *Poems and Letters*, 1971.

Reading List: *Marvell, Poète, Puritain, Patriote* by Pierre Legouis, 1928, revised and translated, as *Marvell, Poet, Puritan, Patriot*, 1965; *Marvell's Poems* by Dennis Davison, 1964; *The Art of Marvell's Poetry* by J. B. Leishman, 1966; *Marvell: Modern Judgements*, edited by M. Wilding, 1969; *"My Ecchoing Song": Marvell's Poetry of Criticism* by Rosalie Colie, 1970; *Marvell's Pastoral Art* by Donald M. Friedman, 1970; *Marvell's Allegorical Poetry* by Bruce King, 1977; *Marvell: His Life and Writings* by John Dixon Hunt, 1978; *Marvell: The Critical Heritage*, edited by Elizabeth Story Donno, 1978.

*   *   *

When Andrew Marvell died, none of his best poetry had been published; and the volume published posthumously in 1681 disappointed the admirers of his satires in prose and verse, since the contents had been written years before in a style that had come to seem old-fashioned. During the next century Marvell was chiefly famous as the friend of Milton, as the champion of toleration, and as the incorruptible member of parliament. Lamb admired his "witty delicacy" and Tennyson persuaded Palgrave to include some of the lyrics in the *Golden Treasury*. Although Marvell shared in the revival of the metaphysicals, Eliot blunted his praise by preferring the poetry of King. Now, perhaps, his reputation as a lyric poet is in danger of overshadowing his splendid prose satires, which Swift acknowledged as his model, and the verse satires, incomparably the best before Dryden's. Like Dryden he had a basic seriousness beneath the wit and banter. Everyone knows the couplet from the satire written during the first Dutch war: "Glad then, as miners that have found the ore,/They with mad labour fish'd the land to shore." Not so well-known are the lines describing Charles II in *Last Instructions to a Painter*, when he attempts to embrace a female apparition:

> But soon shrunk back, chill'd with her touch so cold,
> And th'airy Picture vanisht from his hold.
> In his deep thoughts the wonder did increase,
> And he divin'd 'twas England or the Peace.

The episode neatly combines an attack on Charles's sexual morals with criticism of his policies.

Nevertheless it is mainly on his non-satirical verse that Marvell's reputation now rests. He was not a prolific poet, but the 1681 volume is the most precious collection of lyrics between Milton's 1645 volume and the advent of the great Romantics.

Marvell began as a royalist, and his early work would not be out of place in anthologies of Cavalier poets. He has many echoes of Lovelace, Cowley, Cleveland, and Waller – allusions which gave the thrill of recognition to his contemporaries.

The turning point in Marvell's career came with the execution of Charles I. In 1650, at the age of 29, he wrote the first of his undoubted masterpieces, the Horatian Ode in which, echoing Lucan, he compares Cromwell to Julius Caesar; and from the title we may suspect he was thinking of the way Horace was won over to support Augustus. it is characteristic of Marvell's disinterestedness that in a poem written in celebration of Cromwell the most famous lines are a tribute to Charles's deportment on the scaffold.

Soon afterwards Marvell became tutor to Mary Fairfax, the daughter of the Parliamentary General who had refused to take part in the trial of the King or to fight against the Scots. It was probably on the Fairfax estate in Yorkshire that most of Marvell's best poems were written – "The Garden," the four Mower poems, "The Nymph Complaining," and "Upon Appleton House." The last of these has been seriously undervalued by critics who have failed to appreciate the poet's strategy. It begins as a topographical poem, mingling description with incident, and full of witty absurdities, out-doing Cleveland. It moves from the house to the garden, from the garden to the meadows, and from the meadows to the solitude of the woods. As the poem progresses, Marvell purifies his style, becoming less extravagant in his conceits: he is leading his readers, one might say, from the world of Cleveland to the world of Lovelace, and then to the world of nature untamed by man, a nature right outside the boundaries of fashionable pastoral. Here he can describe birds and trees with loving accuracy, and almost identify with the natural world. The reader has been led by easy stages from the poetic world to which he was accustomed into Marvell's own. Those parts of the poem to which nearly all critics have taken exception are cunningly arranged stepping-stones from the world of fancy to the world of imagination. Marvell was the first real nature poet, and still one of the best.

The quintessence of his nature mysticism is to be found in "The Garden." It is a concentrated and complex poem, with different levels of experience juxtaposed. On one level it is about the sublimation of sex in the creation of art. On another level it is about the fortunate fall, with references to Eden and the fatal apple. But the central stanzas, absent from the Latin "Hortus" which Marvell wrote first, describe the transformation of sensual satisfaction into spiritual ecstasy:

> The Mind, that Ocean where each kind
> Does streight its own resemblance find;
> Yet it creates, transcending these,
> Far other Worlds, and other Seas;
> Annihilating all that's made
> To a green Thought in a green Shade.

In this poem Marvell celebrates solitude – Eden without Eve, "Two Paradises 'twere in one"; but in all the Nun Appleton poems he gives the impression that he knows perfectly well that the retreat from active life is only temporary, and (despite the praise of solitude) he wrote one of the best love poems in the language, "To His Coy Mistress."

Hundreds of poems have been written on this theme. What distinguishes Marvell's are the beautifully articulated argument, the delightful hyperboles of the opening paragraph, the thrilling change of tone when he describes the threat of Time and the "deserts of vast eternity," the continued use of wit when he is most serious – as in the lines "Then Worms shall try/That long preserv'd Virginity:/And your quaint Honour turn to dust" – the ability, which he shared with Shakespeare, to use desperately simple words – "The Grave's a fine and private place,/But none I think do there embrace" – and, above all, his being able to express with absolute precision an emotion he has experienced with singular clarity and intensity.

"The Nymph Complaining for the Death of her Fawn" – despite some weak couplets which remind us that Marvell never prepared his poems for publication – is a good example of his use of multiple levels of meaning. On one level it is a pastoral, based on the episode in the *Aeneid* where Silvia's fawn is killed by Ascanius (a source made obvious by the name of the Nymph's faithless lover, Sylvio). By the reference to "wanton Troopers" it is made to seem an incident of the English civil war. On another level the poem is concerned with a deserted maiden, and her reciprocated love for the fawn. On a third level, the death of an innocent victim, dying "as calmly as a saint," clearly has religious overtones.

The poem serves as a bridge between two other groups of poems, those concerned with young love, and those concerned with religion. In the former group may be mentioned the allusions to Mary Fairfax in the Nun Appleton poem, as when she is said to be sweeter than the flowers and, near the end, the dozen stanzas in which she is paid a whole series of extravagant compliments. Mary was then fourteen; "Young Love" is a charming tribute to a much younger child; and best of all in its unsentimental tenderness is "The Picture of little T.C. in a Prospect of Flowers." In all three Marvell writes of the future conquests of the girls and of their present innocence, and he avoids both the Lolita temptation and the anti-sexual feelings of Lewis Carroll. As with all Marvell's best poetry there is a splendid rightness of tone.

Marvell was described in 1656 as "a notable English Italo-Machiavellian." He was certainly not that, but his religious poems tell us little specific about his basic beliefs. "Bermudas" – one of the most beautiful – shows sympathy with the Puritan emigrants, but is unpuritanical in its celebration of an earthly paradise. "A Dialogue Between the Resolved Soul and Created Pleasure" (which reads like a libretto) is puritanical in spirit; but in the other "Dialogue Between the Soul and Body" Body is given the last word (Leishman thought some lines were missing). "On a Drop of Dew," ingeniously compared with the Soul, is only vaguely Christian. The most impressive of Marvell's religious poems, "The Coronet," has "an intricate and lovely form" which the poet calls his "curious frame." The theme is the difficulty of using his poetic talents, previously devoted to pastoral and erotic poetry, for devotional purposes. Marvell discovers that the Serpent has spoilt his garland of flowers "With wreaths of Fame and Interest." In other words, Marvell realised, however careless he was of fame, that his religious poetry had a mixture of motives, including aesthetic satisfaction.

Nothing has been said here about Marvell's early poems, although "Daphnis and Chloe," "Mourning," and "The Definition of Love" are masterly examples of his early manner. He has a wider range than readers of the half-dozen anthology pieces might suspect. He has been called an amateur, whose poems are nearly all flawed by careless workmanship. It is true that the parts are sometimes better than the whole; but, as we have seen, his longest poem, "Upon Appleton House," should not have its construction misunderstood by the selection of a few stanzas approved by the taste of the anthologist.

—Kenneth Muir

MILTON, John. English. Born in Bread Street, Cheapside, London, 9 December 1608. Educated privately, by a Scottish friend of his father's; St. Paul's School, London; Christ's College, Cambridge, 1625–32, B.A. 1629, M.A. 1632; lived at his father's country house, Horton, Buckinghamshire, devoted to further study, 1632–38; completed his education by travel in France and Italy, 1638–39. Married 1) Mary Powell in 1642 (died, 1652), three daughters; 2) Catharine Woodcock in 1656 (died in childbirth, 1657); 3) Elizabeth Minshull in 1662. Wrote in support of the Puritan cause: appointed Latin (or Foreign) Secretary to Cromwell's Council of State, 1649; went blind, 1652, but continued to serve with the assistance of friends; deprived of office at the Restoration, 1660. Imprisoned and in danger of execution: friends, possibly including the poet Andrew Marvell, intervened, and he escaped with fine and loss of most of his property; thereafter devoted himself to his writing. *Died 8 November 1674.*

PUBLICATIONS

Collections

Works, edited by F. A. Patterson and others. 18 vols., 1931–38.
Poetical Works, edited by Helen Darbishire. 2 vols., 1952–55.
Complete Prose Works, edited by D. M. Wolfe and others. 7 vols. (of 8), 1953–74.
Poems, edited by John Carey and Alastair Fowler. 2 vols., 1971.
The Cambridge Milton, edited by J. B. Broadbent and others. 1972–

Verse

Poems. 1645.
Paradise Lost. 1667; revised edition, 1678; edited by Christopher Ricks, 1968.
Paradise Regained, to Which Is Added Samson Agonistes. 1671; *Paradise Regained* edited by Christopher Ricks, with *Paradise Lost,* 1968.
Poems upon Several Occasions. 1673.

Plays

Comus: A Mask (produced 1634). 1637; edited by F. T. Prince, 1968.
Samson Agonistes, in *Paradise Regained,* 1671. Edited by Michael Davis, 1968.

Other

Of Reformation Touching Church Discipline in England. 1641.
Of Prelatical Episcopacy. 1641.
Animadversions Against Smectymnuus. 1641.
The Reason of Church-Government Urged Against Prelaty. 1641.
The Apology Against a Pamphlet Called a Modest Confutation. 1642; edited by M. C. Jochums, 1950.
The Doctrine and Discipline of Divorce. 1643; revised edition, 1644.
Of Education. 1644; edited by Michael Davis, with *Areopagitica,* 1963.
Areopagitica: A Speech for the Liberty of Unlicenced Printing. 1644; edited by J. C. Suffolk, 1968.
Colasterion: A Reply to a Nameless Answer Against the Doctrine and Discipline of Divorce. 1645.
Tetrachordon: Expositions upon the Four Chief Places in Scripture Which Treat of Marriage, or Nullities in Marriage. 1645.
The Tenure of Kings and Magistrates. 1649; edited by W. T. Allison, 1911.
Observations upon the Articles of Peace with the Irish Rebels. 1649.
Eikonoklastes, in Answer to a Book Entitled Eikon Basilika, The Portraiture of His Sacred Majesty in His Solitudes and Sufferings. 1649; revised edition, 1650.
Pro Populo Anglicano Defensio. 1651; translated by Joseph Washington, 1692.
Pro Populo Anglicano Defensio Secunda. 1654; translated by R. Fellowes, 1806.
A Treatise of Civil Power in Ecclesiastical Causes. 1659.
Considerations Touching the Likeliest Means to Remove Hirelings Out of the Church. 1659.
The Ready and Easy Way to Establish a Free Commonwealth, and the Excellence Thereof Compared with the Inconveniences and Dangers of Readmitting Kingship in This Nation. 1660; edited by E. M. Clark, 1915.
Brief Notes upon a Late Sermon Titled the Dear of God and the King, by Matthew Griffith. 1660.
Accedence Commenced Grammar. 1669.
The History of Britain, That Part Especially Now Called England. 1670; edited by F. Maseres, 1818.
Artis Logicae Plenior Institutio. 1672.
Of True Religion, Heresy, Schism, Toleration, and What Best Means May Be Urged Against the Growth of Popery. 1673.
Epistolarum Familiarum Liber Unus. 1674; translated by J. Hall, 1829; section translated by Phyllis Tillyard, as *Private Correspondence and Academic Exercises,* 1932.

Litera Pseudo-Senatus Anglicani.   1676.
Character of the Long Parliament and Assembly of Divines in MDCXLI.   1676.
A Brief History of Moscovia.   1682; edited by R. R. Cawley, 1941.
Republican Letters.   1682.
Letters of State from the Year 1649 till the Year 1659.   1694; edited by H. Fernow, 1903.
Original Letters and Papers of State Addressed to Oliver Cromwell, edited by J. Nickolls.   1743.
De Doctrina Christiana Libri duo Posthumi, edited by C. R. Sumner.   1825; translated by C. R. Sumner, 1825.
Original Papers, edited by W. D. Hamilton.   1859.
A Common-Place Book, edited by A. J. Horwood.   1876; revised edition, 1877.

Translator, *The Judgement of Martin Bucer Concerning Divorce.*   1644.

Bibliography: *A Reference Guide to Milton from 1800 to the Present Day* by H. F. Fletcher, 1930; *Milton: A Bibliographical Supplement 1929–57* by C. Huckaby, 1960, revised edition, 1969.

Reading List: *The Life of Milton* by David Masson, 7 vols., 1859–94, revised edition, 1881–96; *Milton* by E. M. W. Tillyard, 1930, revised edition, 1949; *This Great Argument* by Maurice Kelly, 1941; *A Preface to Paradise Lost* by C. S. Lewis, 1942; *Paradise Lost and Its Critics* by A. J. A. Waldock, 1947; *The Muse's Method: An Introduction to Paradise Lost* by Joseph H. Summers, 1962; *Milton: A Reader's Guide to His Poetry* by Marjorie Hope Nicolson, 1963; *Milton* by Douglas Bush, 1964; *Milton: A Biography* by Riley Parker, 2 vols., 1968 (includes bibliography); *From Shadowy Types to Truth: Studies in Milton's Symbolism* by W. G. Madsen, 1968; *On Milton's Poetry* edited by Arnold Stein, 1970; *Milton: The Critical Heritage* edited by J. T. Shawcross, 1970; *Milton and the English Revolution* by Christopher Hill, 1977; *Milton Criticism: A Subject Index* by William Johnson, 1978.

*   *   *

John Milton's poetry has been attacked in the 20th century for precisely that quality most admired by the Romantics – its uncompromising idealism. "Strictly speaking, Milton may be said never to have *seen* anything," remarked one modern critic, and T. S. Eliot felt that Milton, in imitating Spenser, had "writ no language." Miltonists have reacted to this criticism by stressing how very similar Milton's poetry is to Eliot's (see C. S. Lewis). In fact Milton's poetry is totally unlike Eliot's: Eliot is the poet of things, the most anti-idealist of poets, and Milton is the greatest English poet of ideas and ideals. Modern taste has preferred "things" to "ideas."

The reader of Milton must begin by accepting his Platonism. His characterization of Plato as "almost divine" is a key to understanding his philosophy. In an early letter to his dearest friend Diodati the *Phaedrus* is invoked:

> For, lest you threaten too much, know that it is impossible for me not to love men like you. What beside God has resolved for me I do not know, but this at least: *He has instilled into me, if into anyone, a vehement love of the beautiful.* Not with so much labor, as the fables have it, is Ceres said to have sought her daughter Proserpina as it is my habit day and night to seek for this *idea of the beautiful...* through all the forms and faces of things ... and to follow it as it leads me on by some sure traces which I seem to recognize. ... You make many anxious inquiries, even as to what I am presently thinking of. Hearken, Theodotus, but let it be in your private ear, lest I blush; and allow me to use big language with you. You ask

what I am thinking of? So may the good Deity help me, – of immortality! And what am I doing? *Growing my wings*. And meditating flight; but as yet our Pegasus raises himself on very tender pinions. Let us be lowly wise.

Milton's discipleship to Spenser and Chaucer follows naturally from his love of Plato. Spenser was for Milton always "Sage and Serious." In his poetry "more is meant than meets the ear." Chaucer had "left half told/The story of Cambuscan bold" (a story from Plato dealing with a tyrant undercut by philosophical wisdom). Chaucer never lacked "high seriousness" for Milton. The attack on ecclesiastical abuses in Milton's works linked him directly to the poet of the *Canterbury Tales*. Chaucer, Spenser, and Milton, later joined by Shelley, constitute the great idealist tradition in English letters, and all were social critics and religious reformers as well as poets.

Milton believed that the great poet had first to be a great man. He also stressed that great art required the hardest kind of labor. And no one ever worked harder to become the great poet. The ideal poet had to combine the learning and wisdom of Plato's "philosopher kings" with the myth-making ability and eloquence of the Homeric poet. When such a combination appeared, then the criticism of poetry in the *Republic* was transcended. The artist was the one who gave society its ideals, and, whether they wish it or not, societies are led by ideals. For Milton, as for the classical tradition in general, these ideas were largely to be found in the literature of the past. Milton's social radicalism was always a *return* to the roots, not the conventional modern rejection of the past and belief in a utopian future. Milton's radicalism is peculiarly relevant to a world that no longer believes in the beneficence of its future.

Comus, an exceptionally difficult work for moderns to read, combines a lesson in chastity, drawn not from St. Paul but from the *Symposium*, with a sensuousness drawn from Shakespeare and Ovid. Comus himself is made physically attractive and his imagery is notably phallic. His arguments are phrased in the most voluptuous imagery possible; his castle contains every luxury, exceeding even that of Keats' St. Agnes. Such a combination of rich language and austere philosophy seems impossible for modern thought. But the great idealist poets have been the most sensual. Sexual appeal lies in ideas, not in things. No poet is less sensual than Donne, for instance, however explicitly sexual his topic.

For Milton, as for the classical writers, the essential task of art was to civilize human society. Orpheus was a mythical exposition of this idea. Men would listen to the poet even against their will. Milton's writings were an attempt to communicate Biblical and classical ideals to the modern world. The poems, the prose works, and the practical duties of the Secretary for Foreign Tongues were all means to the same end. Without the resources of poetic eloquence Milton thought he was writing with only his "left hand" – but it was the hand of a Hercules. Brief as it is, his tractate *Of Education* provides the only viable alternative to the cynical practicality of the modern university. Modern educational thought would dismiss Milton's program as hopelessly utopian. But Milton's education was the one that had produced the greatest of Athenian statesmen, and no society that demanded great leaders could knowingly accept less. Macaulay stressed the great courage required for Milton to publish his writings on divorce, given his own unhappy first marriage – but one must not lose sight of their *incredible* wisdom. In them Milton combined for the first time the practical bourgeois social unit of the family with the highest Platonic ideal of love. He reasoned that the end of love had to be the end of marriage. Met by almost universal outrage at their supposed advocacy of sexual libertinism, the divorce tracts seriously endangered Milton's chances of being taken seriously in any other writings. In them he transcended his own period: they are as fresh today as when they were written.

The *Areopagitica*, in some ways a defense of his right to publish the divorce tracts, has been almost universally admired. Because it was cited in some of the early American trials concerned with the freedom of the press, it is the only work by a poet to have legal stature in American courts. If Milton lost the battle against censorship in the 17th century, he won the war in the 18th. But it is important to note that Milton was less concerned in the tract with ending censorship than with promoting truth through free discussion of ideas.

Milton's political and religious writings were considered far too radical by most of his contemporaries. Already under attack for his divorce pamphlets from both Anglicans and Presbyterians, Milton wrote powerful attacks on tyranny in both state and church which were dismissed as the ravings of a mind that had mastered Latin but not law. But today even the most consummate of Tories would not embrace the ideas that Salmasius, Milton's famous rival, asserted in his works. The Bill of Rights of the U.S. Constitution owes far more to Milton than to John Locke. Freedom of religion and freedom of the press found early expression in Milton's works, and in far more powerful form.

Stripped of all direct political involvement by the Restoration in 1660, and forced "to stand and wait" by his critics, Milton had no choice but to write *Paradise Lost*. This, his great work, can be said to begin with an ending and to end with a beginning. Milton's epic ended the classical epic tradition by making Satan the last of the conventional military heroes. War was seen by Milton not as a form of glory but as a form of death. No writer since Milton has succeeded in writing an epic glorifying war; their hero will always end as a parody of Satan. Milton's epic *makes love, not war*. Men and women in their personal relations, and not arms and the man, became the modern epic subject matter. If it ends the classical epic, *Paradise Lost* begins the modern novel. For here the subject matter of domestic relations is seen as worthy of serious treatment. The heated quarrel that succeeds the Fall is the first full-scale marriage fight in literature, and the world that faces the reconciled couple at the end of Book XII is the world we all now live in: where shall we live? how shall we earn our living? how can we educate the kids? To these questions the heroic posturings of Satan are irrelevant. It is only a slight exaggeration to say that much of later literature is a series of footnotes to Milton. All writers who consider love (Adam and Eve) or evil (Satan) must imitate Milton. If any writer should succeed in transcending him, then that writer would be the next Milton. It is worth remarking that the modern ideas of Eden and of Satan are drawn from Milton, not from the Bible. The religious imagination has been dominated by his poem.

The rejection of classical knowledge in *Paradise Regained* has troubled sensitive readers. Was Milton rejecting his own past work? Ezra Pound ascribed it to Milton's "beastly Hebraism." But the *rejection* is contained in a work that is the purest realization of the Platonic dialogue in poetry. The Christ of *Paradise Regained* is the most eloquent exponent of the ideals of the *Republic*. Satan's Thrasymachus, the eternal apologist for the tyrant, is overthrown by Christ's Socratic wisdom. If *Paradise Lost* is Milton's greatest tribute to the epic tradition of Homer, *Paradise Regained* is his greatest tribute to Plato. Christ is the fullest realization of Plato's ideal of the philosopher-king. Precisely because he understands power and its final corruptions, he does not desire power and so is immune from all of Satan's blandishments.

Samson Agonistes remains, as Goethe perceived, the only successful modern example of classical tragedy. The modern mind makes the same objection to it – it cannot be staged. The simplest answer would be that we will solve the problem of production when we come to appreciate its informing ideals. In Greek tragedy as in Milton's *Samson* the focus is not on simple human heroism displayed through action but upon divine providence that brings wisdom only through suffering. Samson, "eyeless in Gaza," like Oedipus, blind at Colonus, find light through darkness and strength through weakness. The idea was dear to Milton.

There is, as the apostle remarked, a way to strength through weakness. Let me be the most feeble creature alive, as long as that feebleness serves to invigorate the energies of my rational and immortal spirit; as long as in that obscurity, in which I am enveloped, the light of the divine presence more clearly shines, then, in proportion as I am weak, I shall be invincibly strong; and in proportion as I am blind, I shall more clearly see. O that I may thus be perfected by feebleness, and irradiated by obscurity! And indeed, in my blindness, I enjoy in no inconsiderable degree the favor of the Deity, who regards me with more tenderness and compassion in proportion as I am able to behold nothing but himself.

In that sense Samson is Milton, but so is Oedipus. Manoa's great epitaph for his son serves beautifully for John Milton himself: "Samson hath quit himself/Like Samson, and heroically hath finished/A life heroic...."

—Myron Taylor

MONTGOMERIE, Alexander. Scottish. Born, probably at Beith, Ayrshire, c. 1550. Possibly educated in Argyleshire. Married; one son and one daughter. Courtier in the service of the Scottish court of James VI: Chief of the King's "Castilian band" of court poets, and Court Laureate; rewarded with a royal pension. Visited France, Flanders, and Spain, 1586; convert to Roman Catholicism: involved in the Catholic Conspiracy, 1597, and died an outlaw. *Died c. 1599.*

PUBLICATIONS

Collections

   Poems, edited by James Cranstoun.   1887; supplementary volume, edited by George Stevenson, 1910.
   Montgomerie: A Selection from His Songs and Poems, edited by Helena Mennie Shire.   1960.

Verse

   The Cherry and the Slae.   1597; edited by H. Harvey Wood, 1937.
   The Mind's Melody, Containing Certain Psalms of the Kingly Prophet David, Applied to a New Pleasant Tune.   1605.
   The Flyting Betwixt Montgomerie and Polwart.   1621.

Reading List: *Alexander Scott, Montgomerie, and Drummond of Hawthornden as Lyric Poets* by Catherine M. Maclean, 1915.

*   *   *

   Alexander Montgomerie, younger son of a noble Scottish house, was already known as a poet in 1568. Serving abroad as a soldier-of-fortune, he was converted to Catholicism and became a covert partisan of counter-Reform. In 1579 a Catholic diplomat from France gained sway over the young King James VI. Montgomerie was installed at court and taught the King the art of *Scottis Poesie.* He was chief of the King's "Castalian band" of court-poets and musicians, through whose work in translation and imitation and in original composition his

Majesty aimed to make little Scotland matter in the European cultural scene. Montgomerie's share in the programme brought petrarchanism, the sonnet, and the new poetry of France and Spain into Scots writing.

His finest lyrics were made for music. Some matched part-songs from France or England; some were set by Scottish court musicians. He was also a master of the old-style alliterative poetry, using it in his "Flyting" or bardic contest of invective. His fifty sonnets, single-standing or in groups, form a loose-strung life-record, ranging from personal invective to compliment deftly rendered from Ronsard.

His dream-allegory *The Cherrie and the Slae* shows, "darkly," the dreamer journeying towards a choice between the available, bitter berry (of Calvinism) and the delectable inaccessible cherry (the Catholic eucharist). (An early version was interrupted or censored in 1584.) But late in his life Montgomerie, outlawed after being discovered in a Catholic conspiracy, recast the poem, tacitly accusing King James of betraying trust. He died an outlaw in 1599 – and the early truncated version was printed! The intervening years had seen him in and out of royal favour, possibly exploited as secret envoy in the King's devious policies, certainly suffering imprisonment abroad.

On his death King James lamented the loss of "the prince of poets in this land."

—Helena Mennie Shire

NASHE, Thomas. English. Born in Lowestoft, Suffolk, baptized November 1567. Educated at St. John's College, Cambridge (sizar), 1582–88, B.A. 1586. Travelled on the continent, then settled in London, 1588; thereafter a full-time writer; a friend of Greene, Lodge, Daniel, and Marlowe; pamphleteer, engaged in running battle with the Harveys in the 1590's, a controversy suppressed by the Archbishop of Canterbury, 1599; imprisoned for drawing attention to abuses in the theatre (*The Isle of Dogs*), 1597. *Died in 1601.*

PUBLICATIONS

Collections

Works, edited by R. B. McKerrow.   5 vols., 1904–10; revised edition, edited by F. P. Wilson, 5 vols., 1958.
Selected Writings, edited by Stanley Wells.   1964.
The Unfortunate Traveller and Other Works, edited by J. B. Steane.   1972.

Fiction

The Unfortunate Traveller; or, The Life of Jack Wilton.   1594; augmented edition, 1594; edited by John Berryman, 1960.

Play

Summer's Last Will and Testament (produced 1592).   1600.

Verse

The Choice of Valentines, edited by J. S. Farmer.   1899.

Other

The Anatomy of Absurdity.   1589.
An Almond for a Parrot.   1590.
Pierce Penniless His Supplication to the Devil.   1592; edited by G. R. Hibbard, 1951.
Strange News of the Intercepting Certain Letters.   1592; as *The Apology of Pierce Penniless,* 1593.
Christ's Tears over Jerusalem.   1593; revised edition, 1594.
The Terrors of the Night; or, A Discourse of Apparitions.   1594.
Have with You to Saffron Walden; or, Gabriel Harvey's Hunt Is Up.   1596.
Lenten Stuff, with The Praise of the Red Herring.   1599.

Editor, *Astrophel and Stella,* by Sir Philip Sidney.   1591.

Bibliography: *Nashe: A Concise Bibliography* by S. A. Tannenbaum, 1941; *Nashe 1941–65* by R. C. Johnson, 1968.

Reading List: *Two Elizabethan Writers: Nashe and Deloney* by Robert G. Howarth, 1956; *Nashe: A Critical Introduction* by G. R. Hibbard, 1962.

*   *   *

Thomas Nashe, a young Juvenal or an English Aretine according to his contemporaries, seemed something of a literary sport in his own age and has continued to seem so to literary historians. His writings touch on a wide variety of genres – literary criticism, social satire, mock encomia, and short fiction – they represent, in fact, a mixed bag of goods. Furthermore, many pieces seem to have no definite subject matter, depending on the slightest of scaffolding to support adumbrations on a diversity of topics. Yet within this generic and topical variety the recurrence of certain themes may be said to provide a kind of focus.

The first is the high esteem for poetry. Like other Elizabethans, Nashe uses the term broadly to include writing that is fictive in nature and allied to learning since the true poet is a true scholar. Related themes are the niggardliness of patrons (and here Nashe speaks directly out of his own experience as a university graduate earning a scant living by his pen) and the upstart Puritans who have brought both poetry and learning into disrepute.

In his first published work (1589) – a brash critical essay introducing Robert Greene's *Menaphon* – he promises to persecute those idiots and their heirs who have made art bankrupt and sent poetry begging, a promise he in part fulfills in his *Anatomy of Absurdity.* In adopting the term "anatomy," Nashe makes clear that he has taken on the role of a surgeon who is to dissect the diseases of art – broadly interpreted. These include a diatribe against women, a hit and miss attack on Puritans and writers of various sorts, and a defense of poetry and learning. This jumble of topics is set forth in the euphuistic style, but he soon developed his own distinctive manner.

When he arrived in London in the fall of 1588, the Puritan pamphleteer known as "Martin

Marprelate" had just initiated the first of his lively assaults on the Anglican establishment. His technique was to charge his irreverent attacks with all the force and pungency of racy colloquial speech, a technique so successful that the ecclesiastical authorities enlisted professional writers to answer in kind. Although the extent of Nashe's contribution is uncertain, what he learned from this flurry of verbal combat reinforced his own predilection for a seemingly spontaneous, unstudied style. As early as the Preface to *Menaphon* he declared his preference for the man who could achieve the "extemporal vein" in *any* mode to the deliberate rhetorician, and in his most popular work, *Pierce Penniless His Supplication to the Devil*, he boasts, in Latin, that he writes whatever comes into his mouth "as fast as his hand can trot."

Pierce, that is, Purse, Penniless becomes Nashe's long-lived persona. Since the motive for writing is his poverty, stemming from the illiberality of patrons, he addresses his supplication to the devil. This is a recital of the seven deadly sins of London society as they are personified in current social types, a scheme which allows him to satirize foibles and follies by means of sharp caricature and to illustrate them with humorous tales.

Nashe's one extant dramatic text is an occasional piece entitled *Summer's Last Will and Testament* which was privately performed in 1592 during an outbreak of the plague. It is quite simply a pageant of seasonal change where, before yielding up his throne to Autumn, the dying Summer calls on various officers – Ver, Harvest, etc. – to give an account of their stewardship. These seasonal personifications are also representative of social types in a blending of the natural and the human. Appropriately garbed, they sing and dance; yet there is an elegiac undercurrent in the ominous references to death and the plague. *Summer's Last Will* includes Nashe's most poignant lyric as well as jocular songs, but its style is modulated by the deflating, if not abusive, prose comments of – thanks to his name – the ghostly Presenter, Will Summers, Henry VIII's jester.

In 1597 Nashe's share in the scandalous *Isle of Dogs*, a play no longer extant, forced him to skip out of London and take refuge at Yarmouth. As a token of gratitude to the citizens, he wrote *Lenten Stuff*. Taking his cue from scholars of all ages who turned molehills into mountains, Nashe follows up a chronicle history of the city with a mock encomium of the red herring, including an account of its origins by way of a burlesque treatment of Marlowe's *Hero and Leander*. This notably anticipates 17th-century handling of the once popular epyllion.

Nashe also showed his literary gratitude to the Carey family by dedicating his mocking discourse on apparitions, *The Terrors of the Night*, to Sir George's daughter and his fantastical prose treatise, *Christ's Tears over Jerusalem*, to his wife. For the latter piece, though "an infant in the mysteries of divinity," he composes a "collachrymate" oration in which Christ projects the fall of Jerusalem for the sins of the Jews. This is a highly effective, if disconcerting flourish of rhetoric. In its wealth of tropes and figures, its playing on single words in different contexts, its use of classical quotations and instances (Christ cites Herodotus and specifies the height of Mt. Tabor), it suggests spiritual parody. In its stress on the lachrymal, it looks forward to the "tear poetry" of the 17th Century. To this oration Nashe adds a ghastly recital of the desolation of the city through sword, famine, and pestilence. Like a "soul surgeon" he then runs through the sins of the populace.

In *The Unfortunate Traveller*, he essays "a clean different vein." A piece of short fiction, it is a variety show in terms of kind: partly jest book, chronicle history, and travelogue. Its roguish hero, Jack Wilton, a dapper page, attends Henry VIII's wars in France, returns to England as a fop, goes off to Northern Europe where he witnesses the slaughter (in 1534) of the Anabaptists, meets up with his late master the poet Surrey and continues to travel with him, finally reaching Italy, the acme of all European tours. With such a geographical and historical spread, Nashe has ample opportunity to ridicule many intellectual and social pretensions, but most of all he achieves "variety of mirth" by parodying literary styles and genres.

The sensational elements of chronicle history are mocked by the comic treatment of the horrors of war and the sweating sickness. The inanities of Petrarchan love are mocked in the extravagant language of Surrey, who woos a Venetian magnifico's wife as a surrogate for his Geraldine though it is Jack, relying on "simplicity and plainness," who catches the bird and gets her with child. The extremes of symbolic trappings and *imprese* are mocked by the flamboyant tournament in Florence where, on behalf of his beloved, Surrey challenges all comers – Christians, Turks, Jews, or Saracens. When Jack and his courtesan reach Rome, the literary parody becomes more skilful and complex. The travel account – "the shop dust of the sights" he sees – includes a baroque description of the artificial luxuriance of a merchant's summerhouse in a parody of "golden age" literature; the "complaint" of the matron raped on her dead husband's body parodies that form's rhetorical excesses, while the account of Cutwolfe's grisly pleasure in vengeance ("The farther we wade in revenge, the nearer we come to the throne of the Almighty") parodies popular tragedy though its moral value is mockingly acknowledged in that the execution of the revenger persuades Jack to marry his courtesan and flee the Sodom of Italy. Throughout the bewildering multiplicity of action and event, the one constant is the author's concern with manipulating language: rhetorical technique exists for its own sake quite devoid of value judgements. Stressing extravagant manner rather than serious matter in a variety of popular and mixed forms, Nashe illustrates the dilution of humanist theory in the 1590's and forecasts a new emphasis.

—Elizabeth Story Donno

QUARLES, Francis.   English.   Born in Romford, Essex, baptized 8 May 1592. Educated at Christ's College, Cambridge, B.A. c. 1608; Lincoln's Inn, London. Married Ursula Woodgate in 1618; eighteen children. Cup-Bearer to Princess Elizabeth on her marriage to the elector palatine, 1613; abroad, 1615–17; Private Secretary to the Archbishop of Armagh, c. 1626–30; Chronologer of the City of London, 1639–44; wrote in defense of Charles I at the beginning of the Civil War. *Died 8 September 1644.*

PUBLICATIONS

Collections

Complete Works in Prose and Verse, edited by Alexander B. Grosart.   3 vols., 1880–81.

Verse

A Feast for Worms: A Poem of the History of Jonah.   1620.
Hadasa; or, The History of Queen Esther.   1621.
Job Militant.   1624.
Sion's Elegies, Wept by Jeremie the Prophet.   1624.
Sion's Sonnets, Sung by Solomon.   1625.
Argalus and Parthenia.   1629.

The History of Samson.   1631.
Divine Poems.   1630; revised edition, 1634.
Divine Fancies.   1632.
Emblems.   1635.
An Elegy upon Sir Julius Caesar.   1636.
An Elegy upon Mr. John Wheeler.   1637.
Hieroglyphics of the Life of Man.   1638.
Memorials upon the Death of Sir Robert Quarles.   1639.
Sighs at the Deaths of the Countess of Cleveland and Cicily Killigrew, with An Elegy upon the Death of Sir John Wolstenholme.   1640.
Threnodes on Lady Masham and William Cheyne.   1641.
Solomon's Recantation, Entitled Ecclesiastes, Paraphrased.   1645.
The Shepherd's Oracle.   1644; revised edition, 1646.
Hosanna; or, Divine Poems on the Passion of Christ.   1647.

Play

The Virgin Widow (produced before 1649).   1649.

Other

Enchiridion.   1640; selection, as *Observations Concerning Princes and States upon Peace and War,* 1642; as *Institutions, Essays and Maxims, Political, Moral and Divine,* 1695; as *Wisdom's Better Than Money,* 1698.
The Loyal Convert.   1644.
The Whipper Whipt.   1644.
The New Distemper.   1645.
Barnabas and Boanerges; or, Judgment and Mercy for Afflicted Souls.   2 vols., 1644–46.

Bibliography: *Quarles: A Bibliography of His Works to the Year 1800* by John Horden, 1953.

Reading List: *Der Einfluss der Bibel auf die Dichtungen des Quarles* by A. Lohnes, 1909; *Quarles in the Civil War* by Gordon S. Haight, 1939; "The Imagery of Quarles' Emblems" by E. James, in *University of Texas Studies in English,* 1943; *Quarles: A Study of His Life and Poetry* by Masodul Hasan, 1966; Introduction by John Horden to *Hosanna and Threnodes,* 1968, and to *Hieroglyphics of the Life of Man,* 1969.

*   *   *

A voluminous writer who produced Biblical paraphrases, an Arcadian romance, political pamphlets, aphorisms by the hundreds, and a single comedy, Francis Quarles is remembered chiefly for *Emblems* and *Hieroglyphics.* Perhaps "the most popular book of verse published during the century," *Emblems* later gave its author a place in the *Dunciad.* Although recent scholarly attention to emblem books has restored sympathetic attention to Quarles, there is some suspicion that his popularity may have grown from the generally undemanding way in which his poems trace the implications of symbolic and often curiously composed engravings.

The Arcadian romance *Argalus and Parthenia* remains entertaining. Initially, the heroine's ruby lips and pearly teeth seem tediously predictable, but convention is pushed to witty exaggeration in the picture of her breasts as azure-veined spheres: "Which, were they obvious but to every eye,/All liberall Arts would turn Astronomy." Quarles competently handles the suspense of dramatic incidents which retard until Book III the union of hero and heroine. There, deliberately stepping forward as author, he refuses to end the story in the glow of the wedding feast, and, if the final unhappy adventures are even more fanciful than the rest of the plot, they justify the appended poem on mortality: "Delights vanish, the morne o'ercasteth,/The frost breaks, the shower hasteth;/The tower falls, the hower spends;/The beauty fades, and man's life ends."

In the preface to *Argalus and Parthenia*, Quarles promises, "I have not affected to set thy understanding on the Rack, by the tyranny of strong lines." Although "strong lines," the metaphysical compression of metaphor, seem to have a natural affinity with emblematic drawings, Quarles chooses in *Emblems* and *Hieroglyphics* to be clear rather than strenuous. At their blandest, the poems are straightforward exegesis of details in the engravings, but Quarles varies the surface of his verse through elaborate repetition, antithesis, apostrophe, and dialogue, and he experiments with a wide range of metrical patterns. Arrangement of diverse elements creates part of the interest, for each emblem includes a picture, a Biblical motto, the poem, quotations from the Church Fathers, and a four-line epigram. *Emblems* consists of five books, each containing fifteen such units. The engravings were taken from two continental Jesuit collections; most of the pictures are concerned with the soul's struggle for salvation. For *Hieroglyphics*, a single set of fifteen emblems, Quarles obtained plates unified by the image of a candle, and he wrote poems unified partly through recurring images of light and darkness. The final seven emblems on the Ages of Man present a progressively shortened candle; against the movement from infancy to senility which is developed in the engravings and the longer poems, Quarles balances a sequence of epigrams moving in the opposite direction, from dotage to infancy. In emphasizing the brevity and precariousness of man's life, he returns to the theme of his first published work, *A Feast for Wormes*.

—Kay Stevenson

RALEGH, Sir Walter. English. Born in Hayes Barton, Devon, in 1552. Educated at Oriel College, Oxford, 1566–69. Married Elizabeth Throckmorton in 1593. Courtier, diplomatist, soldier and explorer: fought for the Huguenots in France, at Jarnac and Moncontour, 1569; joined expedition of his half-brother Sir Humphrey Gilbert, 1578; fought against the rebels in Ireland, 1580; entered the Court as a protégé of Leicester, 1581, and accompanied him to the Netherlands, 1582; on his return became a great favorite of the Queen; knighted in 1584; appointed Lord Warden of the Stannaries and Vice-Admiral of Devon and Cornwall, 1585; Member of Parliament for Devon, 1585; fitted out an expedition to America, 1584, which discovered and claimed Virginia, 1584; attempted to colonize Virginia with two more expeditions, 1585–87; went to Ireland in an attempt to make his estate there habitable, 1587; returned to court, and involved in organizing resistance to the threatened invasion of the Spanish Armada, 1588, and planning an expedition to seize Spanish treasure ships, 1592; imprisoned in the tower because of the Queen's anger at his secret relationship with her maid-of-honour Throckmorton, 1592–95; explored the coasts of Trinidad, and sailed up the Orinoco, 1595; fought the Spanish at Cadiz, 1596; allowed to resume his place as Captain of the Guard, 1597; involved in the successful attack against

Spain in the Azores, 1597; Governor of Jersey, 1600–03; after James's accession, arrested as "agent of Spain," sentenced to die, but reprieved and imprisoned in the Tower of London, 1603–16; involved in a disastrous expedition to Guiana, 1617; on his return imprisoned and then executed on the former charge. *Died 28 October 1618.*

PUBLICATIONS

Collections

Works.   8 vols., 1829.
Poems, edited by Agnes M. C. Latham.   1929; revised edition, 1951.
Selected Prose and Poetry, edited by Agnes M. C. Latham.   1965.
A Choice of Ralegh's Verse, edited by Robert Nye.   1972.

Verse

Poems, edited by E. Brydges.   1813.

Other

A Report of the Fight about the Isles of the Azores.   1591; edited by H. Newbolt, 1908.
The Discovery of the Large, Rich, and Beautiful Empire of Guiana.   1596; edited by W. H. D. Rouse, 1905.
The History of the World.   1614; abridgement edited by C. A. Patrides, 1971.
The Prerogative of Parliaments.   1628.
Instructions to His Son and to Posterity.   1632; edited by Louis B. Wright, 1962.
The Prince; or, Maxims of State.   1642.
Judicious and Select Essays.   1650; *Apology for His Voyage to Guiana* edited by V. T. Harlow, 1932.
Maxims of State.   1650; augmented edition, 1656.
A Discourse of the Original and Fundamental Cause of Natural War with the Mystery of Invasive War.   1650.
The Sceptic (miscellany).   1657.
Remains.   1657.
Three Discourses.   1702.
A Military Discourse.   1734.
The Interest of England with Regard to Foreign Alliances, Explained in Two Discourses.   1750.
Journal of the Second Voyage to Guiana, edited by R. H. Schomburk.   1848; edited by V. T. Marlow, 1932.

Bibliography: *A Bibliography of Raleigh* by T. N. Brushfield, 1886, revised edition, 1908.

Reading List: *Life, with Letters* by E. Edwards, 2 vols., 1868; *Ralegh, The Last of the Elizabethans* by Edward Thompson, 1935; *Ralegh: A Study in Elizabethan Skepticism* by Ernest A. Strathmann, 1951; "The Poetry of Ralegh" by Peter Ure, in *Review of English Studies,* 1960; *Ralegh, Ecrivain* by Pierre Lefranc, 1968; *Ralegh: The Renaissance Man and His Roles* by Stephen A. Greenblatt, 1973; *Ralegh as Historian* by John Racin, 1974.

*   *   *

A report by Anthony à Wood in 1691 adequately suggests Sir Walter Ralegh's numerous interests and as many personalities. "Authors are perplex'd," Wood stated, "under what topick to place him, whether of Statesman, Seaman, Souldier, Chymist, or Chronologer; for in all these he did excell" (*Athenae Oxonienses*, I, 371). Yet even this list hardly exhausts Ralegh's variegated activities. He was also historian, philosopher, theologian, and poet. Moreover, he pursued commercial enterprises which enriched his country if not himself; he was a noted patron of literature and the sciences; he designed ships; and he was a politician distinguished for his remarkably liberal tendencies. We are also assured that he was "a pioneer in naval medicine, dietetics, and hygiene" (Christopher Hill, *Intellectual Origins of the English Revolution*, 1965).

A staunch supporter of the imperial idea, Ralegh participated in the transatlantic enterprises of his half-brother Sir Humphrey Gilbert. He later sponsored the expedition which occupied the territory he named after the Queen – Virginia – while in 1595 he sailed to South America in search of Eldorado, the fabled city of gold. Active during the threatened invasion of the Spanish Armada in 1588, he rarely lost an opportunity to oppose the Spanish empire, whether at Cadiz in 1596 or off the Azores a year later. Highly favoured by the Queen – save for the period following his secret marriage to Elizabeth Throckmorton in 1593 – he was nevertheless judged much too flamboyant to have merited elevation to the Privy Council. On the Queen's death in 1603, at any rate, his fortunes declined disastrously. Maligned by his enemies who decisively influenced James I, he was arrested on the incredible charge of being an agent of Spain and sentenced to death after a trial generally regarded as "criminal procedure seen at its worst" (Sir John Macdonell, *Historical Trials*, 1927). But the sentence was not carried out. Ralegh was instead conveyed to the Tower where he remained for nearly thirteen years, to 1616. Released, he mounted a disastrous expedition to Guiana where his son Wat was killed in an engagement with Spanish forces alerted to await his arrival. On his return home he was arrested yet again and, without benefit of a trial, was beheaded on 28 October 1618.

Within two days of Ralegh's execution it was said that "his death will doe more hurte to the faction that sought it, then ever his life could have done" (John Pory, edited by W. S. Powell in *William and Mary Quarterly*, 1952, 537). It was a prophetic utterance; for given the mounting opposition to King James, Ralegh was presently canonised as the principal martyr of royal authoritarianism and injustice. Eventually, he was even transmuted into a republican, largely on the basis of the widely circulated report by John Aubrey that upon the death of Elizabeth he had planned to set up a Commonwealth. However mistaken in itself, the claim appeared to have been implicitly advanced in the work Ralegh composed during his confinement in the Tower, *The History of the World*.

Ralegh's few poems encompass the surviving "books" of *The Ocean to Cynthia* – some five hundred lines addressed to Queen Elizabeth – where a series of frequently obscure, highly metaphorical, fragmentary (and fragmented) emotions undulate through remembered joys to currently experienced despair and hysterical hope ("She is gone, she is lost! She is found, she is ever fair!"). His other poems, hardly numerous, have been reduced still further now that the authenticity of one of the finest, "The Lie," has been questioned (see Pierre Lefranc). Yet it is a respectable collection all the same, its high peaks clearly marked by the predominant sombre mood of "Nature that washt her hands in milk," "Methought I saw the grave where Laura lay" (a prefatory poem to Spenser's *Faerie Queene*), and "The Nymph's Reply to the Shepherd" (an answer to Marlowe's "The Passionate Shepherd to His Love"), as well as the exceptionally qualified mood of "The Passionate Man's Pilgrimage." Impressed, we tend to claim with Peter Ure that Ralegh "ranks even better amongst the minor poets of his time," or that his poems are indeed "extraordinary by any standards" (M. C. Bradbrook, *The School of Night*, 1936). But John Aubrey's contrary judgement has the single advantage that it obliges us to reconsider Ralegh's poetic talents. "He was," said Aubrey sourly, "sometimes a Poet, not often."

Ralegh's prose works include the rousing account of Sir Richard Greville's encounter with the Spanish fleet in *A Report of the Truth of the Fight about the Iles of Açores*, the optimistic vision which is *The Discoverie of the Large, Rich, and Bewtiful Empire of Guiana*, and the colossal *History of the World*, which is arguably his principal contribution to English literature. *The History* was on its publication suppressed by King James partly because it was said to censure princes but especially because it appeared to be a veiled denunciation of his reign. What other reason was there for Ralegh's several comparisons of the early seventeenth century with the expired glories of the Elizabethan age? A series of "parallels" compounded the offence, notably the account of the great Queen Semiramis and her incompetent successor Ninias ("esteemed no man of warre at all, but altogether feminine, and subjected to ease and delicacie," I, ii, 1). In fact, however, Ralegh's principal thrust was in another direction. It was conceivably aimed to provide a sustained view of historical events in the light of that expressly Christian view of history which asserts God's constant supervision of the created order (see the introduction to the edition of *The History* by C. A. Patrides, 1971). But it was no less conceivably aimed to deploy "a secular and critical approach" which eventually contributed "to that segregation of the spiritual from the secular which was the achievement of the seventeenth century" (Christopher Hill). Whichever theory persuades in the end, *The History* possesses an impressive unity of style which is the direct result of Ralegh's successful modulation of an infinitely varied tone. As with the polyphonic music of *Paradise Lost*, so here different subjects have different cadences, and in each case, once the cumulative effect is achieved, the measure alters in accord with the new theme. Clarity reigns supreme throughout, in express opposition to the self-conscious obscurity so often encountered in the literature of the same period. *The History of the World*, it is evident, possesses a style answerable to its great argument.

—C. A. Patrides

RICH, Barnaby. English. Born in Essex in 1542. Married in 1586. Soldier for all of his life: enlisted in the Army as a boy, c. 1555; served in Queen Mary's war with France, 1557–58, in the Le Havre siege, 1562, in Ireland, 1570–72, in The Netherlands, 1576, and in Ireland again, 1577–92; rose to the rank of Captain; impoverished during the 1590's; trained soldiers in London, 1600–06; helped put down the Essex rebellion, 1601; returned to Ireland c. 1608; granted pension by King James, 1616. *Died 10 November 1617.*

PUBLICATIONS

Fiction

   A Right Excellent and Pleasant Dialogue Between Mercury and an English Soldier. 1574.
   Rich His Farewell to Military Profession. 1581; revised edition, 1594, 1606; *Apolonius and Silla* edited by Morton Luce, 1907.

The Strange and Wonderful Adventures of Don Simonides.   1581; second part, 1584.
The Adventures of Brusanus, Prince of Hungaria.   1592.

Other

Alarm to England, Foreshowing What Perils Are Procured Where the People Live Without Regard of Martial Law.   1578.
The True Report of a Late Practice Enterprised by a Papist with a Young Maiden in Wales.   1582.
A Pathway to Military Practice.   1587.
Greene's News Both from Heaven and Hell.   1593; edited by R. B. McKerrow, 1922.
A Soldier's Wish to Britain's Welfare.   1604; as *The Fruits of Long Experience,* 1604.
Faults, Faults, and Nothing Else But Faults.   1606; *Room for a Gentleman; or, The Second Part of Faults, Collected for the True Meridian of Dublin,* 1609.
A Short Survey of Ireland Truly Discovering Who Hath Armed the Hearts of the People with Disobedience.   1609.
A New Description of Ireland, Wherein Is Described the Disposition of the Irish Whereunto They Are Inclined.   1610; as *A New Irish Prognostication,* 1624.
A True and Kind Excuse Written in Defence of That Book Entitled A New Description of Ireland.   1612.
A Catholic Conference Between Sir Tady MacMareall a Popish Priest and Patrick Plaine a Student.   1612.
The Excellency of Good Women.   1613.
Opinion Deified, Discovering the Engines, Traps, and Trains That Are Set to Catch Opinion.   1613.
The Honesty of This Age.   1614; edited by P. Cunningham, 1844.
My Lady's Looking Glass, Wherein May Be Discerned a Wise Man from a Fool, a Good Woman from a Bad.   1616.
The Irish Hubbub; or, The English Hue and Cry.   1617; revised edition, 1617.

Translator, *The Famous History of Herodotus.*   1584.

Reading List: *Rich: A Short Biography* by Thomas M. Cranfill and D. H. Bruce, 1953.

*   *   *

Barnaby Rich was a soldier, a government agent, a privateer (briefly), and an author with a passionate social conscience. His first two books sprang from his experience as a soldier, his wide reading, and the strongly anti-Catholic feeling which was to colour much of his writing; essentially they are arguments for national readiness for war with Spain. (He later wrote three more military tracts, one of them, *A Pathway to Military Practice,* containing invaluable descriptions of the different duties of army officers of the period.) Bored in dull Ireland, he turned to story-telling and wrote his most popular work, *Farewell to Military Profession*; three more romances followed, the tediously euphuistic *Don Simonides,* well-accepted enough to permit a second volume, and *Brusanus,* which in part allegorizes with dark humour the author's failure to gain court patronage. The *Farewell,* which had four editions during Rich's lifetime, contains eight tales which draw upon the Italians Cinthio and Strapola and the English writer/translators Golding, Painter, and Pettie. At least nine plays of the period have been shown to be indebted to the *Farewell,* most importantly Shakespeare's *Twelfth Night.* The stories differ in character, but all have realistic detail, a robust joviality, and dialogue which is usually free from the heavily ornamented style of many of Rich's contemporaries. His lightness and humour are at their best in the tales of "Two Brethren" and "Phylotus and Emelia."

Disappointment, poverty, and frustration after 1592 probably led to the aggressively bitter tone of much of his other work. *Faults, Faults* was modishly anti-feminist, *Opinion Deified* and the ironically named *Honesty of This Age* more general in their attack. To those books critical of the government and way of life of the Irish published in his lifetime can be added the confidential reports on the country which he sent to Cecil, Sir Julius Caesar, and King James. Although known best for his fiction, Rich is a valuable source of information and ideas concerning Ireland, military practice, and the society of his day. His vigorous style and lively wit ensure his place in the forefront of the minor Elizabethan prose writers.

—Alan Brissenden

SACKVILLE, Thomas; 1st Earl of Dorset; Baron Buckhurst. English. Born in Buckhurst, Withyham, Sussex, in 1536. Educated at the grammar school in Sullington, Sussex; possibly at Hart Hall, Oxford, or St. John's College, Cambridge; entered the Middle Temple, London; called to the bar. Married Cecily Baker in 1554; four sons and three daughters. Elected Member of Parliament for Westmorland, 1558, for East Grinstead, Sussex, 1559, and for Aylesbury, Buckinghamshire, 1563; toured France and Italy, 1563–66; inherited family estates and returned to England, 1566; served in the House of Lords from 1567; on diplomatic missions for the crown to France, 1568, 1571; Privy Councillor, from 1571, and served as Commissioner at State Trials; sent to the Low Countries by the Queen to survey political affairs after Leicester's return to England, incurred her displeasure, was recalled, confined to his house, then restored to favour, 1587–88; appointed Commissioner for Ecclesiastical Causes, 1588; again sent on an embassy to the Low Countries, 1589; commissioner to sign treaty with France on behalf of the Queen, 1591; with Burghley, unsuccessfully attempted to negotiate peace with France, 1598; appointed Lord Treasurer, 1599, and confirmed in the position for life by James I, 1603; Lord High Steward, presiding at the trial of the Earl of Essex, 1601; a commissioner in the successful negotiation of a new peace treaty with Spain, and pensioned for his services by the King, 1604. Grand Master of the Order of the Freemasons, 1561–67; Chancellor of Oxford University, 1591. M.A.: Cambridge University, 1571; Oxford University, 1592. Knighted, and created Baron Buckhurst, 1567; Knight of the Garter, 1589; Earl of Dorset, 1604. *Died 19 April 1608.*

PUBLICATIONS

Collections

Works, edited by R. W. Sackville-West. 1859.
Poems, edited by M. Hearsey. 1936.

Play

> *The Tragedy of Gorboduc,* with Thomas Norton (produced 1561).   1565; as *The Tragedy of Ferrex and Porrex,* 1570(?); edited by Irby B. Cauthen, 1970.

Verse

> *Induction,* and *Complaint of Henry, Duke of Buckingham,* in *Mirror for Magistrates.*   1563; edited by Lily B. Campbell, 1938.

Reading List: *Sackville* by Normand Berlin, 1974.

*   *   *

In the first edition of *Gorboduc,* the first three acts are attributed to Thomas Norton and the last two to Thomas Sackville, but some current opinion also ascribes the play's first scene to Sackville and its final one to Norton. *Gorboduc,* the first English tragedy properly so called, is based on a story from the British pseudo-history written by Geoffrey of Monmouth. The authors have altered this story (of brother-princes' rivalry, leading to the death of one of them in battle and their mother's murder of the survivor, after which the nobles fall to civil war) by making it begin with the king's abdication of rule in favour of both his sons, by causing the king and queeen to be slain in a popular rebellion which is then put down by the nobles, and by introducing in the last act an ambitious nobleman who covets the vacant throne. Their play is therefore concerned both with tragic passions (which destroy a fated royal house) and with political lessons (particularly the dangers of civil war and the importance of a settled succession): it partakes both of the world of Senecan tragedy and of that of the *Mirror for Magistrates.* In form it resembles classical tragedy, though actually defective in all three unities of time, place, and (finally, when the chief characters are dead) action. It is divided into acts and scenes, with choruses between the acts; there are long speeches containing many *sententiae*; physical action, instead of being shown, is narrated by messengers. From non-classical tradition come the symbolic dumb-shows between the acts. The speeches are in blank verse, the choruses in quatrains (sometimes double) rounded off with couplets.

Sackville also contributed to the 1563 edition of the *Mirror for Magistrates,* supplying one of the tragic narratives (the "Complaint" of the Duke of Buckingham, Richard III's right-hand-man) and a long 76-stanza "induction" to the whole work. In the induction, the poet, musing in a dreary winter landscape, encounters Sorrow personified, who escorts him to the underworld, where he sees various other appropriate personifications – Remorse of Conscience, Dread, Revenge, Misery, Care, Sleep, Age, Malady, Famine, Death, War, and Debate – before crossing in Charon's boat to interview the great men whose falls are the subject of the *Mirror.* Written in rhyme-royal pentameter, this induction powerfully evokes the sombre mood of the collection of "tragedies" by drawing partly on Virgilian and partly on medieval artistic conventions; it looks forward towards Spenser in this mingling, as also in its deliberate use of archaic words for their emotional associations.

—T. W. Craik

SHAKESPEARE, William. English.   Born in Stratford upon Avon, Warwickshire, baptized 26 April 1564. Probably educated at the King's New School, Stratford, 1571–77. Married Anne Hathaway in 1582; two daughters and one son. Settled in London c. 1588, and was well-known as an actor and had begun to write for the stage by 1592; Shareholder in the Lord Chamberlain's Company (after James I's accession, called the King's Men) by 1594, performing at the Globe Theatre from 1599, and, after 1609, at the Blackfriars Theatre; bought New Place in Stratford, 1597, and acquired land in Stratford; retired to Stratford in 1611. *Died 23 April 1616.*

PUBLICATIONS

Collections

> *Comedies, Histories, and Tragedies* (First Folio), edited by John Heming and Henry Condell.   1623.
> *Works* (New Variorum Edition), edited by H. H. Furness and H. H. Furness, Jr.   27 vols., 1871 –
> *Works* (New Cambridge Edition), edited by J. Dover Wilson and A. H. Quiller-Couch.   1921–66.
> *The New Arden Shakespeare,* edited by Una Ellis-Fermor and others.   1951 –.
> *The New Penguin Shakespeare.*   1967 –.

Verse

> *Venus and Adonis.*   1593.
> *The Rape of Lucrece.*   1594.
> *Sonnets.*   1609.
> *Poems.*   1640.

Plays

> *King John* (produced 1589).   In First Folio, 1623.
> *1 Henry VI* (produced 1591?).   In First Folio, 1623.
> *2 Henry VI* (produced 1592?).   1594 (bad quarto).
> *3 Henry VI* (produced 1592?).   1595 (bad quarto).
> *Richard III* (produced 1592?).   1597.
> *The Comedy of Errors* (produced 1593?).   In First Folio, 1623.
> *Titus Andronicus* (produced 1594).   1594.
> *The Taming of the Shrew* (produced 1594).   In First Folio, 1623.
> *Love's Labour's Lost* (produced 1594?).   1598.
> *Romeo and Juliet* (produced 1594–95?).   1597 (bad quarto); 1599.
> *Two Gentlemen of Verona* (produced 1595?).   In First Folio, 1623.
> *A Midsummer Night's Dream* (produced 1595).   1600.
> *Richard II* (produced 1595–96?).   1597.
> *Sir Thomas More,* with Munday (produced 1596?).   Eited by A. Dyce, 1844; edition of W. W. Greg revised by H. Jenkins, 1961.
> *The Merchant of Venice* (produced 1596?).   1600.
> *Henry IV,* part 1 (produced 1596–97?).   1598.
> *Henry IV,* part 2 (produced 1597–98?).   1600.

Much Ado about Nothing (produced 1598?).   1600.
Henry V (produced 1599).   1600 (bad quarto).
Julius Caesar (produced 1599).   In First Folio, 1623.
The Merry Wives of Windsor (produced 1599–1600?).   1602 (bad quarto).
As You Like It (produced 1600?).   In First Folio, 1623.
Hamlet (produced 1601?).   1603 (bad quarto); 1604.
Twelfth Night; or, What You Will (produced 1601–02?).   In First Folio, 1623.
Troilus and Cressida (produced 1602?).   1609.
All's Well That Ends Well (produced 1602?).   In First Folio, 1623.
Measure for Measure (produced 1604?).   In First Folio, 1623.
Othello (produced 1604?).   1622.
King Lear (produced 1605).   1608 (bad quarto).
Macbeth (produced 1606).   In First Folio, 1623.
Antony and Cleopatra (produced 1606?).   In First Folio, 1623.
Coriolanus (produced 1606?).   In First Folio, 1623.
Timon of Athens (produced 1607?).   In First Folio, 1623.
Pericles (produced 1608?).   1609.
Cymbeline (produced 1609?).   In First Folio, 1623.
The Winter's Tale (produced 1610?).   In First Folio, 1623.
The Tempest (produced 1611).   In First Folio, 1623.
Henry VIII, with Fletcher (?) (produced 1613).   In First Folio, 1623.
The Two Noble Kinsmen, with Fletcher (produced 1613).   1634; edited by G. R. Proudfoot, 1970.

Bibliography: *A Shakespeare Bibliography* by Walther Ebisch and Levin L. Schücking, 1931, supplement, 1937; *A Classified Shakespeare Bibliography 1936–1958* by Gordon Ross Smith, 1963.

Reading List: *Shakespeare: A Study of the Facts and Problems* by E. K. Chambers, 2 vols., 1930; *Narrative and Dramatic Sources of Shakespeare* edited by Geoffrey Bullough, 8 vols., 1957–75; *The Printing and Proof-Reading of the First Folio of Shakespeare* by C. Hinman, 2 vols., 1963; *Four Centuries of Shakespeare Criticism* edited by Frank Kermode, 1965; *A Shakespeare Encyclopaedia* edited by O. J. Campbell and E. G. Quinn, 1966; *A New and Systematic Concordance to the Works of Shakespeare* by M. Spevack, 6 vols., 1968–70; *A New Companion of Shakespeare Studies* edited by Kenneth Muir and Samuel Schoenbaum, 1971; *Shakespeare: The Critical Heritage* edited by Brian Vickers, 6 vols., 1973–74; *Shakespeare: A Documentary Life* by Samuel Schoenbaum, 1975, compact edition, 1977.

*   *   *

Shakespeare, "of all modern, and perhaps ancient poets, had the largest and most comprehensive soul." Dryden's tribute, the more generous for coming from an age that prided itself on a superior standard of polish and "politeness," sums up what students of Shakespeare have at all times sought to express. No writer of comparable greatness is more elusive to final definition. None has exercised a more diverse appeal or shown a greater capacity for continual and fruitful renewal in the minds of succeeding generations.

This protean genius came only gradually to full expression. Shakespeare's earliest work is that of a man engaged in exploring, and in some measure creating, the possibilities of his art. The earliest work attributed to him, the three plays on *Henry VI*, show him engaged in shaping chronicle material to dramatic ends. They lead, in *Richard III*, to the creation of a character who stands out by his passionate dedication to the achievement of power against the world of short-sighted time-servers, ambitious politicians, and helpless moralists in which he moves.

Side by side with these early chronicle dramas we find Shakespeare, in a series of plays running from *The Comedy of Errors* though *The Taming of the Shrew* to *Love's Labour's Lost*, shaping the conventions of comedy into an instrument for expressing the finished statements about life – and more especially about love and marriage as central aspects of it – that he was already concerned to make.

In the 1590's Shakespeare also wrote two narrative poems, *Venus and Adonis* and *The Rape of Lucrece*, possibly stimulated by the success of Marlow's *Hero and Leander* of 1593, and he was also at work on his sonnets, though the 1609 *Sonnets* is now generally thought to contain poems from virtually all the periods of his development. Many of the sonnets are exercises in the conventions of the period, addressed to a patron or to an imaginary mistress. But Shakespeare was able to use the thematic conventions in a fresh way, investigating – as he would do in his later plays – the relation of individual experience (in particular the heightened emotions of friendship and love) to time. At the same time Shakespeare developed a distinctively intense and immediate language to meet the strict formal limitations of the sonnet. The stress of feeling informing the language and the exploration of shifting attitudes to a particular emotion are essentially *dramatic*, and mark out linguistic and thematic areas that Shakespeare was to explore in his "problem" plays and later.

His early works led, approximately from 1595 to 1596, to a first remarkable explosion of creative energy. Within a brief period of time, Shakespeare produced his first great tragedy, *Romeo and Juliet*, a comedy of outstanding brilliance, *A Midsummer Night's Dream*, and a historical play, *Richard II*, which gives the chronicle type of drama an entirely new dimension. In *Romeo and Juliet* a pair of young lovers seek to affirm the truth of their mutual dedication in the face of an intolerably hostile world. Their attempt ends, inevitably, in separation and death; but because it is a true emotion, involving an intuition of *value*, of life and generosity, it achieves, even in the doom which overtakes it, a measure of triumph over external circumstance. *A Midsummer Night's Dream* could be regarded as a comic counterpoise to the "romantic" tragedy. Within the framework of a rational and social attitude to marriage, it transports two pairs of youthful lovers to the mysterious woods, where the irrational but potent impulses which men ignore at their peril are released and their capacity to master them tested. By the end of their misadventures, and when the central theme of the play has been presented in the infatuation of Titania, the queen of the fairies, for Bottom the weaver with his ass's head, there is a return to daylight reality and, with it, a resolution of the issues raised by the play in terms of creative paradox. Love is seen at once to be a folly and to contain within itself, absurd indeed but not the less real, a glimpse of the divine element by which human life is imaginatively transformed in terms of "wonder."

The third play of this period, *Richard II*, is the starting-point for a series, continued in *Henry IV*, Parts I and II and *Henry V*, which traces the downfall of a traditional conception of royalty and its replacement by a political force at once more competent, more truly self-aware, and more precariously built on the foundation of its own desire for power. The Lancastrian Bolingbroke, having achieved the crown by deposing and murdering his predecessor, is seen striving to impose unity upon his realm, but foiled in his efforts by the consequences of his original crime. The success which eludes him is finally attained, in *Henry V*, by his son, but in a way which underlines the cost as well as the necessity of his triumph. The presence of Shakespeare's greatest comic creation, Falstaff, and his final rejection, underline the human complexity involved in the new king's necessary choices. As King, he can hardly do otherwise than banish the companion of his youth, and it would surely be wrong to sentimentalize Falstaff in any way; but we are required, in a manner that is very essentially Shakespearean, to weigh the *cost* against the success, and perhaps to conclude that the human and the political orders – both necessary aspects of human life – are in the real world barely to be reconciled.

At about the time that he was writing this second series of history plays, Shakespeare was engaged in developing further his concept of comedy to cover other aspects of human behaviour. In *Much Ado about Nothing* he produced a highly formal comedy which works, through strict conventions and largely in prose, to illuminate facets of truth and illusion in the reality of love. In *As You Like It* the consideration of the basic realities of love and friendship is extended to cover a concept of sociability, of true civilization. The central part of the play, which displaces the action to the Forest of Arden where human relationships are taken temporarily into the state of nature (itself presented in conventional terms) and set in contrast to the corrupt sophistication which prevails at Duke Frederick's court, presents a set of variations on the theme of love. When the various amorous combinations have been sorted out, leading into the concluding "dance" of married harmonies which is a reflection of the universal order of things, the reconciliation at which comedy aims is finally consummated.

The last of these great comedies, *Twelfth Night*, deals in its "serious" part with two characters, Orsino and Olivia, whose lives are initially a blend of sentiment and artifice, and who learn, largely through their relationship with the self-reliant Viola, that the compulsive force of their passions is such as to draw them finally beyond themselves, demanding from each the acceptance of a fuller, more natural and spontaneous way of living. The "lesson" is reinforced by the comic underplot, and more particularly by the exposure of Olivia's steward Malvolio, who is – and remains to the last – "imprisoned" in a darkness which reflects his self-infatuation. Feste, too, the most individual thus far of Shakespeare's clowns, stands rather outside the prevailing mood, answering to the constant tendency of Shakespearean comedy to qualify its imaginative harmonies with a profound sense of relativity, of a final uniqueness and autonomy in human experience.

The period which produced these great comedies was followed by a turning of the dramatist's interest towards tragedy. Two plays of obscure intention and uneven execution – *Troilus and Cressida* and *Measure for Measure* – form the background to *Hamlet* in which many of the same issues were raised to the consistent level of tragedy. The play presents a central figure of unique complexity whose motives penetrate the action at every point, seeking clarification through contact with it and illuminating it in turn by his central presence. In pursuing his duty to avenge his father's death, Hamlet brings to light a state of disease in "Denmark" – the "world" of the play – which affects the entire field presented to his consciousness; and, in the various stages through which the ramifications of this infection are exposed, he finds himself exploring progressively the depths of his own disaffection.

In the great tragedies that followed *Hamlet*, the conflicts there presented are polarized, on an ever-increasing scale, into more clearly defined contrasts. In the earliest of them, *Othello*, the heroic figure of the Moor, tragically compounded of nobility and weakness, is exposed to the critical scepticism of Iago which operates upon his simplicity with the effect of an anarchic and sinister dissolvent. "Perplexed" to the last, betrayed by emotions which he has never really understood in their true nature, Othello makes a last attempt to return, through suicide, to his original simplicity of nature. By then, however, the critical acid supplied by Iago has undermined the structure of his greatness.

In his next tragedy, *King Lear*, Shakespeare embarked upon what is probably the most universal of his conceptions. Lear is at once father and king, head of a family and ruler of a state. As father he produces in his daughters contrasted reactions which reflect contradictions in his own nature; as king, his wilful impulses release in society destructive forces which nothing less than their utter exhaustion can contain. In the central storm scenes, the action of the elements becomes a reflection of Lear's own condition. Man and his environment are seen as organically related in the conflicts of a universe poetically conceived. Human relationships are shattered, and the state of "unaccomodated man" is seen in terms of subjection to the beast of prey in his own nature. Through these overwhelming events we are led step by step to Lear's awakening and recognition of his returned daughter Cordelia. This is the central reconciliation, the restoration of the natural "bond" between father and child, which is seen – while it lasts – as the resolution of the ruin caused by passion and egoism in the most intimate of human relationships. It is not, however, lasting. Since we are engaged in an exploration of the human condition under its tragic aspect, not elaborating the supposedly beneficial effects of suffering in promoting moral understanding, the armies of France are defeated by the "Machiavellian" realist Edmund; and though he dies in meeting the challenge of his disguised half-brother Edgar, his death cannot reverse the hanging of

Cordelia by his orders. As the play ends, Lear returns with her dead body in his arms and, in a world dominated by returning darkness, the curtain falls.

The next great tragedy, *Macbeth*, deals with the overthrow of harmony not merely in an individual of tragic stature, but in an ordered realm. Macbeth murders, not only a man and a kinsman, but order, sanity, life itself. From the moment of the execution of his deed his character and that of his wife develop on lines of rigid determinism. One crime leads logically, by a dreadful and pre-determined process, to another; and the career that began by following the illusion of "freedom," mastery of circumstance, ends by an inexorable development in a complete enslavement from which defeat and death provide the only conceivable release.

Close in time to the writing of these great tragedies, a series of plays on Roman themes represents Shakespeare's final effort in this kind. The earliest, *Julius Caesar*, is one of his most effective studies of public behaviour. The central character, Brutus, the nearest approach to a truly consistent figure which the play offers, is flawed by the self-consciousness of his determination to be true to his ideals. His need to live up to an acceptable image of himself makes him the victim of those who appeal to him in the name of friendship and devotion to freedom, but who are moved in no small part by resentment and envy. The other principal agent in the tragedy, Mark Antony, combines genuine feeling with the ability to exploit mob emotion, and ends by disclaiming responsibility for the destruction and brutality he has unleashed. Finally, after Caesar's death, the world which survives him is shown separating into its component elements of selfish "realism" and disillusionment.

The next Roman play, *Antony and Cleopatra*, is among Shakespeare's greatest masterpieces. His Cleopatra is at once the Egyptian queen of history and something more: a woman experienced in the ways of a corrupt and cynical world and ready to use her fascination over men in order to survive in it. Antony's love for her is, at least in part, the fascination of a man no longer young, who has chosen to give up his public responsibilities to become the dupe of an emotion that he knows to be unworthy. Side by side with the moral judgment that is unrelentingly pressed throughout the tragedy, the implication remains that the measure of the passion which has led this pair to accept death and ruin may be correspondingly universal in its value. It is the play's achievement to convey that *both* judgments contain a measure of truth, that neither can be suppressed without distorting our sense of the complete human reality which the play offers.

After *Coriolanus*, the disconcerting study of a gauche and inflexible hero whose unnatural desire for revenge upon his city leaves him at the last disoriented and ruined in a world that he is incapable of understanding, the last stage of Shakespeare's development consists of a series of "romances," written from 1607 onwards, which represent an effort to give dramatic form to a new "symbolic" intuition. After two plays – *Pericles* and *Cymbeline* – which can be thought of as experiments, *The Winter's Tale* presents the story of two kings whose life-long friendship is broken up by the jealous conviction of one of them – Leontes – that his friend Polixenes has replaced him in the affection of his wife Hermione. By the end of an action in which the passage of time has an essential part to play, the estranged monarchs are reconciled through the spontaneous love of their children, the divisions introduced by disordered and self-consuming passion into the harmony of life have been healed, and winter has passed through spring into the summer of gracious fulfilment.

The Tempest, which some have seen, perhaps a little over-schematically, as Shakespeare's farewell to the stage, takes us to an island in which the normal laws of nature are magically suspended. Prospero can be seen as a figure of the imaginative artist, bringing together on his island stage the men who, in another world, have wronged him and whom he now subjects to a process of judgment and reconciliation. He is accompanied by his servants Ariel and Caliban, the former of whom may represent the imaginative, creative side of his nature, the latter the passionate instincts which, as a human being, he keeps uneasily under control. By the end of the play, as in *The Winter's Tale*, a measure of reconciliation has been born out of the exposure to tragic experience. Prospero's daughter Miranda marries Ferdinand, the son of his former enemy, whom she first saw in her inexperience as a vision proceeding from a "brave new world," but whom she has learned to love as a man. The "brave new world" is seen as an ennobling vision of love in the light of an enriched experience, and upon it the "gods" are invited to bestow the "crown" which raises a new-born vision of humanity into a symbol of royalty. The "crown" they bestow is a sign of the "second," the redeemed and "reasonable" life which Prospero's action has made accessible. At this point, if anywhere, and always within the limits of the imaginative action which has created a *play*, the design presented by Shakespeare's work is substantially complete.

—Derek A. Traversi

SIDNEY, Sir Philip. English. Born in Penshurst, Kent, 30 November 1554. Educated at Shrewsbury School, Shropshire, 1564–68; Christ Church, Oxford (left without a degree). Married Frances Walsingham in 1583. Travelled in France, Germany, and Italy, as Gentleman of the Bedchamber to Charles IV, 1572–75; Member of Elizabeth's court: Ambassador to Emperor Rudolf and then to the Prince of Orange, 1577; in disfavor with the Queen, retired to his sister's estate at Wilton, 1580; Member of Parliament, 1581; knighted, 1582; Governor of Flushing, 1585; accompanied Leicester to the Netherlands to fight against Spain, and died in battle there. *Died 17 October 1586.*

PUBLICATIONS

Collections

Complete Works, edited by Albert Feuillerat.   4 vols., 1912–26.
Poems, edited by William A. Ringler, Jr.   1962.
Selected Poetry and Prose, edited by David Kalstone.   1970.

Verse

Astrophel [i.e., Astrophil] and Stella (includes sonnets by other writers), edited by Thomas Nashe.   1591; revised edition, in *Arcadia,* 1598; edited by M. Putzel, 1967.
The Psalms of David, with the Countess of Pembroke, edited by S. W. Singer.   1823 edited by J. C. A. Rathmell, 1963.

Fiction

The Countess of Pembroke's Arcadia.   1590; revised edition, including material from earlier version, 1593; edited by Albert Feuillerat, in *Complete Works,* 1922; earlier version, edited by Albert Feuillerat, in *Complete Works* 1926; as *The Old Arcadia,* edited by J. Robertson, 1973; 1590 edition edited by Maurice Evans, 1977.

Other

> *The Defense of Poesy.*   1595; as *An Apology for Poetry,* 1595; edited by Jan van Dorsten,
> 1966.
> *The Countess of Pembroke's Arcadia* (miscellany; includes *Certain Sonnets, Defense of
> Poesy, Astrophel and Stella, The Lady of May*).   1598; augmented edition, including
> *A Dialogue Between Two Shepherds,* 1613.
> *Miscellaneous Prose,* edited by Katherine Duncan-Jones and Jan van Dorsten.   1973.

Bibliography: *Sidney: A Concise Bibliography* by S. A. Tannenbaum, 1941, supplement by G.
R. Guffey, 1967; *Sidney: An Annotated Bibliography of Modern Criticism, 1941–1970* by
Mary A. Washington, 1972.

Reading List: *Sidney and the English Renaissance* by J. Buxton, 1954; *Sidney* by Kenneth
Muir, 1960; *Symmetry and Sense: The Poetry of Sidney* by R. L. Montgomery, Jr., 1961;
Sidney's Poetry: Contexts and Interpretations by David Kalstone, 1965; *The Epic Voice:
Arcadia* by R. Delasanta, 1967; *Heroic Love: Studies in Sidney and Spenser* by Mark Rose,
1968; *Sidney* by Robert Kimbrough, 1970; *Young Sidney 1572–1577* by James M. Osborn,
1972; *The Poetry of Sidney: An Interpretation in the Context of His Life and Times* by John G.
Nichols, 1974; *Sidney: A Study of His Life and Work* by A. C. Hamilton, 1977; *Sidney: The
Maker's Mind* by Dorothy Connell, 1978.

*   *   *

The keynote of Sir Philip Sidney's work is self-conscious artistry in the service of
psychological exploration. In his *Defense of Poesy*, he defined poetry as an art of imitation, as
did theorists before him; but he insisted that the object of imitation exists not in nature but in
the poet's mind, so that poetry becomes the giving form or image to ideas. Thus the poet
becomes a maker of fictions, and fiction becomes the exercise of hypothesis, whereby the
poet, "freely ranging within the zodiac of his own wit," explores "the divine consideration of
what may be, or should be." The end of knowledge for Sidney is the repair of the Fall by
implanting self-knowledge and action; and poetry does that better than philosophy or history,
not only because it presents precepts of virtue in apprehensible images, but also because, by
so doing, it causes delight which moves men to "take that goodness in hand which, without
delight, they would flee as from a stranger." By casting his treatise into the form of a
delightful classical oration – with its changes of tone from the relaxed humor of the opening
to the passionate exhortation of the ending – Sidney made the defending of poetry itself an
imaginary action, whereby his persuasion to love poetry became analogous to poetry's
persuasion to embrace virtue.

Sidney's great prose romance, *Arcadia*, exists in two different forms. The *Old Arcadia* (ca.
1579–80) is a straightforward narrative in five "books" or "acts" following the five-act
structure of Terentian comedy; the books are separated by four verse interludes or
entertainments by the Arcadian shepherds, each with its special theme which both ties
together the various actions preceding it in the narrative and contrasts the main action
tonally. The romance belongs to the pastoral tradition, with its concerns over humility,
figured as man's harmony with nature, and pride, as man's attempt to rise above nature. It
centers around questions of human control over events, and these dilate into parallel actions
of love, in the private, and order, in the political, realms, book-by-book. Sidney's
sophisticated narrative persona views these actions with objectivity and, frequently, with wry
comedy.

The comic tone disappears in the incomplete *New Arcadia*, an extensive revision of the first
two and one-half books (ca. 1583–4) which elaborated characterization, ideas, style, and
especially plot. Sidney added thirteen new episodes that showed events in the main plot from

a variety of angles and created thematic density whereby the three books of the revised romance became small disquisitions on love, reason against passion, and the nature of marriage. By focusing on a clearly articulated ideational structure thus, Sidney forged the pastoral romance into an ethical and psychological tool, according to the aims of poetry set out in the *Defense*. The verse interludes of both *Arcadias* are marked by interesting experiments with classical meters and Romance forms. Some of them – the sapphic "If mine eyes can speak," the great double sestina "Ye goatherd gods" – are really accomplished poems.

In *Astrophil and Stella* Sidney made his most telling experiments. He made the sonnet psychologically dramatic by emphasizing conflict in the form, specifically by polarizing octave and sestet to dramatize the clash of different states of mind. In sonnet 15 the octave parodies bookish modes of composition, while the sestet reverently presents the natural emergence of poetry from love. The stylistic clash in this and other sonnets suggests the replacement of a less by a more valid perception of a situation, usually an external viewpoint by an internal one. In sonnet 31, the contrast between the sentimental octave and the satiric sestet frames a dramatic action whereby the sentimental lover gradually reaches contact with the whole moral man. The histrionics of the Sidneyan sonnet come out strikingly in sonnets like 47, which reads like a soliloquy in a play, the internal argument of Astrophil suddenly crumbling with the appearance of Stella, and 74, wherein, after Astrophil's presentation of himself as bumbling poet, he suddenly emerges as the sophisticated lover-poet who teases the simple reader.

In the 108 sonnets and 11 songs of *Astrophil and Stella* we observe an anatomy of the mind of the lover in its infinite variety. When read consecutively, the collection outlines a psychological action, in a series of lyric moments, describing the influence of love on the relation between the self and reality. The first 22 sonnets lay out themes of love and poetry in a dispersed manner; with the twenty-third sonnet, interrelations become firmer by contiguous themes and rhyme links, and the action settles into the rejection of external reality for the sake of love. Sonnets 31 to 40 explore the precise nature of this love, its difficulty in the face of a real-life husband for Stella and the desire to retreat from it in sleep and dream. With Sonnet 41, we move from the "prospective musings" internal to Astrophil outward to his experience of the reality of life in love; sonnets are now directly addressed to Stella and describe experiences with her. From Sonnet 52 through the first Song (the songs presenting public events in the love experience), sensuality enters the sequence, and for a while external action determines the progress of the affair, first in a series of linked sonnets on hope (66–67), joy (68–70), and desire (71–72), then by a stolen kiss described in the Second Song and celebrated in the ensuing sonnets (79–82). This external action is shown directly in the Fourth through Ninth Songs describing a meeting, Astrophil's open declaration, and Stella's firm rejection of him. The sequence then returns to internal experience in a group of sonnets on absence (87–92) wherein Astrophil turns inward and Stella becomes abstract to him; the final movement shows Astrophil alone, bound up in his mind once more; night characterizes his state, as do images of the self as prison.

Sidney's works offer various hypotheses about love's influence on the mind. In both prose and verse he experimented with form as a means of conveying psychological insight. Whereas in the two *Arcadias* he infused fiction with poetic and dramatic devices, in *Astrophil and Stella* he welded lyrics together into a psychological fiction. The effects of such bold experimentation were quick to be grasped by Sidney's contemporaries, especially after the publication of his works in the early 1590's, and they can be seen especially in the fiction of Greene and Lodge, and in the poetry of Spenser, Grenville, Campion, Daniel, Drayton, and Jonson.

—Walter R. Davis

SOUTHWELL,   Robert.   English.   Born   in   Horsham   St.   Faith,   Norfolk,   in
1561.   Educated by English jesuits in Douai; also studied in Paris and Rome; Jesuit novice,
Rome,   1578;   ordained   priest,   1584;   returned   to   England,   with   Father   Garnet,   as
missionaries, 1586: sheltered by various Catholic families, and became chaplain to the
Countess of Arundel. Betrayed, and imprisoned in the Tower of London, 1592–95, and then
executed. Canonized, Roman Catholic Church, 1970. *Died 21 February 1595.*

PUBLICATIONS

Collections

> *Prose Works,* edited by W. J. Walter.   1828.
> *Poems,* edited by J. H. McDonald and Nancy Pollard Brown.   1967.

Verse

> *Saint Peter's Complaint; Other Poems.*   1595; revised edition, 1595, 1602; edited by W.
>   J. Walter, 1817.
> *Moeniae; or, Certxs609–1805ain Excellent Poems and Spiritual Hymns.*   1595.

Other

> *An Epistle of Comfort to the Reverend Priests.*   1587(?); edited by Margaret Waugh,
>   1966.
> *Mary Magdalen's Funeral Tears.*   1591.
> *The Triumphs over Death; or, A Consolatory Epistle.*   1595; edited by J. W. Trotman,
>   1914.
> *A Humble Supplication to Her Majesty.*   1595 (1601?); edited by R. C. Bald, 1953.
> *A Short Rule of Good Life.*   1596(?); edited by Nancy Pollard Brown, in *Two Letters
>   and Short Rules of a Good Life,* 1972.
> *Spritual Exercises and Devotions,* edited by J. M. de Buck, translated by P. E.
>   Hallett.   1931.

Bibliography: *The Poems and Prose Writings of Southwell: A Bibliographical Study* by J. H.
McDonald, 1937.

Reading List: *Southwell* by R. Bastian, 1931; *The Life of Southwell* by Christopher Devlin,
1956; *The Poetry of Southwell* by Joseph D. Scallon, 1975.

*   *   *

For his short, heroic life Robert Southwell provides an explanation in *An Epistle of
Comfort:* "When England was Catholic, it had many glorious confessors. It is now for the
honour and benefit of our country that it be also well stored with the number of martyrs."
For his poetry, he offers a programme in his prefatory epistle to *Saint Peters Complaint,*
deploring the unworthy subjects of secular poets and proposing "to weave a new webbe in
their owne loome."
His subject-matter is always religious, sometimes Biblical, sometimes gnomic, sometimes

introspective. Within this range, he draws on a variety of metrical and rhetorical patterns, and his writing is informed by a curious mixture of influences: Ignatian meditation, the Italian poetry both secular and religious which he read during his Jesuit training in Rome, the popular English collections such as *Tottel's Miscellany* which he would refine to higher use. In the ballad stanzas of "The Burning Babe" he combines apparent naivety, a startling vision, and ingeniously fused conceits for love, pain, and purification. In the sequence of lyrics on the Virgin Mary he develops the paradoxes proper to her story. In "Looke home" he works with a quiet series of definitions: "Mans mind a myrrour is of heavenly sights,/A breefe wherein all marvailles summed lye." Nourished on meditation, Southwell can unite emotion with the exercise of a subtle mind, expressed with colloquial force or simplicity. In "Sinnes heavy load," he attributes Christ's fall to the ground (in Gethsemane or on the way to Calvary) solely to "my sinne"; "But had they not to earth thus pressed thee,/Much more they would in hell have pestred mee."

The longest of his poems, *Saint Peters Complaint*, grew slowly through at least four versions, beginning as a partial translation of Luigi Tansillo's *Le Lagrime di San Pietro* and ending as a dramatic monologue, passionate and analytical, in 132 stanzas. Together with *Mary Magdalens Funerall Teares*, in prose, this work introduced into England the "literature of tears" of the Counter-Reformation, a line of penitential writing taken up by authors from Lodge and Nashe to major metaphysical and baroque poets of the seventeenth century, including Herbert, Crashaw, and Vaughan.

In the half-century after Southwell's execution, at least twenty editions of his various poems appeared, both evidence and vehicle for his influence on seventeenth-century writers. His prose was equally popular, and like his verse it has immediate, and not merely historical, interest. The sweetness and the rigour of his mind are expressed in beautifully cadenced sentences, as in *An Humble Supplication to Her Majestie*, and in *An Epistle of Comfort* he writes movingly of the plight of English Catholics, or in *A Short Rule of Good Life* he counsels scrupulous attention to detail, whether in devotion or in dress.

—Kay Stevenson

SPENSER, Edmund. nglish. Born, probably in East Smithfield, London, c. 1552. Educated at Merchant Taylors' School, London, 1561–69; Pembroke Hall, Cambridge (sizar, i.e., poor scholar), 1569–76, B.A. 1573, M.A. 1576. Married 1) Machabyas Chyld in 1579 (died by 1591); 2) Elizabeth Boyle in 1594. Secretary to John Young, Bishop of Rochester, 1578–79; entered the household of the Earl of Leicester, 1579, and became acquainted with Sidney; appointed Secretary to Lord Grey of Wilton, Lord Deputy of Ireland, 1580, and thereafter held various official posts in Ireland; in return for services was given Kilcolman Castle in Cork, where he settled in 1586; visited London with Ralegh, 1589; revisited London, 1596; made Sheriff of Cork, 1598; Kilcolman burned down, 1598, and he returned to London. *Died 16 January 1599.*

PUBLICATIONS

Collections

Works: A Variorum Edition, edited by Edwin Greenlaw, and others. 10 vols., 1932–58.

Verse

The Shepherd's Calendar, Containing Twelve Eclogues Proportionable to the Twelve Months.   1579.
The Faerie Queene, Disposed into Twelve Books, Fashioning XII Moral Virtues (6 books completed).   2 vols., 1590–96; revised edition, with *Mutability Cantos,* 1609; edited by A. C. Hamilton, 1977.
Complaints, Containing Sundry Small Poems of the World's Vanity.   1591.
Daphnaida: An Elegy upon the Death of the Noble and Virtuous Douglas Howard.   1591; revised edition, in *Four Hymns,* 1596.
Amoretti and Epithalamion.   1595; *Epithalamion* edited by E. Welsford, with *Four Hymns,* 1969.
Colin Clout's Come Home Again.   1595.
Four Hymns.   1596; edited by E. Welsford, with *Epithalamion,* 1969.
Prothalamion; or, A Spousal Verse in Honour of the Double Marriage of Lady Elizabeth and Lady Katherine Somerset.   1596.

Other

A View of the Present State of Ireland, in *The History of Ireland,* edited by J. Ware.   1633; edited by W. L. Renwick, 1970.
Three Proper and Witty Familiar Letters; Two Other Very Commendable Letters, with Gabriel Harvey.   1580.

Translator, *Axiochus,* by Plato.   1592.

Bibliography: *A Critical Bibliography of the Works of Spenser Printed Before 1700* by F. R. Johnson, 1933; *Two Centuries of Spenserian Scholarship 1609–1805* by J. Wurtsbaugh, 1936; *Spenser: An Annotated Bibliography 1937–1972* by Waldo F. McNeir and Foster Provost, 1975.

Reading List: *The Life of Spenser* by A. C. Judson, in *Works,* 1945; *Spenser and the Faerie Queene* by Leicester Bradner, 1948; *The Allegorical Temper* by Harry Berger, Jr., 1957; *The Allegory of the Faerie Queene* by M. P. Parker, 1960; *Spenser and the Numbers of Time* by Alastair Fowler, 1964; *Spenser's Image of Nature: Wild Man and Shepherd in the Faerie Queene* by D. Cheney, 1966; *The Poetry of the Faerie Queene* by Paul J. Alpers, 1967, and *Spenser: A Critical Anthology* edited by Alpers, 1969; *Spenser's Anatomy of Heroism: A Commentary on the Faerie Queene* by Maurice Evans, 1970; *The Faerie Queene: A Companion for Readers* by Rosemary Freeman, 1970; *The Prophetic Moment: An Essay on Spenser* by Angus Fletcher, 1971; *A Preface to Spenser* by Helena Mennie Shire, 1978.

*   *   *

"The best poets are astronomical poets."
Gabriel Harvey

Spenser made for Elizabethan England the heroic poem hoped for by each emergent nation-state of renaissance Europe. He brought to the reading Englishman, in print and in his own tongue, fresh and lovely verses – and a chance to participate in the new poetry from Italy, its great themes, its philosophy of love, its re-envigorated sense of language. (Sir Philip Sidney had written earlier in "the sweet new style" – but his poems remained unprinted, a private pleasure among friends.)

Spenser had won himself a fine education by his own talents; as scholar and poet he must make his career. By 1579 in the household of Lord Leicester, the Queen's favourite, he published – if under a pseudonym – *The Shepheardes Calender*. This major poem of sparkling originality gave a virtuoso display of verse-rhythms and forms in a language no longer plain-style Tudor, but coloured by country speech or rising to eloquence in words from poetry abroad. It was a pastoral – but with a difference. A series of eclogues like Vergil's were now given cosmic form, being fashioned as a calendar of months, each month with its traditional character and zodiac sign; and there were pictures (woodcuts) – another innovation. Thus a calendar made of poetry interpreted in universal terms the year 1579 as it passed, its crises and its personalities. The work was an immediate success. But the poet had carried pertinence of comment too far. Offence was taken in high places and the poet was removed from the scene – to Ireland.

Spenser was appointed Secretary to the Lord Governor of Ireland, whose thankless task it was to keep peace in the portion of that island under English settlement and to defend it from the determined efforts of the native Irish to end that colonisation. Elizabeth would not adequately support her Deputy and would not recognise the dire threat of Irish "rebels" now supported by Catholic powers in Europe. As civil servant – and later as himself settler and land-holder – Spenser wrote his first-hand experiences, his informed anxieties of some sixteen-years' residence, into a political treatise *A Vue of the Present State of Ireland*. The mounting danger he announced in 1596 was not heeded. General rebellion two years later proved him justified – but destroyed his home. He returned to London to die.

Spenser's heroic poem *The Faerie Queene* was planned on a grand scale in his Cambridge days: from the court of Gloriana (figuring Elizabeth) twelve Knights should ride out, each champion of a Virtue, each on a quest to overcome that Virtue's vicious foes. At some point he foreclosed his plan to a sequence of seven Books. As Alastair Fowler has argued, he gave to a recognised *genre* a new cosmic form, the seven days of the week each under its planet. Knight, Virtue and the terrain through which his adventures lead him all "belong" in their character to the Book's number and planet.

This sense of an indwelling potency or significance in each phenomenon of nature making up a vast harmonious whole (the sacral universe) is a sense we have lost – but can recapture through study and alert response to the poem's persuasive power. Artistic involvement in cosmic form is itself "formative": we participate in harmony. We progress with the Knight through his Book, learning to tell false from true, to defeat enticements or menaces by evil powers, to discern and to will the good to prevail. So we today can be fashioned "in virtuous and gentle discipline" as Spenser intended. All the time there are clues to historical events, which provide instances of profound issues under discussion. *The Faerie Queene* Books I to III, printed in 1590, won Spenser fame and a royal pension – but no post in England. Later Books conceived from Ireland under Elizabeth's misgovernment show a darkening image of the Queen, as lady of the Book. As Defender of the Faith she had shone in Una of Book I, Of Holinesse. As Astraea, heavenly maid of Justice, she has departed from the earth in Book V and she appears ambiguously in figures of female tyranny and qualified mercy. The Quest is for Irena – peace and Ireland, inbuilt irreconcileables. The Irish colouring deepens in the Book of Courtesie – and of "the savage man." The fragment of Book VII shows the enemy of cosmic harmony, mutability in nature and rebellion in man, arraigned before a council of Olympian gods – on Arlo Hill, visible from Spenser's Irish domain. Though the issues of this Elizabethan heroic poem are with us today sometimes in identical gear, luckily so is the vision of cosmic harmony, mankind and the graces dancing to the poet's piping, vouchsafed us still.

Spenser's major poems on love are similarly illuminating and "formative": love is the creating principle of the universe, flowing from God to man and returning upwards in aspiration towards true love through perception of true beauty. His last printed volume was *Fowre Hymnes* of such love and beauty. His single eclogue, *Colin Clout's Come Home Againe*, treats of varieties of love, of incestuous lust, and of never ending devotion for his own beloved, of false and true in sophisticated love-service of the sovereign lady, Elizabeth. His sonnet sequence, *Amoretti*, traces the psychic discipline of courtship on the outline of his own for Elizabeth Boyle, his second wife. It culminates in a celebration of marriage, *Epithalamion*, an ode. Here cosmic rhythm at its zenith of solar power at midsummer informs the record of the marriage day and night, a dance of the hours in a polyphonic pattern of number symbolism and delightful sounds. The modern reader is drawn in to participate fully as he learns to discern the harmony of intellectual concepts. (No other sonnet sequence had this climax of marriage, of cosmic joy and harmony.)

Prothalamion, his last poem, celebrates the espousal of two noble sisters, held at Essex House on Thames-side (where Spenser had served Lord Leicester). The brides made their way there by water and they are figured as swans, while the swan image also voices the poet's farewell singing. Symbolism of number in line and stanza gives cosmic orientation. Venus's blessing is asked for the brides and cosmic harmony is conjured between Cynthia/ Elizabeth and Lord Essex, for the moment in royal displeasure.

The minor poems offer "complaints" on mutability (a renaissance concern), a beast-fable mirroring personalities at court, several gracious trifles for presentation to noble patronesses and a fabled apology – written long since to Leicester, now dead – for that early offence.

Spenser made the experience of poetry universal in a new way. We can perceive the "profit and delight" it offers and learn to share it.

—Helena Mennie Shire

STANLEY, Thomas.   English.   Born in Cumberlow, Hertfordshire, baptized 8 September 1625. Educated at Pembroke Hall, now Pembroke College, Cambridge, matriculated 1639, M.A. 1642. Married Dorothy Enyon; nine children. After several years spent travelling on the Continent he retired to lodgings in the Middle Temple, London: his wealth allowed him to live as a man of letters and classical scholar and to act as patron to numerous writers; after collapse of the Royalist cause in 1649, continued this way of life in Cumberlow. Fellow of the Royal Society, 1663. *Died 12 April 1678.*

PUBLICATIONS

Collections

Poems and Translations, edited by Galbraith Miller Crump.   1962.

Verse

Poems and Translations.   1647; as *Poems*, 1651.
Psalterium Carolinum.   1657.

Other

*The History of Philosophy, Containing the Lives, Opinions, Actions, and Discourses of the
Philosophers of Every Sect.*   3 vols., 1655–62.

Bibliography: "Stanley: A Bibliography of His Writings in Prose and Verse" by M. Flower,
in *Transactions of the Cambridge Bibliographical Society,* 1950.

*   *   *

Thomas Stanley's main achievements are scholarly, but he was also a poet and translator,
and as such, he has a place among the Cavalier lyrists, together with his cousin Lovelace and
his friends Shirley and Hall.

Stanley's importance as a translator is partly historical, for his choice of subjects such as
Anacreon and Marino reflects the interests of his age. His graceful translations are not
conspicuously different from his own compositions, employing similar conceits and
paradoxes and the same vocabulary of hearts, flames, roses, ashes, stars, and snow. The
majority of Stanley's own poems are brief lyrics describing or addressed to a mistress whose
love he seeks, enjoys, or with quiet bitterness forgoes. These surpass not only his dull
excursion into political comment, *Psalterium Carolinum*, but also his "Register of Friends"
and other pieces addressed to male acquaintances, which – for all the value Stanley sets on
friendship – do not contain particularly memorable verse. Yet his love-lyrics, metrically
skilled and neatly constructed as they are, lack urgency, and while the plaintive cadences or
muted Platonism of individual pieces can be moving, read as a whole the collection gives the
impression of underlying languor. A poem to his friend Hammond contains an open
statement of preference for emotional non-involvement, which bears out the impression
given by his poetry as a whole. When translating he tends to tone down passages which
display a vigour or physicality not found in his own poems, of which Saintsbury remarked
with truth in his edition (*Minor Poets of the Caroline Period*, 1921): "There is a very little of
the *exercise* about them." Moreover, while Stanley's phraseology or material is at times
reminiscent of some of his contemporaries, the converse is hardly true, for no strongly
marked identity can be found in his work; nor does he ever achieve one of those golden
moments that lift so many of the minor poets of this age temporarily above themselves in one
or two poems of exceptional felicity.

Inasmuch as any personality at all emerges from the poems, it is a slightly schizoid one,
that prefers to avoid vulnerability by suppressing feeling, and suffers the inevitable
consequence of emotional flattening, a stoical dreariness devoid of hope. Hence while most of
his poems make their impact through the prettiness of the conceit on which they are based, or
the neatness of the conclusion, or the swell and fall of the verse which Stanley can contrive so
admirably, a number of his most effective pieces draw their strength from a grim preference
for suppression, a strongly willed refusal to participate, to be involved, to live. "The
Divorce," "The Repulse," "The Exequies," "Despair" – which rejects both pain and any
possibility of joy – and the heavily ominous "Expectation" are among the poems which show
this attitude most clearly. For all the charm of his lighter lyrics it is in these sombre pieces that
Stanley is most moving, for here the withholding of his full energies ceases to be a trivialising
inhibition, and becomes instead a source of genuine tension and power.

—Margaret Forey

STRODE, William.   English.   Born at Shaugh Prior, near Plympton, Devon, c. 1601. Educated at Westminster School, London (King's Scholar); entered Christ Church, Oxford, 1617, B.A. 1621, B.D. 1631, D.D. 1638. Married the sister-in-law of Bishop Skinner; one daughter. Public Orator, and Proctor, Oxford University, 1628. Ordained, 1628: Chaplain to Richard Corbett, Bishop of Oxford; held livings of East Bradenham, Norfolk, 1632–37; Blackbourton, Oxfordshire, from 1638; Badley, Northamptonshire, 1638–42; South Stoke, Oxfordshire, from 1641. *Died 11 March 1645.*

PUBLICATIONS

Collections

Poetical Works, edited by Bertram Dobell.   1907.

Play

The Floating Island (produced 1636).   1655; in *Poetical Works,* 1907.

Other

A Sermon Concerning Death and the Resurrection.   1644.
A Sermon Concerning Swearing.   1644.
A Sermon at a Visitation at Lynn.   1660.

Reading List: "The Poetry of Strode" by H. Morris, in *Tulane Studies in English,* 1957; *A Critical Edition of the Poetical Works of Strode* edited by Margaret Forey, unpublished B. Litt. thesis, 1966.

*   *   *

The poetry of William Strode was popular in his time, and was printed anonymously in miscellanies to the end of the century; the virtual extinction of his reputation after his death is probably largely due to the lack of any contemporary edition of his verse, much of which is still unpublished. His main affinities are with the courtly lyrists – indeed some of his poems have often been ascribed to Carew – and he shows interest in trying his hand at currently fashionable modes of writing, such as the mock-song and the "sic vita" poem; but, though he never attempted an original poem of any length, in some respects his range is wide, and another poet whom he often resembles is one very different from Carew, namely his patron Bishop Corbett. Strode shares Corbett's enjoyment of popular culture, and writes sympathetically of ordinary people and everyday events. His lively ballads and colloquial accounts of local affairs are humorous rather than witty; his tone is normally rollicking and genial, as in his thanks to a friend "For your good looks [i.e., welcoming expression] and for your claret,/For often bidding, 'Do not spare it,' " or his rueful complaint to his shoemaker, "How is't I pay to you/One groat for ev'ry toe in Spanish shoe?" Yet Strode was also capable of great delicacy, as in the recurrent bird-imagery which adds softness and even a touch of warmth to the gently falling snow in his most successful piece, the charming "I saw fair Cloris walk alone." Elsewhere the homeliness and simplicity of his imagery, his delight in what is neat and seemly, the spontaneity and naturalness of his manner, and the gentle dignity of his most successful treatments of serious topics give his work individuality and quiet charm. Unfortunately the quality of his poems is uneven, and such faults as flatness, forced wit, confused syntax, or the metrical weakness of his favourite enjambed couplets, mar pieces which contain fine lines or passages. Nevertheless his poetry deserves more attention than it has received. The sermons on the whole are of less value, though parts of *On Death and the Resurrection* are quietly moving.

Strode is also of interest as an anti-Puritan satirist. The influence of his staunchly Parliamentarian family (which included one of the Five Members, and was related by marriage to Pym), may be seen in the kindlier pieces, but his attack on Puritan hypocrisy in "The Town's New Teacher" – described by Firth in *Transactions of the Royal Historical Society*, 1912, as the best example of its kind – is scathing. Equally bitter, but less successful, was Strode's allegorical play *The Floating Island*, performed before the king in 1636. Strode was no dramatist, and although the performance was marked by Inigo Jones's introduction of movable wings to the English stage, the tedious piece was a failure with the court. However, the timing of its attack on Burton, Bastwick, and Prynne, whom Laud was shortly to arrest, makes it of some historical importance, since it was under Laud's aegis that the play was produced.

—Margaret Forey

SUCKLING, Sir John. English. Born in Whitton, Middlesex, baptized 10 February 1609. Educated at Trinity College, Cambridge, 1623–26, left without taking a degree; Gray's Inn, London, 1626–27. Inherited large estates on the death of his father, 1627, and attended court, 1627–29; travelled on the continent, returned to England and knighted, 1630; served in the English embassy to Gustavus Adolphus, 1631; returned to England, 1632, and became a court poet and attendant to Charles I; with his followers took up the King's cause in the first Bishops War, 1639, and served as a captain of carabineers in the second Bishops War, 1640; Member of the short Parliament, 1640; took part in the "Army Plot," 1641: when the plot was discovered, forced to flee to Paris, where he died. *Died in 1641.*

PUBLICATIONS

Collections

Works, edited by Thomas Clayton and L. A. Beaurline.   2 vols., 1971.
Cavalier Poets, edited by Thomas Clayton.   1978.

Plays

The Sad One (produced 1632?).   In *Last Remains,* 1659.
Aglaura (produced 1637; revised version, produced 1638).   1638.
The Goblins (produced 1637–41?).   In *Fragmenta Aurea,* 1646.
The Discontented Colonel.   1642; as *Brennoralt* (produced 1639–41?), in *Fragmenta Aurea,* 1646.

Other

A Letter Written to the Lower Houses of Parliament.   1641.
A Letter Found in the Privy Lodgings at Whitehall.   1641.
Fragmenta Aurea (miscellany).   1646.
Last Remains.   1659.

Bibliography: in *Works* 1971.

*   *   *

In comparison with other luminaries at the court of Charles I such as William Davenant, Richard Lovelace, and Edmund Waller, Sir John Suckling was clearly the most naturally gifted, versatile, and undisciplined. His posthumous collection *Fragmenta Aurea* contains four plays, numerous love lyrics, verse satires, several political and religious tracts, and almost fifty personal letters, many of them as well-written and interesting as Byron's. An excellent critic, he was an avid reader of Shakespeare, Jonson, and Donne, but his own careless verses only rarely reflect their patience with language. In such occasional sparks of lyricism as his famous song from *Aglaura* ("Why so pale and wan, fond lover?") he is a worthy disciple of Jonson, but such flashes of genius are rarely sustained.

Suckling's play *Aglaura* was performed at court in 1637 by the King's Men, and when it failed to please as a tragedy Suckling gave the last act a happy ending and showed it again the following year to great royal applause. *The Goblins* is Suckling's only comedy and possibly his best play for its lively presentation of a band of Robin Hood bandits. In 1639 he returned to tragedy with *Brennoralt*, a thinly-disguised political allegory attacking the Scots. His unfinished tragedy, *The Sad One* is, like his other plays, slipshod in construction and inconsistent in characterization, but occasionally illuminated by brilliant dialogue and graceful songs.

Suckling's best-known verses are "A Ballad upon a Wedding" and his satiric poem "The Wits" ("A Sessions of the Poets"), in which he wittily portrays poets like Jonson, Carew, and Davenant competing for the laurel. His love poems are typical of his generation of cavalier lyrists – cynical, witty, derisively anti-Petrarchan in the manner of the young Donne's "Go and catch a falling star," but without Donne's complex metaphors and iron-hard language. The love lyrics were calculated to convey the impression of a cynical rake, a pose belied by many of Suckling's personal letters and his eminently earnest anti-Socinian treatise "An Account of Religion by Reason."

—James E. Ruoff

SYLVESTER, Joshua(h).   English.   Born in the Medway region of Kent in 1563. Educated at the school of Adrian à Saravia, Southampton, 1573–76. Married to Mary Sylvester; five or six children. Businessman and merchant; later associated with the Earl of Essex; Groom to the Chamber of Prince Henry, 1606; Secretary to the merchant adventurers, and lived at Middleburg, 1613–18. *Died 28 September 1618.*

PUBLICATIONS

Collections

Works, edited by A. B. Grosart.   2 vols., 1880.

Verse

A Canticle of the Victory Obtained by Henry the Fourth at Ivry, from Du Bartas.   1590.
The Triumph of Faith, The Sacrifice of Isaac, The Ship-Wreck of Jonas, A Song of the Victory, from Du Bartas.   1592.
The Profit of Imprisonment: A Paradox, from Odet de la Noue Lord of Teligni.   1594.
Monodia: An Elegy in Commemoration of Dame Helen Branch, Widow.   1594.
The Second Week or Childhood of the World.   1598.
Bartas His Divine Weeks and Works.   1605; revised edition, 1621; edited by Susan Snyder, 2 vols., 1978.
Posthumous Bartas: The Third Day of His Second Week.   1606.
Posthumous Bartas: The Fore-Noon of the Fourth Day of His Second Week.   1607.
Lachrimae Lachrimarum.   1612; with *Other Elegies,* 1613.
The Parliament of Virtues Royal, from Jean Bertaut and others.   1614; *Second Session,* 2 vols., 1615.
The Sacred Works.   1620.
The Maiden's Blush; or, Joseph, from Girolamo Fracastoro.   1620.
The Wood-Man's Bear.   1620.
Panthea; or, Divine Wishes and Meditations.   1630.

Play

Nebuchadnezzer's Fiery Furnace, edited by M. Rösler.   1936.

Other

Translator, *A Panegyric of Henry the Fourth,* by Pierre Matthieu, with *The Heroic Life of Henry the Fourth* by E. Grimeston.   1612.

Reading List: *Du Bartas en Angleterre* by H. Ashton, 1908; *Milton's Use of Du Bartas* by G. C. Taylor, 1934.

*   *   *

Preceded by Sir Philip Sidney and King James, among others, Joshua Sylvester turned into English the ambitious religious poetry of the French Protestant, Guillaume de Salluste du Bartas (1544–1590), and published the most complete translation of his *Sepmaines* as *Bartas His Devine Weekes and Workes*, which ran through half a dozen editions by the mid-seventeenth century. The first "week," in seven "days" and seven books, expands the first chapter of Genesis through surveys of knowledge from mineralogy to morality. Thus, in the Third Day, on the division of the Earth and Sea, the poet proposes to discuss both the "Bounds of the ocean's rage" and "Why it is salt," along with "Mines, Metals, Gemms of price:/Right use of Gold: the Load-stone's rare effects:/The Country-life preferr'd in all respects." The second, unfinished week undertakes the entire sacred history of the world, and proceeds in four "days" from Adam through David.

As Sylvester turns the hexameters of du Bartas into thousands of heroic couplets, there are inevitably some anticipations of eighteenth-century moral essays in verse. Thus the *Devine Weekes* sometimes suggests Pope in epigrammatic neatness and in moral stance, as in scorn for mortals who proudly speculate in theology until "th'Author's praise they in themselves eclipse."

Milton and the young Dryden were among Sylvester's readers, although Dryden in his later years scorned the verse as "fustian." Admirers of the translation are apt to appreciate precisely those qualities which Sylvester and du Bartas share: large enthusiasm, quaint simile, exuberant diction. Sylvester can parallel du Bartas' wordplay as deftly as in turning "Bruyant, courant, errant, terrible, horrible, rible," into "They jumble, tumble, rumble, rage, and rave." His additions to du Bartas are usually no more than adaptation of references to French history or geography so that they become familiarly English.

Although he wrote a substantial volume of devotional, complimentary, satiric, and (somewhat obscurely) autobiographical verse of his own, Sylvester's positive reputation rests on his translations. His original compositions are seldom reprinted, read, or praised, despite the ingenuity of anagrams, the visual allure of shaped poems, or the enticement of such titles as "Tobacco Battered and the Pipes Shattered (about their Ears that idlely Idolize so base and barbarous a Weed; or at least-wise over-love so loathsome Vanitie)."

—Kay Stevenson

TOWNSHEND, Aurelian. English. Born, possibly in Norfolk, c. 1583. Nothing is known of his early life and education. Married in 1622; three sons and two daughters. Steward to Sir Robert Cecil, afterwards Earl of Salisbury; a friend of Ben Jonson; accompanied Lord Herbert of Cherbury on a tour abroad, 1608; resident in London in the 1620's and was prominent as a court poet: probably held the post of gentleman of the privy chamber; succeeded Ben Jonson as composer of court masques, 1631–32; granted freedom from arrest for debt by the House of Lords, 1643; possibly in the service of the Earl of Dorset at Knole in 1640's. *Died c. 1651.*

PUBLICATIONS

Collections

Poems and Masks, edited by E. K. Chambers. 1912.
Poems and Masques, edited by Cedric C. Brown. 1977

Plays

Albion's Triumph (produced 1632). 1632.
Tempe Restored (produced 1632). 1632.

*   *   *

Although poems have turned up since E. K. Chambers's edition of 1912, the canon of Aurelian Townshend's verse is still small, and many surviving datable poems come from his middle and later years. Clearly, some lyrics must precede the time at which he was chosen to write verses for court masques in 1631/2, but there is little sign that Townshend saw himself publicly as a notable poet, even after he was taken up by the Caroline court and found serviceable for dramatic and celebratory verses. Only his masques and a few occasional poems were printed in his lifetime. A few lyrics found their way into songbooks from 1651 onwards. Otherwise, the verse survives in manuscript anthologies.

The songs in *Albions Triumph* and *Tempe Restored* are neat but lack the variety of tone or declamatory energy of Jonson or Carew. The opening verses of *Albions Triumph* are laboured. Those who have noticed Townshend have usually commented on an individual lyrical quality in his poetry, and it is true that one or two of his non-lyrical poems (e.g., the elegy on the Countess of Bridgewater) have flat passages. Even at his best and wittiest, Townshend rarely surprises in sentiment: the best of his occasional and celebratory verse is a decorous and direct, if sometimes conceited, expression of the obvious.

Nevertheless, in the poem on Venetia Digby he proclaimed that he delighted "most in unusual ways." Perhaps a striving for originality can be found in his attempt to emulate the display of Donne, for example in "The Paradox" and "Hide not thy love." These longer poems achieve distinguished lines and stanzas that are Donne-like, though finally they lack the dramatic compression, immediacy, and calculated obliqueness of Donne. Townshend's originality may also be seen in the variety of genuinely lyrical measures and forms he tries. Some poems which seem rhythmically overdetermined to the mere reader, or awkward because of disparate stanza-forms, were written with an eye chiefly on the conventions of song-writing and song-setting. Fortunately, the music for eight songs survives. Seven were set by Henry Lawes. Within lyrical kinds, Townshend's range is broad and indicates Caroline courtly fashion, from the delicate parody of Herrick's "Amidst the myrtles" ("Thou shepherd whose intentive eye") to the stout bacchanalian ditty, "Bacchus, I-acchus," a chorus-song written for the court revival of Cartwright's *The Royal Slave*. There are signs also that his range could have extended further outside the lyrical: his verse-letter to Carew on the death of Gustavus Adolphus convinces in the closing heroic and elegiac imagery, nicely set off by the opening section of relaxed colloquialism. At his finest Townshend judges well the tone for aristocratic and courtly occasions. The success of "Victorious Beauty" as a poem addressed to a noble patroness lies in the balance between witty impudence and subservient social grace. In this kind of delicacy Townshend is strikingly representative of the more refined manners of the Caroline court.

—Cedric C. Brown

TRAHERNE, Thomas. English. Born in Hereford c. 1638. Educated at Brasenose College, Oxford, B.A. 1656, M.A. 1661, B.D. 1669. Took holy orders: Rector of Credenhill, Herefordshire, 1657; Chaplain to Sir Orlando Bridgeman, Lord Keeper of the Great Seal, 1667. *Died 27 September 1674.*

PUBLICATIONS

Collections

Centuries, Poems, and Thanksgivings, edited by H. M. Margoliouth.   2 vols., 1958.
Poems, Centuries, and Three Thanksgivings, edited by Anne Ridler.   1966.

Verse

Poems of Felicity, edited by H. I. Bell.   1910.
Poetical Works, Now First Published from the Original Manuscripts, edited by Bertram Dobell.   1903.
Felicities (includes prose), edited by Arthur Quiller-Couch.   1934.

Other

Roman Forgeries.   1673.
Christian Ethics; or Divine Morality Opening the Way to Blessedness.   1675; edited by G. R. Guffey and C. L. Marks, 1968.
A Serious and Pathetical Contemplation of the Mercies of God.   1699; edited by Roy Daniells, 1941.
Hexameron; or, Meditations on the Six Days of Creation, in *A Collection of Meditations and Devotions.*   1717; edited by G. R. Guffey, 1966.
Centuries of Meditations, Now First Published from the Author's Manuscript, edited by Bertram Dobell.   1908; edited by J. Farrar, 1960.
Of Magnanimity and Charity, edited by J. R. Slater.   1942.

Reading List: *Traherne* by Q. Iredale, 1935; *Traherne* by G. I. Wade, revised edition, 1946; *Three Metaphysical Poets* by Margaret Willy, 1961; *The Paradise Within: Studies in Vaughan, Traherne, and Milton* by Louis J. Martz, 1964; *Traherne: Mystic and Poet* by K. W. Salter, 1964; *The Mystical Poetry of Traherne* by A. L. Clements, 1969; *Mystical Symbolism in the Poetry of Traherne* by Alison J. Sherrington, 1970; *The Expanded Voice: The Art of Traherne* by Stanley Stewart, 1970; *The Temple of Eternity: Traherne's Philosophy of Time* by Richard D. Jordan, 1972.

*   *   *

When Thomas Traherne's work was rediscovered, by chance, two-and-a-half centuries after his death, its author was at first thought to be Henry Vaughan. There are striking resemblances in the style and spirit of their work, and in their irradiating imagery of light, and, above all, in the affinity of their attitude towards childhood.

For Traherne, as for Vaughan, "The first Impressions are Immortal all" ("Dumnesse"). In poems like "The Salutation," "Eden," "Wonder," and "Shadows in the Water," and his prose masterpiece *Centuries of Meditations*, we are reminded also of Blake and Wordsworth. The same luminous intensity of vision evokes the child's innocence of "the Dirty Devices of this World," the freshness of his delight, and that sense of limitless horizons which made "All Time ... Eternity, and a Perpetual Sabbath." Perceiving the kinship between the "Infant-eye" view of the universe, with its intuitions of a world beyond the visible one, and the mystic's intimations of harmony and happiness, Traherne believed that these held the key to the most fundamental realities of human life and its relationship with God. Only through regaining that wisdom "unattainable by Book," and becoming "as it were a little Child again," could a man enjoy the world in communion with his Creator: through those praises which, Traherne declared, are "the Marks and Symptoms of a Happy Life ... the very End for which the World was created."

"Enjoy" is perhaps the most frequent verb in Traherne's work. Its objects are marvellously comprehensive, ranging from sea, sky, stars, and the "lovely lively air" to Blake's grain of sand and "evry Spire of Grass"; from the diverse personalities of his fellow men to the simple fulfilment of daily material needs. In his profound conviction of the interdependence of the worlds of sense and spirit, each enriching and intensifying the other, the senses are seen – in the metaphor of "News" – as ambassadors, bringing tidings from a foreign country which houses man's true treasure. To this "Christian epicurean," as he termed himself, an ascetic rejection of the divinely planned universe seemed a denial of that desire implanted in him as positive proof of his immortal soul and its destination. Savouring life to the utmost on both planes, the natural and the transcendental, Traherne is indeed – in his own phrase – "Felicity's perfect Lover."

Traherne's is a poetry of scattered felicities: his impetuous, exuberant urgency tends too often to spill over into repetitive diffuseness. Apart from a handful of completely achieved pieces, he lacks as a poet the verbal discipline of his spiritual autobiography, *Centuries of Meditations*. Here, as nowhere else, he achieves a harmonious fusion of form with content, of the sonorous splendours of the older style with the vigorous simplicity of the new. This eloquent and impassioned testament to his creed of dedicated joy places Traherne among the masters of English religious prose.

—Margaret Willy

TURBERVILE, George. English. Born in Whitchurch, Dorset, c. 1543. Educated at Winchester School (scholar); New College, Oxford; resided at one of the Inns of Court, 1562. Married in 1574. Fellow of New College, 1561; Secretary to Thomas Randolph, Ambassador to Russia, 1568–69; retired to an estate in Shapwick, Dorset, 1577. *Died c. 1597.*

PUBLICATIONS

Collections

Poems, edited by John Erskine Hankins.   1952.

Verse

The Eclogues of Mantuan Turned into English.   1567; edited by Douglas Bush, 1937.
The Heroical Epistles of Ovid, with Aulus Sabinus' Answers.   1567; edited by F. S. Boas, 1928.
Epitaphs, Epigrams, Songs, and Sonnets, with a Discourse of the Affections of Tymetes to Pyndara.   1567; edited by J. P. Collier, 1867.
A Plain Path to Perfect Virtue Devised by Mancinus.   1568.

Other

Tragical Tales Translated out of Sundry Italians, with Some Other Broken Pamphlets and Epistles Sent to Certain of His Friends in England, at His Being in Moscovia.   1576(?); edited in part by L. E. Berry and R. O. Crummery, in *Rude and Barbarous Kingdom,* 1969.

Editor, *The Book of Falconry or Hawking.*   1575.
Editor, *The Noble Art of Venery or Hunting.*   1575(?); edited version, 1908.

Reading List: *Life and Works* by John Erskine Hankins, 1940; Introduction by Richard J. Panofsky to *Epitaphes, Epigrams, Songs, and Sonets,* 1977.

*   *   *

George Turbervile belonged to the energetic generation of young writers who set about at the start of Elizabeth's reign to build a vernacular library for England by the wholesale importation of ancient and foreign works. Scion of a prominent Dorsetshire family, he was educated at important centers of the New Learning, Winchester School and New College, Oxford. A facility for making verses put him much in demand among his fellows as a source of love letters; Turbervile made it the basis of a prolific career as a poet and translator. He englished a variety of works, from Ovid's *Heroicall Epistles* through *A Plaine Path to Perfect Vertue* by Mancinus to a pair of elegant treatises on falconry and hunting compiled "out of the best aucthors." He favored English schoolboys with a useful version of Mantuan's eclogues, and his versifications of melodramatic Italian novelle catered to still another segment of Elizabethan taste.

The volume of "Tragicall Tales" also contained a miscellany of original work, including reports on a 1568 trip to Muscovy that Hakluyt reprinted. The bulk of Turbervile's own poetry appeared in his *Epitaphes, Epigrams, Songs, and Sonets.* A bookish poet, he loaded his verses with his learning. The copious enlargement and over-precious rhetorical artifice that passed for stylistic elegance in his day are likely to displease a modern ear – as they already displeased Turbervile's younger contemporaries less than two decades later. Whether reciting Ovid at length to his mistress, expanding apothegms by grammar-school schemes, or praising deceased nobles by comparing them to every god in the pantheon, Turbervile too often smothers his poems with pedantry. Only when pursuing a different stylistic ideal, such as the clarity of the song set to music or the efficiency of the epigram, does he merit Yvor Winters's praise as "one of the most minute stylists of the century." Among his imitations of poems from the Greek Anthology are to be found Turbervile's most readable and appealing productions.

Like many poets of his generation who were affected by the ethical tone of their humanist education, Turbervile experienced some discomfort with poetic love. He insisted on the inconsequentiality of his love poems, calling them trifles and toys, and he reached toward an urbane detachment from the follies of conventional *amour.* When he strung a number of poems together into a continuous narrative and offered it to his young readers as "a Glasse & Myrror for them to gaze vpon" to teach them "to flee that fonde and filthie affection of poysoned & vnlawful loue," he discovered the characteristic Elizabethan mode of love poetry, the amatory sequence, and was the first to commit one to print.

Turbervile experimented with dozens of verse forms, and with subjects, tones, and stylistic devices of every description. Though his work was rapidly superseded by that of later poets, he laid down a broad foundation for them to build upon, and his contribution has too frequently been overlooked.

—William E. Sheidley

TUSSER, Thomas.   English.   Born in Rivenhall, Essex, c. 1524. Trained as a singer: chorister at Wallingford College, Berkshire, then at St. Paul's Cathedral, London; educated at Eton College; King's College, and Trinity Hall, Cambridge. Married twice; second wife, Amy Moon, by whom he had three sons, one daughter. Resided at court as musician to Lord Paget for ten years; thereafter settled as a farmer at Cattiwade, Suffolk; after death of his first wife lived variously in Norfolk, Essex, and London, and then Cambridge: matriculated as a servant of Trinity Hall. Died in debtor's prison, London. *Died 3 May 1580.*

PUBLICATIONS

Verse

> *A Hundred Good Points of Husbandry.*   1557; augmented edition, with *A Hundred Good Points of Huswifery,* 1570; augmented edition, as *Five Hundred Points of Good Husbandry United to as Many of Good Huswifery,* 1573; augmented edition, 1580; edited by W. Payne and S. J. Herrtage, 1878; 1571 text edited by Dorothy Hartley, 1931.

*   *   *

Thomas Tusser's fame rests entirely upon one extremely popular farmer's almanac in doggerel verse, first published in 1557 by Richard Tottel as *A Hundred Good Points of Husbandry* and thereafter much augmented. Its final version, as *Five Hundred Points of Good Husbandry* in 1573, contains additional illustrations, a section of good housewifery, and autobiographical verses of Tusser's experiences as a farmer in Suffolk. *Five Hundred Points* provides practical advice on planting, tillage, forestry, animal husbandry, home economics, and weather. Like Benjamin Franklin's Poor Richard, Tusser embellishes his instructions with gossipy antecdotes, jokes, pious truisms, and homespun observations on men and manners. An execrable poet, Tusser endeared himself to generations of readers for his sustained tone of rustic common sense and congeniality rather than for any aesthetic qualities, yet his work clearly illustrates that before the Industrial Revolution ordinary people found poetry and the most practical subjects entirely compatible. Among the most popular books of the sixteenth century, *Five Hundred Points* was reprinted almost consistently down to the modern period, with introductions by Sir Walter Scott in 1810 and Rudyard Kipling in 1931.

—James E. Ruoff

VAUGHAN, Henry.   Welsh.   Born in Newton-by-Usk, Llansaintfraed, Brecknockshire, 17 April 1622. Privately educated at Llangattock, 1632–38, then at Jesus College, Oxford, matriculated 1638, left without taking a degree; studied law in London, then medicine, and qualified as a physician. Served in Colonel Price's Royalist Company, as a surgeon, 1645.

Married 1) Catherine Wise c. 1646 (died, 1653), three daughters and one son; 2) his first wife's sister Elizabeth Wise c. 1655, three daughters and one son. Practised medicine in Brecknock. 1645–50, and in Newton-by-Usk, 1650 until the end of his life. *Died 23 April 1695.*

PUBLICATIONS

Collections

Works, edited by L. C. Martin.   2 vols., 1914; revised edition, 1957.
Complete Poems, edited by Alan Rudman.   1976.

Verse

Poems, with the Tenth Satire of Juvenal Englished.   1646.
Silex Scintillans; or, Sacred Poems and Private Ejaculations.   1650; revised edition, 1655.
Olor Iscanus: A Collection of Some Select Poems and Translations.   1651.
Thalia Rediviva: The Pass-Times and Diversions of a Country-Muse, in Choice Poems on Several Occasions, with Some Learned Remains.   1678.

Other

The Mount of Olives; or, Solitary Devotions.   1652.

Editor, *Flores Solitudinis: Certain Rare and Elegant Pieces Collected in His Sickness and Retirement.*   1654.

Translator, *Hermetical Physic*, by Henry Nolle.   1655.

Bibliography: *A Comprehensive Bibliography of Vaughan* by E. L. Marilla, 1948, *Supplement* by Marilla and James D. Simmonds, 1963.

Reading List: *Vaughan: A Life and Interpretation* by F. E. Hutchinson, 1947; *Vaughan* by E. W. Williamson, 1953; *Vaughan: Experience and Tradition*, 1959, and *The Unprofitable Servant in Vaughan*, 1963, both by Ross Garner; *Of Paradise and Light: A Study of Vaughan's Silex Scintillans* by E. C. Pettet, 1960; *Three Metaphysical Poets* by Margaret Willy, 1961; *On the Mystical Poetry of Vaughan*, 1962, and *Masques of God: Form and Theme in the Poetry of Vaughan*, 1972, both by R. A. Durr; *The Paradise Within: Studies in Vaughan, Traherne, and Milton* by Louis J. Martz, 1964.

*   *   *

Henry Vaughan's phrase about one who "sees Invisibles" epitomizes his own mystical insight and exaltation. In all his mature work the influence of George Herbert, in subject, spirit, and even language, is pervasive and profound. Yet Vaughan is no mere imitator of the man he acknowledged as master in his poetry and religious life alike. Lacking Herbert's sense of form and verbal economy, Vaughan at his best soars to a lyrical rapture which is distinctively his own.

On all his books after the first, Vaughan inscribes himself with the title of "Silurist" – a reference to the ancient tribe of Silures which had once inhabited the south-eastern district of his native Wales. His early verse is not remarkable, consisting mainly of derivative love-songs in the manner of contemporaries like Donne. Throughout the 1650's he was publishing various prose translations and contemplative works. His volume *Thalia Rediviva*, sub-titled "The Pastimes and Diversions of a Countrey-Muse," includes an "Elegiac Eclogue" between two shepherds, possibly written for the death in 1648 of his younger brother William, and afterwards adapted for that, in 1666, of Thomas his twin.

According to a mutual friend, Henry and Thomas Vaughan resembled each other as closely in spirit as in body: "Not only your *faces*, but your *wits* are *Twins*." Both brothers were keenly interested in the art of alchemy, and published translations and prose treatises on Hermeticism. The traditions of this occult philosophy, which attracted other seventeenth-century writers like Donne and Sir Thomas Browne, furnished Henry Vaughan with various apt and fruitful analogies for his poems.

It is, however, essentially as a Christian poet that Vaughan seeks to communicate his apprehensions of spiritual reality. In his greatest work, *Silex Scintillans*, two contrasting themes are clearly defined. One is a desolating sense of alienation from God, caused by man's "black self-wil" and "hard, stonie heart." A prisoner in "sad captivity" on earth, the exiled spirit yearns for its true home, now "so far/That he hath quite forgot how to go there." Although disgusted with "impure, rebellious clay" and the "dark Confusions" it houses, Vaughan does not regard material substance as intrinsically evil. Otherwise he could not have expressed that frank and lyrical delight in nature which forms the other main theme of *Silex Scintillans*.

The mounting, exultant surge of praise in "The Morning Watch" expresses the central idea of prayer as "the world in tune." In many other poems Vaughan sees the wonders of creation as the outward proof and pledge of God's power and love, actively proclaiming that Presence which animates and illumines it. For him the visible, finite beauties of cloud and flower, "purling Corn," "primros'd" spring path, and the snow that "*Candies* our Countries wooddy brow," which he celebrates with such delicate precision and felicity of phrase, are divinely infused embodiments of invisible and infinite Beauty which show man "heaven ... and point him the way home." God's "wondrous Method" in ordering the universe is echoed in man's spiritual processes. One of Vaughan's favourite images for the soul is that of a flower or plant: shaken by the storms of sin, thirsting for dew and aspiring upwards "as flow'rs do to the Sun"; or sensing, like the child in "The Retreate," "through all this fleshly dresse/Bright *shootes* of everlastingnesse."

It is, Vaughan believes, in that "first, happy age;/An age without distast and warrs," before the spirit is separated from its source or has "walkt above/A mile, or two, from its first love," that man is nearest the state of his primal innocence. He laments that, distracted by the world's insistent claims and clamour, "I find my selfe the lesse, the more I grow." In poems like "Childe-hood," "Looking Back," and "The Retreate" – the most perfect and poignant expression of that regret – he yearns no less passionately than Wordsworth in the Immortality Ode to regain the lost clarity and purity of vision which were his when he "Shin'd in [his] Angell-infancy."

The verb is characteristic. Images of light irradiate Vaughan's most memorable poems as symbols of spiritual illumination. "The World," with its famous opening,

> I saw Eternity the other night
> Like a great *Ring* of pure and endless light,
>   All calm, as it was bright,

opposes the light of God to the darkness of mundane preoccupations. God's "deep, but dazling darkness," in "The Night," is matched in "They are all gone into the world of light!"

by the metaphor of death as "the Jewel of the Just,/Shining nowhere, but in the dark," and sight of the dead walking "in an Air of glory,/Whose light doth trample on my days." Many lesser-known poems, too, make light synonymous with man's experience of God, whose "beams, and brightnes" are invoked to

> brush me with thy light, that I
> May shine unto a perfect day....
> Rove in that mighty, and eternall light
> Where no rude shade, or night
> Shall dare approach us.

Vaughan is, however, a disconcertingly uneven writer. Too many of his poems are as trite and commonplace in sentiment and expression as the average hymn; and his capacity to sustain a single poem at a consistently satisfying level is comparatively rare. Yet where he does (to adapt his title image) strike sparks from the flint, the illumination is unforgettable. These isolated splendours which haunt the inward ear, as much as the impact of such unified and wholly realized poems as "Man," "The Retreat," and "The Morning Watch," assure Vaughan his permanence among the English religious poets.

—Margaret Willy

WALLER, Edmund.   English.   Born in Coleshill, Hertfordshire, now Buckinghamshire, 3 March 1606. Educated at Eton College; King's College, Cambridge, matriculated 1620, may have left without taking a degree; admitted member of Lincoln's Inn, London, 1622. Married 1) Anne Banks in 1631 (died, 1634); 2) Mary Bracey in 1644 (died, 1677). Wealthy landowner: inherited large estate at Beaconsfield, Buckinghamshire, 1616. Served in Parliament: Member for Amersham, 1621, Ilchester, 1624, Chipping Wycombe, 1626, and Amersham, 1628–29, and St. Ives, in the Long Parliament, 1640; defended episcopacy, and conducted the impeachment of Sir Francis Crawley, 1641; opposed raising of troops by Parliament, 1642; appointed commissioner to treat with Charles I at Oxford, 1643; involved in an attempt to seize the City of London for Charles ("Waller's Plot"), 1643: expelled from Parliament, 1643, imprisoned in the Tower of London, 1643–44, then banished from the country; lived in France, 1644 until the banishment was revoked by the House of Commons, 1651; returned to England, appointed a commissioner of trade, 1655; elected to Parliament as Member for Hastings, 1661, and sat in the House of Commons until his death. Member of the Royal Society, 1661. *Died 21 October 1687.*

PUBLICATIONS

Collections

Works in Verse and Prose, edited by E. Fenton.   1729.
Poems, edited by G. Thorn Drury.   2 vols., 1893.

Verse

To the King's Most Excellent Majesty.   1642.
Poems.   1645; Second Part, 1690.
A Panegyric to My Lord Protector.   1655.
Upon the Late Storm, and the Death of His Highness.   1658.
The Passion of Dido for Aeneas, with Sidney Godolphin.   1658.
To the King, upon His Majesty's Happy Return.   1660.
To My Lady Morton.   1661.
A Poem on St. James's Park.   1661.
To the Queen, upon Her Majesty's Birthday.   1663.
Instructions to a Painter.   1666.
Of the Lady Mary.   1677.
A Poem on the Present Assembling.   1679.
A Poem upon the Present Assembly of Parliament.   1685.
Divine Poems.   1685.

Plays

Pompey the Great, with others, from a play by Corneille (produced 1664).   1664.
The New Masque for The Maid's Tragedy by Beaumont and Fletcher.   1683(?).
The Maid's Tragedy, from the play by Beaumont and Fletcher (produced 1689).   In
    Poems, 1690.

Other

The Works of Waller in This Parliament.   1644.
The Life and Death of William Laud.   1645.

Reading List: Towards an Augustan Poetic: Waller's "Reform" of English Poetry by A. W.
Allison, 1962; The Poetry of Limitation: A Study of Waller by W. L. Cherniak, 1968.

*   *   *

To the generation of poets that succeeded him, Edmund Waller appeared one of the most
important writers of the seventeenth century. Dryden, in his preface to Walsh's Dialogue
Concerning Women, 1691, even said that if Waller had not written "none of us could write."
Although Waller also anticipated the Augustan age in attitudes and diction, it was primarily
his versification that made him so important an influence on Dryden and later on Pope. It was
Waller who, together with Denham, first made conspicuous and extensive use of a balanced,
end-stopped couplet, discarding the slackly-rhymed enjambed couplet, often metrically
rough, favoured in the early part of the century. He makes frequent use of parallel or
antithetical phrases: "A prince with such advantages as these,/Where he persuades not, may
command a peace"; "The valiant Duke! whose early deeds abroad/Such rage in fight and art
in conduct showed./His bright sword now a dearer interest draws,/His brother's glory and
his country's cause." Syntactical patterning is also achieved by inversion: "Light was the
wound, the prince's care unknown." Diction is abstract, Latinate and elevated – where
Donne had said "Till age snow white hairs on thee," Waller speaks of "the violation/Of
coming years." Epithets are appropriate, not startling. The result is poetry essentially
civilised, showing manners, order, control. It is better suited to public occasions than to
intimate exchanges, and Waller employed it frequently in celebrating public events. The

blandness of his style extended to his matter: though his successors were to use his shapely couplet for satiric purposes, Waller himself devoted it to heroic panegyric. As times changed, his subject-matter changed; praise of Cromwell was succeeded by praise of Charles II; the tone and style, however, remained constant.

Yet the poems that influenced the Augustans are not those which have survived. Greater masters of the couplet followed and eclipsed his achievements in versification, and Waller is now remembered mainly as the author of the exquisite lyric, "Go, lovely rose." Even here, where his subject-matter was most Caroline, we find him using effects that Pope was later to adopt and transform, for "Tell her that wastes her time and me" gains its poignancy from the zeugma which replaces the expected "her time and mine," so drawing attention to the double meaning of "waste." Other lyrics derived from the Caroline tradition have retained their power: "On a girdle," "To a very young lady," and "It is not that I love you less." "Of the last verse in the book," which Waller wrote in his eighties, treats of old age and approaching death with a grave dignity quite unlike the graceful playfulness of the earlier lyrics. The theme is summarised in its most famous couplet: "The soul's dark cottage, battered and decayed,/Lets in new light through chinks that time has made." Augustan in its powerful generalisations, impressive in its dignified serenity, Waller's last poem shows a life not conspicuous for nobility attaining a noble close.

—Margaret Forey

WALTON, Izaak.   English.   Born in Stafford, 9 August 1593. Married 1) Rachel Floud in 1626 (died, 1640), seven children; 2) Anne Ken in 1647 (died, 1662), one daughter and two sons. Apprenticed to a London sempstress c. 1610; set up as a draper in Fleet Street, 1614; Freeman of the Ironmongers' Company, 1618; retired, 1644; lived with Bishop George Morley at Farnham, Surrey, 1662–78, and with his son-in-law at Winchester, 1678 until his death. *Died 15 December 1683.*

PUBLICATIONS

Collections

The Compleat Walton, edited by Geoffrey Keynes.   1929.

Prose

The Life of John Donne.   1658; revised edition, in *Lives,* 1670.
The Compleat Angler; or, The Contemplative Man's Recreation.   1653; revised edition, 1658, 1661; in *The Universal Angler,* 1676.
The Life of Mr. Rich. Hooker.   1665; revised edition, in *Lives,* 1670.
The Life of Dr. Sanderson, with tracts by Sanderson and a sermon by Hooker.   1678; edited by W. Jacobson, in *Works of Sanderson,* vol. 6, 1854.

The Lives of Dr. John Donne, Sir Henry Wotton, Mr. Richard Hooker, Mr. George Herbert. 1670; revised edition, 1675; edited by George Saintsbury, 1927.
Love and Truth. 1680.

Editor, *Reliquiae Wottonianae; or, A Collection of Lives, Letters, Poems,* by Sir Henry Wotton. 1651; revised edition, 1654, 1685.

Bibliography: in *The Compleat Walton,* 1929.

Reading List: *Walton* by Margaret Bottrall, 1955; *The Making of Walton's Lives* by D. Novarr, 1958; *Biography in the Hands of Walton, Johnson, and Boswell* by J. E. Butt, 1966; *The Art of the Compleat Angler* by J. R. Cooper, 1968.

*   *   *

Chance rather than design led Izaak Walton to a literary career. He was a London tradesman who had enjoyed no educational advantages. A man of great integrity, a traditionalist in religion and politics, he must have possessed a genius for friendship. It was through the encouragement of such high-ranking friends as Sir Henry Wotton, Bishop Morley, and Charles Cotton that he became a writer of real distinction.

Walton was a pioneer in biography, and his *Lives,* particularly those of Herbert and Donne, are small masterpieces; but by far his most famous book is *The Compleat Angler.* It was not, however, until its pastoral charm caught the fancy of Charles Lamb and other Romantic critics that it became something of a best-seller as well as a classic. His original readers certainly welcomed the book, and Walton revised it several times; but to them it was primarily a fishing manual, though diversified by many songs and poems, anecdotes and snatches of moralising. Only posterity could fully appreciate the idyllic quality of Walton's portrayal of innocent country pastimes and pleasures in an unspoilt English landscape, or relish the quaintness of his credulity in matters of natural history.

To the author, the book was a recreation, written during the Cromwellian interregnum to solace himself for the loss of happier bygone times. He had already published his lives of Donne and Wotton. Both men had been personally known to him. He had gone fishing with Wotton, and was familiar enough with the Dean of St Paul's to receive one of his emblematic seals and to be present at his death-bed. Izaak Walton devoted much patient labour to the compilation of these and three subsequent biographies (Hooker, Herbert, and Sanderson). They were published collectively in 1670, a proof that they were quickly recognised as possessing merits quite beyond those of the ordinary prefatory life or commemorative eulogy. Dr. Johnson, himself a master of the brief biography, regarded Walton's *Lives* as one of his favourite books.

Izaak Walton's standards of accuracy naturally differ greatly from those of modern academic researchers. He did, however, set down straightforwardly what he took to be facts, and he relied whenever possible on personal testimony, thus achieving an impression of intimacy that is particularly engaging. When occasion required it, he could be impressively eloquent, and he handled both narrative and digression with great skill. Walton has been criticised for treating his subjects with too much veneration, and for reducing them all to a sameness of gentle piety. The charge is not unfounded. He was himself a pious conformist, and a rather sententious moralist. His experience of public life was limited. But if the testimony of his extant portraits can be trusted, he was, as all his writings suggest, a strong, genial and intelligent man, who deserved the appellation of "honest Izaak." Few seventeenth-century writers of prose have left behind them a more attractive legacy.

—Margaret Bottrall

WARNER, William.   English.   Born in London in 1558. Educated at Magdalen Hall, Oxford; studied law. Practised as an attorney in London; a friend of Marlowe and Drayton. *Died 9 March 1609.*

PUBLICATIONS

Verse

> *Albion's England: Books 1–4.*   1586; *Books 1–6,* 1589; *Books 1–9,* 1592; *Books 1–12,* 1596; *Books 1–13,* 1602; *Books 14–16,* 1606.

Play

> *Menaechmi,* from the play by Plautus (produced 1592?).   1595; edited by Geoffrey Bullough, in *Narrative and Dramatic Sources of Shakespeare,* 1957.

Fiction

> *Pan His Syrinx or Pipe: Seven Tragical and Comical Arguments.*   1584; revised edition, as *Syrinx; or, A Sevenfold History,* 1597; edited by W. A. Bacon, 1950.

*   *   *

William Warner, much praised and often quoted in his own day, owed his reputation entirely to *Albion's England*, his long narrative poem of myth, history, fiction, and moral truths told in rollicking and, frequently, halting "fourteeners":

> I tell of things done long ago, of many things in few:
> And chiefly of this clyme of ours, the accidents pursue.
> Thou high director of the same, assist my artlesse pen,
> To write the gests of Bruton's stout, and actes of English men.

First published in four books (1586), the poem was augmented in several subsequent editions up to 1606, when it reached its final state of sixteen books and a prose abstract. Its last contemporary re-issue in 1612 marked not only a quarter-century of popular success against comparable verse histories (e.g., Samuel Daniel's *Civil Wars* and Michael Drayton's *Mortimeriados*) but also the end of the genre itself in an age grown philosophically skeptical and culturally and politically more sophisticated. Warner's work had appealed to the same instincts in its readership as did the immensely popular *A Mirror for Magistrates* – pride in nation, an interest in its past, and the enjoyment of a good tale. *Albion's England* first appeared only a year before the last sixteenth-century edition of *A Mirror for Magistrates*, and it was current during the surge of national pride occasioned by the defeat of the Armada – these facts seem to have been enough to insure its success throughout the century. Warner's *Pan His Syrinx* is a lengthy prose romance comprised of seven interwoven exotic tales whose style, influenced by John Lyly's *Euphues*, left no legacy. His reputation, which had been secured only by his long poem, waned as the genre of verse "history" became less central to English culture. Perhaps Drayton's kind assessment (in "To Henry Reynolds") written some years after Warner's death, remains acute:

Then *Warner* though his lines were not so trim'd,
Nor yet his Poem so exactly lim'd
And neatly joynted, but the Criticke may
Easily reproove him, yet thus let me say;
For my old friend, some passages there be
In him, which I protest have taken me,
With almost wonder, so fine, cleere, and new
As yet they have bin equalled by few.

—Frank Fabry

WATSON, Thomas. English. Born in London c. 1557. Possibly educated at Oxford University; studied law in London. Married a Miss Smith. Visited Paris, 1581, and met Sir Francis Walsingham, thereafter his patron; returned to England and became a prominent figure in London literary society; in his last years employed in the household of William Cornwallis, probably as a tutor. *Died* (buried) *26 September 1592.*

PUBLICATIONS

Collections

Poems, edited by E. Arber. 1870.

Verse

The Hecatompathia; or, A Passionate Century of Love. 1582; edited by S. K. Heninger, Jr., 1964.
An Eclogue upon the Death of Sir Francis Walsingham. 1590 (also a Latin version *Meliboeus*, 1590).
The First Set of Italian Madrigals Englished. 1590; edited by E. H. Fellowes, in *English Madrigal Verse*, 1967.
Amintae Gaudia (in Latin). 1591; translated by I. T. as *An Old Fashioned Love*, 1594.

Other

Compendium Memoriae Localis. 1585(?).
A Gratification unto John Case for His Book in Praise of Music. 1586(?); edited by M. C. Boyd, in *Elizabethan Music and Musical Criticism*, 1940.

Translator, *Antigone* (in Latin), by Sophocles . 1581.
Translator, *Tebani Helenae Raptus* (in Latin), by Coluthus. 1586.
Translator, *Amyntas* (in Latin), by Tasso. 1587; translated by Abraham Fraunce, 1587; both versions edited by W. F. Staton, Jr., and F. M. Dickey, 1967.

Reading List: *Primi Studi su Watson,* 1964, and *Watson e la Tradizione Petrarchista,* 1969, both by C. G. Cecioni.

*   *   *

Thomas Watson, translator and poet, friend to such Elizabethan worthies as John Lyly, Christopher Marlowe, and Thomas Nashe, enjoyed a high reputation during his lifetime for his knowledge of ancient and Continental languages and for his poetry written in the Petrarchan manner. Today Watson is little read, but he remains interesting to the student of cultural change and the literary historian. His major work, *Hecatompathia; or, A Passionate Century of Love,* a collection predominantly of eighteen-line "sonnets," published about the time that Sidney was writing his sonnet cycle, *Astrophel and Stella,* antedates by a decade the vogue of sonneteering in England. His *Italian Madrigals Englished,* a substantial anthology of contemporary Italian art-songs with English adaptations to the Italian text (together with two pieces "composed after the Italian vaine" by William Byrd), is one of two such collections which appeared in England just prior to the assimilation and naturalization of Italian polyphonic music by English composers. Though Watson was no inventive genius – nearly his entire canon is comprised of translations, paraphrases, and adaptations – his use of up-to-date Continental poetry and music to underpin his own creative abilities, limited though they were, helped to stimulate and form an audience for the creative activity that so distinguishes the last decade of the sixteenth century in England.

In addition to Watson's general influence upon the literary and musical taste of his time, he occupies a place of some importance in the history of lyric poetry as a reformer of English prosody, and, were it not for the more obvious technical achievements of Sidney's *Astrophel and Stella,* Watson's reputation would be higher than it is. Yet when we recall that the verses of the early Elizabethan poets are characterized by a metrical rigidity, an unfailing *caesura,* inevitable end-stopping, and non-functional alliteration, we can better realize by how far Watson's supple line (in imitation of Petrarch's) could transcend them, as in *Hecatompathia,* 39:

> When first these eyes beheld with great delight
> The phoenix of this world, or second sun,
> Her beams or plumes bewitched all my sight,
> And love encreas'd the hurt that was begun,
> Since when my grief is grown so much the more
> Because I find no way to cure the sore.

From the evidence of his most influential work Watson appears to have been as interested in educating his readers as he was in writing poetry. Each of the *Hecatompathia* poems is prefaced with a notation (sometimes of considerable length) in which the poet acknowledges a source, points out a classical allusion, notes the similarity of this or that motif to a classical or Continental work, narrates a myth, or explains his method. By thus calling attention to the significance of historical knowledge to an appreciation of his poems, Watson seems as much the humanist who would use art to unite past with present as the poet intent upon anatomizing the vagaries of love.

Of Watson's Latin translations (Sophocles's *Antigone*; Tasso's *Aminta,* an activity which earned him the respect of his most learned contemporaries, little need be said except to note that the act of translation again points to the humanistic bent of this scholar-poet who did not stay at Oxford for his degree. His obvious commitment to the Latin language chimes with his intention to educate the readers of his "passions" to the continuities of the literary tradition.

—Frank Fabry

WHETSTONE, George. English. Born in London c. 1544. Courtier: spent his inheritance in extravagant living, and thereafter supported himself by writing and soldiering: served as an officer in the army, fighting against the Spanish in the Low Countries, 1572–74; accompanied Sir Humphrey Gilbert on his expedition to Newfoundland, 1578–79; visited Italy, 1580; accompanied the English forces to Holland, 1585–86, and fought at the Battle of Zutphen, 1586. *Died c. 1587.*

PUBLICATIONS

Verse

The Rock of Regard (includes fiction).   1576; edited by J. P. Collier, 1870.
A Remembrance of George Gascoigne.   1577; edited by E. Arber, with *Notes of Instruction* by George Gascoigne, 1868.
A Remembrance of Sir Nicholas Bacon.   1579; edited by A. Boswell, in *Frondes Caducae 1,* 1816.
A Remembrance of Sir James Dier.   1582 (?); edited by A. Boswell, in *Frondes Caducae 1,* 1816.
A Remembrance of Thomas, Late Earl of Sussex.   1583; edited by A Boswell, in *Frondes Caducae 1,* 1816.
A Mirror of the Life of Francis, Earl of Bedford.   1585; edited by T. Park, in *Heliconia 2,* 1815.

Play

Promos and Cassandra, from a story by Giraldi Cinthio (produced 1578).   1578; edited by Geoffrey Bullough, in *Narrative and Dramatic Sources of Shakespeare,* 1958.

Fiction

An Heptameron of Civil Discourses.   1582; as *Aurelia the Paragon of Pleasure,* 1593.

Other

A Mirror for Magistrates of Cities; A Touchstone for the Times.   1584; as *The Enemy to Thriftiness,* 1586.
The Honourable Reputation of a Soldier.   1585.
The English Mirror.   1586.
The Censure of a Loyal Subject, edited by Thomas Churchyard.   1587; edited by J. P. Collier, in *Illustrations of Early English Popular Literature 1,* 1863.
Sir Philip Sidney His Honourable Life.   1587; edited by A. Boswell, in *Frondes Caducae 1,* 1816.

Reading List: *Whetstone: Mid-Elizabethan Gentleman of Letters* by T. C. Izard, 1942.

*   *   *

Although George Whetstone wrote voluminously in a variety of genres – conduct books, travel accounts, pastorals, moral treatises, and amorous verse complaints – he is remembered chiefly as author of the ten-act tragicomedy *Promos and Cassandra*, which provided Shakespeare with his principal source for *Measure for Measure*. Whetstone's own source was the fifth novel of the eighth decade of Giraldi Cinthio's *Hecatomithi* (1565). Although Whetstone in his preface describes his play as a "history" and a "comical discourse," it is the first English play to deal seriously with a domestic conflict, and is thus a significant landmark in the development of domestic drama. Of slender poetic talent, Whetstone wrote the play in limping poulter's measure, followed his source closely, and maintained a humorless tone. In writing *Measure for Measure*, Shakespeare found little to appropriate from Whetstone except the bare bones of the plot, and even here Shakespeare wisely altered certain details to suit his own purposes. Four years after writing the play, Whetstone reworked it into a prose tale, *An Heptameron of Civil Discourses*. This change of genre enabled Whetstone to embellish the original story with lengthy digressions on one of his favorite subjects, the customs and manners of Italian nobility.

Whetstone's earliest work, *The Rock of Regard* (1576), consists of several prose tales with verse "complaints" of dissolute women like Cressida. Some of the verses are vigorous and brilliant, particularly his "Invective Against Dice." This work indicates that penchant for didacticism characteristic of such later works as *The Enemy to Unthriftiness*, essentially a sermon inveighing against vices, and *The English Mirror*, a systematic analysis in prose of a catalogue of wicked and worthy behavior. Another prose work, *The Honourable Reputation of a Soldier*, is a conduct book worthy of note for its firm, direct style and its psychological treatment of military life. One of Whetstone's last works was *The Censure of a Loyal Subject*, a dialogue castigating the condemned conspirators of the Babington Plot. In summary, Whetstone's strength as a writer would appear to be in his prose style, which is often vigorous and occasionally vivid when not dulled by sermonizing.

—James E. Ruoff

WITHER, George.   English.   Born in Bentworth, Hampshire, 11 June 1588. Educated at Magdalen College, Oxford, 1604–06; entered Lincoln's Inn, London, 1615. Imprisoned for *Abuses Stript and Whipt*, 1613–14, and for *Wither's Motto*, 1621. Served as a captain of horse in the First Bishops' War, 1639; sold estate to raise a regiment for the Puritan cause, 1642; Governor of Farnham Castle, 1642, captured by the Royalists but released at Denham's request; Justice of the Peace for Hampshire, Surrey, and Essex, 1642–58; Major-General of the forces in Surrey, 1643; briefly imprisoned for *Justitiarius Justificatus*, 1646; Commissioner for the sale of the King's goods, 1653; Master of the Statute Office, 1655; lost positions and property at the Restoration; imprisoned for unpublished satire against Parliament, *Vox Vulgi*, 1660–63. *Died 2 May 1667.*

PUBLICATIONS

Collections

Miscellaneous Works.   6 vols., 1872–73. (10 other volumes of reprints of Wither's works also published by the Spenser Society).
Poetry, edited by F. Sidgwick.   2 vols., 1902.

Verse

Prince Henry's Obsequies; or, Mournful Elegies upon His Death.   1612.
Epithalamia; or, Nuptial Poems.   1612.
Abuses Stript and Whipt, The Scourge: Epigrams.   1613.
A Satire, Dedicated to His Most Excellent Majesty.   1614.
Fidelia.   1615.
The Shepherd's Hunting.   1615; edited by William B. Hunter, Jr., in *The English Spenserians*, 1977.
Exercises upon the First Psalm, Both in Prose and Verse.   1620.
Works, Containing Satires, Epigrams, Eclogues, Sonnets, and Poems.   1620.
The Songs of the Old Testament, Translated into English Measures.   1621.
Wither's Motto: Nec Habeo, Nec Careo, Nec Curo.   1621.
Juvenilia.   1622; revised edition, 1633; selection, as *Extracts from Juvenilia*, edited by A. Dalrymple, 1785; revised edition, as *Juvenilia*, edited by J. M. Gutch, 4 vols., 1820.
Fair-Virtue, The Mistress of Phil'arete.   1622.
The Hymns and Songs of the Church.   1623.
Britain's Remembrancer.   1628; selections, as *Mr. Wither His Prophecy*, 1642, *Wither's Remembrancer*, 1643, *Mr. Geo. Wither Revived*, 1683.
The Psalms of David Translated into Lyric Verse.   1632.
A Collection of Emblems, Ancient and Modern.   4 vols., 1635.
Halleluiah; or, Britain's Second Remembrancer.   1641; selections included in *Wither's Remembrancer*, 1643.
Campo-Musae; or, The Field-Musings of Captain George Wither.   1643.
The Great Assizes Holden in Parnassus by Apollo.   1645.
Vox Pacifica: A Voice Tending to the Pacification of God's Wrath.   1645.
What Peace to the Wicked?   1646.
Amygdala Britannica.   1647.
Carmen Expostulatorium.   1647.
Carmen-Ternarium Semi-Cynicum.   1648.
A Si Quis; or, Queries.   1648.
Prosopopoeia Britannica: Britain's Genius, or Good-Angel, Personated.   1648.
The Tired Petitioner.   1648; edited by J. M. French, in *Four Scarce Poems*, 1931.
A Thankful Retribution.   1649.
An Alarum from Heaven; or, A Memento to the Great Council.   1649.
Vaticinium Votivum; or, Palaemon's Prophetic Prayer.   1649.
Carmen Eucharisticon: A Private Thank-Oblation.   1649.
Three Grains of Spiritual Frankincense.   1651.
The British Appeals, with God's Merciful Replies.   1651.
A Timely Caution.   1652.
The Dark Lantern, Containing a Dim Discovery; The Perpetual Parliament.   1653.
Westrow Revived.   1653.
Three Private Meditations.   1655.
The Protector.   1655.
Vaticinium Causuale.   1655.
Boni Ominis Votum: A Good Omen to the Next Parliament.   1656.
The Sudden Flash Timely Discovering Some Reason Wherefore the Style Protector Should Not Be Deserted by These Nations.   1657.
A Cause Allegorically Stated.   1657.
Epistolium-Vagum-Prosa-Metricum; or, An Epistle at Random.   1659.
A Cordial Confection, to Strengthen Their Hearts Whose Courage Begins to Fail.   1659.
Salt upon Salt, Made Out of Certain Ingenious Verses upon the Late Storm and the Death of His Highness Ensuing.   1659.

Speculum Speculativum; or, A Considering Glass, Being an Inspection into the Present and Late Sad Condition of These Nations.   1660.

Furor-Poeticus Propheticus.   1660.

A Triple Paradox, Affixed to a Counter-Mure Raised Against the World, the Flesh, and the Devil.   1661.

An Improvement of Imprisonment, Disgrace, Poverty, into Real Freedom, Honest Reputation, Perdurable Riches.   1661.

Verses Intended to the King's Majesty.   1662.

Tuba-Pacifica, Seasonable Precautions.   1664.

A Memorandum to London, Occasioned by the Pestilence.   1665.

Sighs for the Pitchers.   1666.

Echoes from the Sixth Trumpet.   1666; as *Nil Ultra; or, The Last Works*, 1668; as *Fragmenta Prophetica; or, The Remains*, 1669.

Vaticinia Poetica.   1666.

Divine Poems (By Way of Paraphrase) on the Ten Commandments.   1688.

A Strange and Wonderful Prophecy.   1689.

Wither's Redivivus.   1689.

A Paraphrase of the Ten Commandments.   1697.

Select Lyrical Passages, Written about 1622, edited by E. Brydges.   1815.

Vox Vulgi: A Poem in Censure of the Parliament of 1661 (sic), edited by W. D. Macray.   1880.

The History of the Pestilence 1625, edited by J. M. French.   1932.

Other

A Preparation to the Psalter.   1619.

The Scholar's Purgatory.   1625(?).

Read and Wonder: A War Between Two Entire Friends, the Pope and the Devil.   1641.

Se Defendendo: A Shield, and Shaft, Against Detraction.   1643.

Mercurius Rusticus; or, A Country Messenger.   1643.

Letters of Advice, Touching the Choice of Knights and Burgesses for the Parliament.   1644.

The Speech Without Door.   1644.

Prophecy of the Downfall of Antichrist.   1644.

To the Most Honourable the Lords and Commons: Petition.   1646.

Justitiarius Justificatus: The Justice Justified.   1646.

Opobalsamum Anglicanum: An English Balm, Lately Pressed Out of a Shrub and Spread upon These Papers.   1646.

Major Wither's Disclaimer.   1647.

Articles Presented Against This Parliament.   1648.

Respublica Anglicana; or, The History of Parliament in Their Late Proceedings.   1650.

The Modern States-Man.   1653.

To the Parliament of the Common-Wealth: The Humble Petition of G. W.   1654.

The Petition and Narrative of Wither.   1659.

Fides-Anglicana; or, A Plea for the Public-Faith of These Nations.   1660.

Predictions of the Overthrow of Popery.   1660.

The Prisoner's Plea.   1661.

Joco-Serio, Strange News, of a Discourse Between Two Dead Giants.   1661.

Parallelogrammaton: An Epistle to the Three Nations of England, Scotland and Ireland.   1662.

A Proclamation in the Name of the King of Kings, to All the Inhabitants of the Isles of Great Britain (includes verse).   1662.

Meditations upon the Lord's Prayer.   1665.

The Grateful Acknowledgement of a Late Trimming Regulator.   1668.

Translator, *The Nature of Man,* by Nemesius.   1636.

Reading List: "Wither: The Poet as Prophet" by Allan Pritchard, in *Studies in Philology,* 1962; *The Later Career of Wither* by C. S. Hensley, 1969; *The Spenserian Poets* by Joan Grundy, 1969.

*   *   *

George Wither was a voluminous poet who went on writing long after his poetic light was extinguished. His later works, produced in the mistaken belief that he was God's prophet, chosen to denounce the coming reign of Antichrist, can mostly be dismissed as "poetical prosings." It is on his earlier works, up to and including *Britain's Remembrancer* (1628), that his reputation as a poet must rest. These too are effusions: Wither despised "method" and had a fatal facility for producing smooth and quite readable but seemingly interminable couplets. But unlike the later outpourings, these poems have genuine charm and interest.

Fair-Virtue could be described as Wither's *Testament of Beauty*: in it he engagingly expatiates on his love of beauty in woman, virtue, Nature, and poetry itself. *Fidelia,* a verse-epistle from a forsaken woman, is delicately feminist in its sympathies, and is well, sometimes movingly, written. *The Shepherd's Hunting,* a dramatization in pastoral form of his imprisonment in the Winchilsea, addressed to his friends and fellow-poets, notably William Browne, is an appealing piece of self-portraiture. His imprisonment arose out of the publication of *Abuses Stript and Whipt,* a collection of satires, vigorously attacking vice and immorality in all the estates of the realm. Despite the satiric persona Wither adopts, the spirit and manner of this work are closer to the moral essayist than the satirist, and this is even more apparent in the enormously popular *Wither's Motto.* Here Wither simply takes the stage and holds forth about himself and his opinions, painting a self-satisfied portrait of a man humble but content. The portrait is intended to be a model for others: if in Wither's eyes poetry both delights and teaches, the delight is in the first place for himself (coming from the sheer joy of "making") and the teaching for his reader. Didacticism and self-expression were the two poles on which his work always turned. *Britain's Remembrancer* both teaches and preaches: it finds in the Plague of 1625 an opportunity to combine vivid, detailed description with an exhaustive analysis of the abuses of the day, for which the Plague is seen as a punishment. This poem is valuable to historians, as indeed are parts of the later polemics, for its social and political comment. As the watch-dog of liberty, Wither's incessant barking is irritating but sometimes not entirely unjustified.

Other works deserving to be remembered are Wither's prose work, *The Scholar's Purgatory,* a lively account of the confrontations between author and printer (i.e., the Stationers' Company); his *Epithalamia* for Princess Elizabeth, which has a pleasing freshness; his *Hymns and Songs of the Church* and, still more, his *Haleluiah,* which provides the reader with hymns for every conceivable occasion, written in simple language, employing a variety of stanzas, and indicative of a tender, pastoral concern and sympathetic heart. His fine *Collection of Emblems* is a valuable cultural document of the times. Most memorable, and indeed remembered, of all, are his delightful lyrics, "Shall I wasting in despair," "I loved a lass, a fair one," and "So, now is come our joyfullest Feast."

—Joan Grundy

WOTTON, Sir Henry.   English.   Born in Broughton Malherbe, Kent, 30 March 1568. Educated at Winchester School; New College, Oxford, 1584, moved to Queen's College, Oxford, B.A. 1588; Middle Temple, London, 1595. Courtier and diplomat: travelled on the Continent, 1588–95; returned to England and became Secretary to the Earl of Essex, 1595–1601; lived in Italy, 1601–03; knighted, 1603; Ambassador to Venice, 1604–12, 1616–19, 1621–24, and went on additional diplomatic missions to France, 1612, The Hague, 1614, and Vienna, 1620; Member of Parliament for Appleby, 1614, and Sandwich, 1625; Provost of Eton College, 1624–39; ordained deacon, 1627. *Died in December 1639.*

PUBLICATIONS

Collections

> *Poems,* edited by Alexander Dyce.   1843.
> *Poems by Wotton and Others,* edited by J. Hannah.   1845.

Other

> *The Elements of Architecture.*   1624; edited by F. Hard, 1968.
> *Ad Regem e Scotia Reducem Wottoni Plausus et Vota.*   1633.
> *A Parallel Between Robert Late Earl of Essex and George Late Duke of Buckingham.*   1641; edited by E. Brydges, 1814.
> *A Short View of the Life and Death of George Villiers Duke of Buckingham.*   1642.
> *A Panegyric of King Charles.*   1649.
> *Reliquiae Wottonianae: or, A Collection of Lives, Letters, Poems,* edited by Izaak Walton.   1651; revised edition, 1654, 1685; *A Philosophical Survey of Education; or, Moral Architecture, and The Aphorisms of Education,* edited by H. S. Kermode, 1938.
> *The State of Christendom; or, A Discovery of Many Hidden Mysteries of the Times.*   1657.
> *Letters to Sir Edmund Bacon.*   1661.
> *Letters and Dispatches, 1617–1620,* edited by George Tomline.   1850.

Reading List: *Life and Letters of Wotton* by L. P. Smith, 2 vols., 1907; *Wotton, with Some General Reflections on Style in English Poetry* by H. H. Asquith, 1919.

*   *   *

Although he sometimes appears in library catalogues as "Sir Henry Wotton, *poet*," it is by hardly more than a dozen poems that he merits the label. Friend of Izaak Walton (who was later to write his biography), ambassador to Venice, and in his last years provost of Eton College, Wotton is relished for his letters, his treatise on architecture, his humane though unfinished *Philosophical Survey of Education; or, Moral Architecture*, and a handful of anthology pieces, notably "You Meaner Beauties of the Night," written for Elizabeth of Bohemia.

Reliquiae Wottonianae, edited by Izaak Walton, is as charming a collection of works and fragments as its long subtitle promises: "A Collection of Lives, Letters, Poems; with Characters of Sundry Personages, and Other Incomparable Pieces of Language and Art." Unfinished as it is, the treatise on education is admirable and moving as an early attempt to base an educational system on sympathetic observation of "the Naturall Capacities and Inclinations of Children."

Wotton's enthusiasm in *The Elements of Architecture* for "the secret power of proportion" informs his poems as surely as it shapes his appreciation of Italian buildings and his ideal of the English country house. While the group of poems he produced is small, poise and polish, a pervasive classical spirit, characterize his moral verse, the delicacy of his best known lyric, and the precise quietness of his epitaph for the wife of his nephew, Sir Albertus Morton: "He first deceased; she for a little tried/To live without him, liked it not, and died." Drummond of Hawthornden reports that Ben Jonson had by heart "The Character of a Happy Life," and, dates apart, Wotton would qualify as a most authentic son of Ben.

—Kay Stevenson

NOTES ON CONTRIBUTORS

BERRY, Francis. Professor of English, Royal Holloway College, University of London. Author of several books of verse, the most recent being *Ghosts of Greenland*, 1966, and of critical works including *Poets' Grammar*, 1958, *Poetry and the Physical Voice*, 1962, and studies of Herbert Read, Shakespeare, and John Masefield. **Essay**: Sir John Denham.

BOTTRALL, Margaret. Biographer and Critic. University Lecturer, Department of Education, and Senior Tutor, Hughes Hall, Cambridge University, until 1972. Author of *George Herbert*, 1954, and *Every Man a Phoenix: Studies in Seventeenth-Century Autobiography*, 1958. Editor of *Personal Records*, 1961, and *Songs of Innocence and Experience*, by Blake, 1970. **Essays**: Richard Crashaw; Lord Herbert of Cherbury; Izaak Walton.

BRISSENDEN, Alan. Senior Lecturer in English, University of Adelaide, Australia; Joint General Editor, Tudor and Stuart Text series. Author of *Rolf Boldrewood*, 1972. Editor of *A Chaste Maid in Cheapside* by Thomas Middleton, 1968, *Shakespeare and Some Others*, 1976, and *The Portable Boldrewood*, 1978. **Essay**: Barnaby Rich.

BROWN, Cedric C. Member of the Department of English Language and Literature, University of Reading, Berkshire. Editor of *The Poems and Masques of Aurelian Townshend*, 1977. **Essay**: Aurelian Townshend.

CRAIK, T. W. Professor of English, University of Durham. Author of *The Tudor Interlude*, 1958, and *The Comic Tales of Chaucer*, 1964. Joint General Editor of *The Revels History of Drama in the English Language*, and editor of plays by Massinger, Marlowe, and Shakespeare. **Essay**: Thomas Sackville.

DAVIS, Walter R. Professor of English, University of Notre Dame, Indiana. Author of *A Map of Arcadia*, 1965, and of articles on Surrey, Lodge, Spenser, Drayton, Bacon, and Browne. Editor of *The Works of Thomas Campion*, 1967, *Idea and Act in Elizabethan Fiction*, 1969, and *Twentieth Century Interpretations of "Much Ado about Nothing,"* 1969. **Essays**: Francis Bacon; John Cleveland; Richard Lovelace; Sir Philip Sidney.

DONNO, Elizabeth Story. Professor of English, Columbia University, New York; Editor of *Renaissance Quarterly*. Editor of *Metamorphosis of Ajax* by Sir John Harington, 1962; *Elizabethan Minor Epics*, 1963; *The Complete Poetry of Andrew Marvell*, 1972; *An Elizabethan in 1582: The Diary of Richard Madox*, 1976; *Marvell: The Critical Heritage*, 1977. **Essays**: Michael Drayton; Thomas Nashe.

DONOVAN, Dennis G. Professor of English, University of North Carolina, Chapel Hill; Editor of *Renaissance Papers*. Editor of bibliographies of Sir Thomas Browne and Robert Burton, and of checklists on other seventeenth-century writers. **Essay**: Robert Burton.

DOWNIE, J. A. Lecturer in English Literature, University of Leeds. Author of "Political Characterization in *Gulliver's Travels*," in *Yearbook of English Studies 7*, 1977; *Robert*

Harley and the Press: Propaganda and Public Opinion in the Age of Swift and Defoe (forthcoming). **Essay:** Thomas Hobbes.

DOYNO, Victor A.   Associate Professor of English, State University of New York, Buffalo. Editor of *Parthenophil and Parthenophe* by Barnabe Barnes, 1971. **Essay:** Barnabe Barnes.

DUNLAP, Rhodes.   Member of the Department of English, University of Iowa, Iowa City. Editor of *The Poems of Thomas Carew*, 1949. **Essays:** Thomas Carew; William Habington.

FABRY, Frank.   Professor of English, University of South Florida, Tampa; Assistant Editor of *Seventeenth-Century News*. Author of articles on Sidney and on satire in *Renaissance Quarterly, English Literary Renaissance*, and *Seventeenth-Century News*. **Essays:** Richard Barnfield; Nicholas Breton; William Warner; Thomas Watson.

FOREY, Margaret.   Examiner and part-time teacher; currently editing a work by William Strode. Formerly Lecturer at the University of Durham. Author of "Cleveland's 'Square Cap': Some Questions of Structure and Date" in *Durham University Journal*, 1974. **Essays:** Edward Benlowes; Richard Corbett; Thomas Stanley; William Strode; Edmund Waller.

GILL, Roma.   Member of the Department of English, University of Sheffield. Editor of *The Plays of Christopher Marlowe*, 1971, *William Empson: The Man and His Work*, 1974, and of works by Middleton and Tourneur. **Essays:** Giles Fletcher the Elder; Thomas Lodge; Christopher Marlowe.

GORDON, Ian A.   Professor of English, University of Wellington, 1936–74. Has taught at the University of Leeds and the University of Edinburgh. Author of *John Skelton*, 1943; *The Teaching of English*, 1947; *Katherine Mansfield*, 1954; *The Movement of English Prose*, 1966; *John Galt*, 1972. Editor of *English Prose Technique*, 1948, and of works by William Shenstone, John Galt, and Katherine Mansfield. **Essays:** Robert Greene; John Lyly.

GRUNDY, Joan.   Reader in English Literature, Royal Holloway College, University of London. Author of *The Spenserian Poets*, 1969. Editor of *The Poems of Henry Constable*, 1960. **Essays:** Henry Constable; Giles Fletcher the Younger; Phineas Fletcher; George Wither.

HEATH-STUBBS, John.   Writer and Lecturer. Author of several books of verse, the most recent being *The Watchman's Flute*, 1978, a book of plays, and of *The Darkling Plain: A Study of the Later Fortunes of Romanticism*, 1950, *Charles Williams*, 1955, and studies of the verse satire, the ode, and the pastoral. Editor of anthologies and works by Shelley, Tennyson, Swift, and Pope; translator of works by Giacomo Leopardi, Alfred de Vigny, and others. **Essay:** William Drummond.

HUGHEY, Ruth.   Professor Emeritus of English, Ohio State University, Columbus. Author of *John Harington of Stepney, Tudor Gentleman*, 1971, and of articles on Harington, Elizabeth Grymeston, and Elizabeth I. Editor of *The Correspondence of Lady Katherine Paston*, 1941, and *The Arundel Harington Manuscript of Tudor Poetry*, 2 vols., 1960. **Essay:** Sir John Harington.

KENDLE, Burton.   Associate Professor of English, Roosevelt University, Chicago. Author of articles on D. H. Lawrence, John Cheever, and Chekhov. **Essays:** Sir John Davies; Thomas Deloney.

LYLE, A. W.   Lecturer in English, University of Sheffield. **Essays:** William Browne; George Gascoigne; Joseph Hall.

MACKERNESS, E. D.   Member of the Department of English Literature, University of Sheffield. Author of *The Heeded Voice: Studies in the Literary Status of the Anglican Sermon 1830–1900*, 1959, *A Social History of English Music*, 1964, and *Somewhere Further North: A History of Music in Sheffield*, 1974. Editor of *The Journals of George Sturt 1890–1927*, 1967. **Essay:** Thomas Campion.

MUIR, Kenneth.   Professor Emeritus of English Literature, University of Liverpool; Editor of *Shakespeare Survey*, and Chairman, International Shakespeare Association. Author of many books, including *The Nettle and the Flower*, 1933; *King Lear*, 1952; *Elizabethan Lyrics*, 1953; *John Milton*, 1955; *Shakespeare's Sources*, 1957; *Shakespeare and the Tragic Pattern*, 1959; *Shakespeare the Collaborator*, 1960; *Introduction to Elizabethan Literature*, 1967; *The Comedy of Manners*, 1970; *The Singularity of Shakespeare*, 1977; *Shakespeare's Comic Sequence*, 1978. Editor of several plays by Shakespeare, and of works by Wyatt and Middleton; translator of five plays by Racine. **Essay:** Andrew Marvell.

PATRIDES, C. A.   Professor of English Literature, University of Michigan, Ann Arbor. Formerly, Professor of English, University of York, England. Author of *Milton and the Christian Tradition*, 1966, and *The Grand Design of God: The Literary Form of the Christian View of History*, 1972. Editor of *Approaches to Paradise Lost*, 1968; *The Cambridge Platonists*, 1969; *History of the World* by Sir Walter Ralegh, 1971; *English Poems* by George Herbert, 1974; *Selected Prose* by Milton, 1974; *Major Works* by Sir Thomas Browne, 1977; *Approaches to Marvell*, 1978. **Essays:** Sir Thomas Browne; Sir Walter Ralegh.

PERRY, John J.   Member of the Department of English, State University of New York, Brockport. **Essay:** Alexander Hume.

PRESS, John.   Area Officer, British Council, Oxford. Author of three books of verse – *Uncertainties*, 1956, *Guy Fawkes Night*, 1959, and *Troika* (with others), 1977 – and several critical books, including *Rule and Energy*, 1963, *A Map of English Verse*, 1969, *The Lengthening Shadows*, 1971, and *John Betjeman*, 1974. **Essay:** Robert Herrick.

REES, Joan.   Member of the Department of English Language and Literature, University of Birmingham. Author of *Samuel Daniel*, 1964, *Fulke Greville: A Critical Biography*, 1971, and *Jane Austen, Woman and Writer*, 1976. Editor of *Selected Writings* by Greville, 1973. **Essays:** Samuel Daniel; Sir Fulke Greville.

RUOFF, James E.   Associate Professor of English, City College of New York. Author of *Elizabethan Poetry and Prose*, 1972, *Crowell Handbook of Elizabethan and Stuart Literature* 1973, and *Major Shakespearean Tragedies* (with Edward G. Quinn), 1973. **Essays:** Thomas Churchyard; Abraham Cowley; Sir John Suckling; Thomas Tusser; George Whetstone.

SALGĀDO, Gāmini.   Professor of English, University of Exeter, Devon. Author of *Eyewitnesses of Shakespeare: Firsthand Accounts of Performances, 1590–1890*, 1975, and *The Elizabethan Underworld*, 1977. Editor of *Sons and Lovers: A Collection of Critical Essays*, 1969, *Cony Catchers and Bawdy Baskets*, 1973, works by D. H. Lawrence and Shakespeare, and collections of Jacobean and Restoration plays. **Essay:** Ben Jonson.

SELL, Roger D.   Member of the Department of English, Abo Academy, Finland. Editor of *The Shorter Poems of Sir John Beaumont*, 1974. **Essay:** Sir John Beaumont.

SHADY, Raymond C.   Member of the English Department, St. John Fisher College, Rochester, New York. Editor of *Love's Mistress* by Thomas Heywood, 1977. **Essay:** John Marston.

SHEIDLEY, William E.   Associate Professor of English, University of Connecticut, Storrs. Co-Editor of the journal *Children's Literature*, 1974–77. Author of articles on Marlowe, George Turbervile, Barnabe Googe, and Shakespeare in *Concerning Poetry*, *Journal of English and Germanic Philology*, *Studies in Philology*, and *Modern Language Quarterly*. **Essays:** Barnabe Googe; George Turbervile.

SHIRE, Helena Mennie.   Fellow of Robinson College, Cambridge. Former Senior Research Fellow in the Arts, Carnegie Trust for the Universities of Scotland. Author of *Song, Dance and Poetry of the Court of Scotland under King James VI*, 1969, and *A Preface to Spenser*, 1978. **Essays:** Sir Robert Ayton; Alexander Montgomerie; Edmund Spenser.

STEVENSON, Kay.   Lecturer in Literature, University of Essex, Colchester. **Essays:** William Alabaster; Francis Quarles; Robert Southwell; Joshua Sylvester; Sir Henry Wotton.

SUMMERS, Joseph H.   Professor of English, University of Rochester, New York. Author of *George Herbert: Religion and Art*, 1954, *The Muse's Method: An Introduction to Paradise Lost*, 1962, and *The Heirs of Donne and Jonson*, 1970. Editor of *Selected Poems* by Andrew Marvell, 1961, *The Lyric and Dramatic Milton*, 1965, and *Selected Poetry* by George Herbert, 1967. **Essays:** George Herbert; Henry King.

TAYLOR, Myron.   Associate Professor of English, State University of New York, Albany. Author of articles on Shakespeare in *The Christian Scholar*, *Studies in English*, and *Shakespeare Quarterly*. **Essay:** John Milton.

TRAVERSI, Derek A.   Professor of English Literature, Swarthmore College, Pennsylvania. Author of *An Approach to Shakespeare*, 1938 (revised, 1968); *Shakespeare: The Last Phase*, 1954; *Shakespeare: From Richard II to Henry V*, 1957; *Shakespeare: The Roman Plays*, 1963; *T. S. Eliot: The Longer Poems*, 1976. **Essay:** William Shakespeare.

WADDINGTON, Raymond B.   Professor of English, University of Wisconsin, Madison; Member of the editorial boards of *Sixteenth Century Journal* and *Literary Monographs*. Author of *The Mind's Empire: Myth and Form in George Chapman's Narrative Poems*, 1974, and of articles on Shakespeare, Chapman, Milton, and others. Co-Editor of *The Rhetoric of Renaissance Poetry*, 1974. **Essay:** George Chapman.

WHEELER, Thomas.   Professor of English, University of Tennessee, Knoxville. Author of *Paradise Lost and the Modern Reader*, 1974, and of articles on Milton and Thomas More. **Essays:** Joseph Beaumont; Sidney Godolphin.

WILLY, Margaret.   Free-lance Writer and Lecturer. Author of two books of verse – *The Invisible Sun*, 1946, and *Every Star a Tongue*, 1951 – and several critical works, including *Life Was Their Cry*, 1950; *Three Metaphysical Poets: Crashaw, Vaughan, Traherne*, 1961; *Three Women Diarists: Celia Fiennes, Dorothy Wordsworth, Katherine Mansfield*, 1964; *A Critical Commentary on "Wuthering Heights,"* 1966; *A Critical Commentary on Browning's "Men and Women,"* 1968. Editor of two anthologies and of works by Goldsmith. **Essays:** John Donne; Thomas Traherne; Henry Vaughan.